RAILWAY MAN

MITCHELL DEAVER

AuthorHouse™
1663 Liberty Drive
Bloomington, IN 47403
www.authorhouse.com
Phone: 1-800-839-8640

© *2013 Mitchell Deaver. All rights reserved.*

The moral right of the author has been asserted.

No part of this book may be reproduced, stored in a retrieval system, or transmitted by any means without the written permission of the author.

Published by AuthorHouse   01/10/2013

ISBN: 978-1-4772-9972-2 (e)
ISBN: 978-1-4772-9973-9 (sc)

Library of Congress Control Number: 2012923654

Any people depicted in stock imagery provided by Thinkstock are models, and such images are being used for illustrative purposes only.
Certain stock imagery © Thinkstock.

This book is printed on acid-free paper.

Because of the dynamic nature of the Internet, any web addresses or links contained in this book may have changed since publication and may no longer be valid. The views expressed in this work are solely those of the author and do not necessarily reflect the views of the publisher, and the publisher hereby disclaims any responsibility for them.

*To
My Dear Wife*

PREFACE

The years 1962 to 1988 were marked by a series of sharply differing experiences. To portray events during those disparate periods, this true story necessarily passes through several moods, ranging from a detailed and serious study of railway operations to a whimsical approach not normally associated with the subject, from an emotional account of the end of steam engines on British Railways to the dryness of a government report on events that followed, from candid disclosures of misspent youth to sombre recollection of years alone.

Events from my past have been described exactly as they happened as far as memory will permit, though some names have been changed to protect privacy of those concerned. Conversations have been reproduced as I remember them, save that any strong language in original exchanges has been replaced by milder forms. Where memory is inadequate, a best guess has been made at actual words spoken. Dialogue may appear quotidian. That was the manner in which we spoke; to change the record would put words into people's mouths they did not say and render the account false.

M.D.
December 2012

PART ONE

STEAM

CHAPTER ONE

The heartbeat quickened as landscape I had not seen for eight years raced into view. I deplored immediate transportation the motor car offered; the pilgrimage deserved more than the mad dash of which the vehicle was capable. Despite constant braking, the car's speed allowed no opportunity to savour moments before arrival at my old haunt, it permitted no time to enjoy a myriad hues of roadside vegetation that would tax even the most gifted artist's palette, a kaleidoscope of colour I may or may not have appreciated as a boy. The impatient vehicle disallowed enjoyment of meandering country lanes that, shepherded by fierce hawthorn hedges, criss-crossed this green and pleasing part of the North Riding, now North Yorkshire. It sped through one village, then another, allowing little time to identify neatly kept cottages where one-time school chums lived. Each field, each dwelling rapidly brought me closer to the goal of the day's journey, the village of Bickle.

When I left Bickle at age eleven I thought I would never return. Since boyhood I had studiously avoided returning to the village because that period of life belonged to the past, because priceless memories were parcelled away and sealed with sealing wax, because childhood was childhood and I was now an adult. But owing to an undeniable contribution Bickle had made to the character of a person who, in 1965, was now nineteen years old, sundry distractions that habitually placed themselves in the way of a man at that age were no longer capable of damming a flood of desire to go back. A return to Bickle had become imperative.

I broke into a sudden, nervous sweat as the car took me closer. A looming double bend prompted a fugacious recollection of the place-name Starbeck, a name I had given to this twist in the road where I used to play trains as a lad. Though Starbeck fled the mind as quickly as it had entered, the boyhood memory triggered in turn a snap review of the entire four years spent in Bickle. A busy double-tracked railway line running through the village had provided endless hours of interest, entertainment, instruction and inspiration. It had produced the happiest four years of childhood as I first became beguiled by those striking monuments to Victorian railway technology, semaphore railway signals, whose bright reds, yellows, blacks and whites had splashed colour over the flat green agricultural vale through which railway passed. Workings of the signal box at Bickle station (a rare signal box in that it was open to the public because train tickets were dispensed there) had fascinated me as a boy. Crashing of signal levers and ringing of mysterious bell codes as steam engines thundered by belching copious amounts of sulphurous smoke had left a profound impression on a young mind.

    Still perspiring, I concentrated on the remaining few hundred yards of highway. The last time I had gazed down this road had been through the open rear door of a removals van when, in 1957, it had whisked our family away from Bickle to another place. As I slowed the car to a crawl, I saw with immense delight Bickle signal box's tubular steel Up Main starting signal poking above tree tops, its red enamelled semaphore arm jutting towards the highway like some proud standard held in a breeze, its steadfastness defying the years.

CHAPTER TWO

I halted the motor car, then made one or two backwards and forwards moves to squeeze the white and blue Ford Anglia Super, still shiny and still with its bouquet of fresh upholstery, hard against a narrow grass verge. The white metal post of the Up Main starting signal stretched into the sky to my right. Immediately beyond stood Bickle station platforms sealed off from the village road by the same high smoky-bricked secretive wall I had admired as a boy. Directly ahead lay a level crossing flanked by opened, gleaming white gates. To the left stood the brick-built signal box. I got out, locked the vehicle, and strode to a position in the middle of the road. I looked up at the signal box. As I did, a large ginger handle-bar moustache appeared at the window immediately followed by its owner in the form of round face and substantial frame of my old friend and mentor signalman Dan Patterson. The man who had, when I was young, taught me so much about railways was still there. A window noisily slid open. I stood in shock for a fraction of a second, then, regaining composure, spoke.

"Hello," I began, "I don't know if you remember me, but I used to come here when I was a boy."

"Way, aye, 'course ah do," replied the beaming signalman. "Come on up."

We remembered each others' names without difficulty and immediately exchanged platitudes as if only a week had passed since last seeing one another. Then Dan Patterson said, "Pity yer didn't come about 'alf an 'our sooner, we 'ad a steam special go by. Yer know, one of them enthusiasts' specials."

I hung my head in disappointment at narrowly missing the steam locomotive. So many times at this very location had I been enthralled by the drama of motion, the heady aroma, the thundering sound of steam traction. I had just missed a chance to enjoy it once again. After a moment's pensiveness I recovered. "Ah, well," was all I could utter. I consoled myself with the thought that to have arrived just as the special train was going by would have been a chance in a million, and that had that happened, I might have swooned in disbelief.

Dan Patterson had changed little since last I saw him, his ginger hair a little wispier, an inch or two added about his girth - the extra pounds pressing hard against blue-black railway uniform. But his magnificently groomed handle-bar moustache, which he occasionally dressed with forefinger and thumb to maintain a sharp curl, still dominated his appearance. Though I was now fully grown, the large and impressive man still towered over me. He urged me to sit down and make myself comfortable. Without ceremony and without comment, I took up the position I used to occupy as a boy: on an old wooden bench in the corner of the signal box. I could have remarked to the signalman how many times I had sat there as a boy, but too many enquiries about today elbowed out banalities about yester-year.

The most significant changes to the signal box, Dan Patterson told me, were loss of the public delivery siding and of the crossover, resulting in levers 11, 12, 13 and 14 being painted white signifying out-of-use. The signalman reported all freight workings had been diverted to another route with the exception of one short goods train running in the Down direction (northwards) only. All other trains comprised diesel multiple unit passenger trains tearing up and down the line no longer stopping at Bickle nor other local stations. Owing to reduction in traffic, the night shift at Bickle signal box had gone. Dan Patterson, as senior man, had been given choice of the box's retaining two day-time shifts, or of reducing the work to one ten-hour shift; he had chosen the latter. In thus fashion he became the only signalman stationed there, working six ten-hour shifts Monday to Saturday.

On the shelf carrying telegraph signalling equipment, the block shelf, I noticed a new item, a black box with numbered lights and switches, and asked what it was.

In reply Dan Patterson said, "This thing 'ere is daft. It's supposed to let yer know if a light 'as gone out in one of t'signals. It's instead of t'indicators that used to be fixed to t'front of 'shelf. D'yer remember?"

I nodded. In the North Riding version of Yorkshire dialect, the signalman explained that the device detected drop in temperature, which it interpreted as the paraffin lamp having gone out, and to which it drew attention by sounding a buzzer. Unfortunately, on a breezy day any wind that entered the lamp housing also had the effect of reducing temperature even though the lamp was still burning, resulting in the buzzer sounding on and off all day long. The signalman had switched the device off.

"And this," said Dan Patterson pointing to a small oval contraption with a handle on the front, "is a Welwyn Control." In the circumstances of, say, a train having been cancelled, the handle had to be wound numerous times before a second Line Clear could be given on the block indicator. Dan Patterson demonstrated by grabbing the small handle and furiously spinning it for about a minute until an indicator slowly came into view showing he had completed the cycle. Red in face from the pointless exercise and grinning foolishly, he explained the device had been installed in signal boxes to establish thinking time before a signalman could give a second Line Clear. A tragic mistake had occurred at Welwyn Garden City, Hertfordshire, which place gave its name to the device, where the signalman mistakenly had indicated Line Clear when in fact the line was not clear since there was already a train between two signal boxes. As consequence of a simple but dreadful error of turning a block indicator commutator handle when it should not have been turned, one train rammed into the back of another with terrible loss of life. The Welwyn Control was designed to prevent such a disaster recurring.

Explanation of Welwyn Control completed review of key physical changes that had occurred over the last eight years. Sitting on a bench on which I had first sat eleven years ago at an old green-painted kitchen-like table at which I had first sat eleven years ago, I looked round the signal box to see that it remained substantially unaltered. A white earthenware kitchen sink, still unconnected to running water, occupied the corner by the entrance door. A serried row of sixteen levers filled space at the rear of the box. A gate wheel, formerly at the left-hand end of the lever frame, had disappeared as level crossing gates were now opened and closed by hand necessitating a journey outside on each occasion. Above the frame seven assorted telegraph block instruments – comprehensible only to the initiated - adorned the block shelf. Each encased in polished wood and approximately the size of a large shoe box, they comprised four block indicators, two bells and a block switch to close the box should there ever be need. To continue clockwise round the box, the Dickensian train register book desk, gleaming electrical cabinet and telephone to Control occupied the next corner, green-painted signalmen's lockers the next. A coal stove in the middle of the box front brought the survey back to the corner in which I was sitting. As the signalman and I bathed in warmth created by both the auspiciousness of two old friends meeting again and by inherent coziness of a small country signal box, conversation took a personal turn.

CHAPTER THREE

"Where d'yer work then, Mitch?"

I replied that I had taken a position in public service.

"Yer didn't get a job on t'railway, then," said Dan Patterson with a tinge of sadness to his voice.

"No," I sighed. "I wanted to be a signalman, but my family persuaded me not to do it. Dead end job, they said."

The prevailing feeling at the time was that the railways were a declining industry, a not inaccurate assessment in the mid-1960s. This anti-railway sentiment was most pronounced in older people who had vivid memories of widespread unemployment amongst blue-collar workers between the wars. My paternal grandparents were particularly forceful in their objections to working on the railway. They urged me to enter relatively secure public service.

"'Ow did yer get on at school, then?" asked Dan Patterson. "Did yer pass yer eleven-plus?"

I shook my head. "I got as far as an interview."

"Interview?"

"All places at the grammar school were filled except two, and there were three of us left who had actually passed the examination, so they had to interview the three of us," I explained.

"An' yer didn't get in," said Dan Patterson.

"Nope."

I dwelt briefly and privately over what I had just said, and was troubled by the parallel between failing the eleven-plus examination by a whisker and just missing the steam engine earlier that day. But I would sometimes just as narrowly squeeze by to good fortune. On the day I bought the Ford Anglia, hire purchase interest rates went up to a level I could not afford, but the sale propitiously went through by back-dating the transaction to the previous day. It was, and would continue to be, a fact of life that from time to time I would find myself teetering on the knife-edge of fate.

"When we got to senior school," I continued, "the class I was in was

6

the top stream in the secondary modern part (grammar school kids were the very top class) and after the first year they decided to start us on 'O' level GCE courses. That put us a year behind, so we were at a bit of a disadvantage," I said.

"'Ow did yer do?"

"Not too bad," I said. "I got six passes."

"That's very good," said Dan Patterson. His face brightened on hearing his one-time protégé had achieved at least modest scholastic success.

"Thanks. But there were some in the grammar school who got eight 'O' levels, and they said they didn't study much. I had to start studying about ten weeks before the exams to try to remember the stuff. I've got a rotten memory. One lad said he just glanced through his notebooks the night before, that's all the studying he did."

"'E might 'ave just been saying that," said Dan Patterson.

"Dunno," I said reflectively.

An unfortunate reluctance of the brain to readily absorb large amounts of information, such as that necessary to pass Ordinary Level General Certificate of Education examinations, would limit the author's progress through life. Noetic inflexibility would restrict choice of vocations to those where instant recall was not of paramount importance. These mental shortcomings were offset at school by an incisive, analytical mind that could tear through algebraic and geometric problems with ease. Nevertheless, after weeks and weeks of self-enforced torture studying for "O" levels I vowed never again to inflict such hardship on myself. That vow meant of course that I would leave school at age sixteen, much to the dismay of schoolmasters who felt I was sixth form material, and possibly much more. An affinity for algebra paradoxically played a role in the decision to leave school. As a youngster in Bickle I had briefly worked on a farm for pocket money, an episode that taught me a simple equation: work = money. To stay on at school would mean having no job which in turn multiplied both sides of the above equation by zero. Our family never did have a great deal of money; I would be virtually penniless if I continued formal education.

My old friend saw fit moment to change the subject. "Are yer courting?" he asked.

"Nah," I replied. "I was going out with this girl...'n...like, she lived in Halifax. It was too far."

Owning a motor car allowed me to wander far and wide, and had resulted in striking up a relationship with a young woman who lived forty miles away. The strain of long-distance courtship had prevented it from flourishing, and not unsurprisingly, the friendship withered. As upset as I may have been over the failed romance, absence of an amourette had released the mind from preoccupation with the opposite sex, had allowed review of a childhood love of railways which in turn had prompted today's journey. I struggled for words to make light of losing the girlfriend from afar.

"Well, there's plenty o' fish in t'sea," said the signalman interrupting my faltering account.

I nodded in concurrence. It was now my turn to switch subjects. "I would have come here on my bike, you know, but I would have hated to have come all this way on the bike and found the signal box gone."

"You ride a bike!" exclaimed Dan Patterson.

"Yeh, I ride all over, or I used to anyway, till I bought the car," I said.

"I have to ride a bike to work, now," said the signalman. "'Doctor said I needed to get more exercise on account of me health, yer know." He patted his bulging midriff. "So I ride to work 'n back every day."

"I cycle eight miles to and from work myself most days," said I, surprised to learn someone else did the same thing.

"You mean you bike to work!" said Dan Patterson, his face suddenly illuminating like an arc-light.

"Most days," I replied. "If it's really bad weather, I'll catch the bus or use the car, but I try not to use the car to save on petrol, and so as not to wear it out."

"By Jove! you've just given me a new lease of life," enthused Dan Patterson, his countenance radiating with irrepressible joy. He leapt out of the old, worn armchair, and sprang about the wooden floor excitedly as if he were ten, nay, twenty years younger. For all his size the man was still nimble. "I thought I was t'only bloke who rode a bike to work. I never see anyone else riding a bike nowadays. You've just given me new heart, Mitch."

The man's animated delight on learning he was not the only person in Yorkshire who still rode a bicycle to work far exceeded my own feelings of encouragement on receiving the same intelligence. Though many clad in athletic attire rode racing bicycles for sport, very few in the late 1960s rode traditionally built sit-up-and-beg bicycles with straight handlebars, the kind Dan Patterson and I possessed. Even fewer used them as a means of transport to and from work. I had been told large numbers used to cycle a decade or two ago to the government offices where I worked; now I was the only one.

In truth, I considered, and still consider, the motor car an atrocious waste of resources. From the moment of purchase an inexorable decline in value begins. Even if a motor car saw very little use, as mine did, or was not used at all, it would still eventually rust away to worthlessness. The wastefulness of petrol at five shillings a gallon pumped into cylinders only to be blasted into oblivion by a series of tiny explosions to produce valueless and harmful waste seemed even more appalling. But shunning the car for work in favour of exercise and negligible cost of cycling raises the question: why did I buy the car in the first place? Many a young man bought an automobile through love of mechanics, only to discover in vehicle ownership a side effect of attracting women. I bought a car through love of the opposite sex, only to discover, despite assurances an internal combustion engine was just a collection of simple artifices joined together, that I was Laodicean about the science of mechanics.

CHAPTER FOUR

A loud ding came from one of the block telegraph instruments. The instrument was a single-beat bell (as opposed to a continuously ringing door bell) comprising a bell dome mounted on a box with a Morse code type key, or tapper, protruding from the front. The one beat signified Call Attention, and came from Pellerby North signal box. Dan Patterson replied one beat on the key. The signalman at Pellerby North then sent the train's code, which may have been five beats, I cannot remember. Dan Patterson replied with the same code on the key. On an adjacent instrument, a block indicator, which looked vaguely like a mantelpiece clock, Dan Patterson rotated a handle on the front (called a commutator handle) 120 degrees from the Line Blocked position to the Line Clear position, a movement copied by a dial in the upper part of the instrument.

"This is that freight I was telling yer about," said Dan Patterson.

Soon, two beats of the Train entering Section bell signal announced the train's passing Pellerby North. Dan Patterson replied two beats and turned the commutator handle a further 120 degrees to the Train on Line position, again copied on the dial above. There then followed bell code exchanges with the next signal box down the line, Kewlby, identical to the first exchanges with Pellerby North. Another block indicator subsequently displayed Line Clear.

After going outside to close the level crossing gates, Dan Patterson effortlessly pulled red lever number 10 to work a tall tubular steel Down Main home signal located on the opposite side of the tracks from the signal box. The signal had replaced a wooden version a few years ago. Perched on the side of an embankment a quarter-mile away, the number 9 starting signal, a squat North Eastern Railway design with the semaphore arm passing through the lower quadrant for the "off" indication, demanded more effort. After number 9, Dan Patterson used his full strength and weight to drag yellow distant lever number 8 out of the frame, the lever completing its movement with a monstrous crash against black ironmongery holding the whole assembly together. He flung a duster over the polished steel handle of number 8 lever, and watched an alarm clock-like arm repeater dial hesitatingly flick over to "off". The raised fish-tailed yellow arm of the distant signal, about three-quarters-of-a-mile away, told the train driver that both home and starting signals were showing the all-clear and that he could proceed with all speed.

"That distant's a begger," said Dan Patterson. "T'drivers complained it was too close to t'crossing, so they moved t'signal back, so far back yer can 'ardly get it 'off'. In between trains I walked down 'track and put a drop of oil on t'pulleys, did a few each day yer know, now it's a lot better than it was. They say yer not supposed to put oil on t'pulleys, but ah did it all t'same."

"What would have happened if there had been a train?" I asked.

The signalman waved his hand dismissively. "There wouldn't be any trains. If there was anything extra they'd send a special notice," he said confidently. Turning to the other yellow lever in the frame, the signalman said, "That number 6 Up distant, yer know, they renewed that 'n motorized it and shoved it further back round t'bend."

I remembered well the lower quadrant distant close to a farm on the way to Kewlby. "Is that why the top of the lever has been cut off?" I asked, looking at the truncated lever.

"Yes," said Dan Patterson. "They 'ad to do summat about that signal. T'wire used to go back 'n forth under 'tracks, 'n everything was getting worn, it was about impossible to get 'off'."

A short train hauled by a diesel locomotive soon loomed into view, and in little time, raced by with four measly vehicles. Such an uneconomic train would not have done in the 1950s when all trains (except the pick-up train that, entertainingly to a young boy, served local sidings such as that at Bickle) were a quarter-mile in length. This contrast in loading was naught when compared to the drop in total number of freight trains using the line over the eight-year period. Bickle signal box at one time saw, perhaps, fifty goods trains – all steam hauled of course – in a twenty-four hour period. Now it saw only one sad little freight train a day, and that was diesel hauled.

Yellow lever number 8 was slammed back, followed by return of red levers number 10 and 9. As the apology for a train disappeared from view beyond the Down Main starting signal, Dan Patterson called attention with one beat on the tapper to Pellerby North. After a one-beat reply, the signalman rang 2-1 for Train out of Section and turned the commutator handle back to the vertical position of Line Blocked. After a few minutes, the sequence of signalling the freight train was completed by Kewlby ringing 2-1 bell code to Bickle and by the needle on the block indicator concerned swinging back to Line Blocked.

Traincrews on this isolated freight working, said the signalman, were rumoured to occasionally make a brief stop at Grington station to pick apples from the former station master's orchard. From this anecdote I inferred Grington station, a station that once boasted a staff of five including station master, to be now abandoned. Poignant memories briefly stabbed at the mind of happy times spent chatting to men who worked at that bustling place. But all such recollections were trod underfoot by the auspiciousness of revisiting Bickle, by the celebration of two old friends meeting again after an eight-year hiatus. Mawkish preoccupation with former glories would have been as out of place as discussing bereavement at a wedding.

Though conversation flowed easily and entertainingly between two people who were now both adults as opposed to one being an adult and one a child, two hours would elapse before another train was due, so we agreed the day would end at that point, and that I would call by to see him again.

After turning round the Ford Anglia, mentally drained, I drove home. Grass verges which at one time offered up their variety for children to admire and pick at now raced by in an indiscriminate smudge of verdant rises and falls. The head swam with joy of seeing Dan Patterson, with the phenomenon of two lives that had unfolded separately yet identically in the form of cycling eight miles to and from work, with delight of seeing Bickle signal box's semaphore signals again, with sadness at the decline in freight traffic, with disappointment at just missing the steam train. From this cauldron of mixed emotions there nevertheless rose a determination to keep alive the renewed association with Dan Patterson and Bickle signal box, and it was that sentiment that chiefly occupied the mind on the drive home.

CHAPTER FIVE

Whilst the return to Bickle signal box was an event of great import, it was but one of many to occur after leaving school. Another milestone, though of quite different character, deserves more than passing mention, the discovery of rewards and pitfalls of alcohol. Drinking beer would become aligned with pursuit of the opposite sex, often to a background of popular music. Wine, women and song, plus the motor car that facilitated indulgence therein, conspired to shut out nobler activities, particularly interest in railways. I did not deliberately shun the railway, for I would still visit Dan Patterson from time to time at Bickle signal box, and would admire other signal boxes and signals I should happen across. No, it was more a case that combined demands of work and newly-found excesses left little time for anything else.

A number of boys had been friends as far back as I can remember - we were toddlers together and had been in the same infants' school class. We had re-met at secondary modern school, and a handful of us re-grouped yet again around 1964 to embark on what seemed to be a mission to drink the maximum amount of beer in as little time as possible in the greatest number of public houses. Of all brews sampled, the now defunct Cameron's brewery must have had special significance because I still dream about Cameron's beer. Wherever we went, we habitually referred to a public house by the name of the village in which it was situated rather than by the inn's real name. This misuse of village names violated the Yorkshire of youth by converting the county from a spread of delightfully named picturesque villages to a map of licensed premises.

One evening when we were undecided, a friend declared spontaneously: "Let's go to Bickle!" Desecration upon desecration, I would now be drinking on hallowed ground. Four of us raced by car to Bickle, tearing by the signal box with such speed I could not even steal a glance. The haste with which we tumbled into the bar even disallowed looking at the council house opposite where I had lived eight years ago. As we drank I did not bring up proximity of the childhood home, nor did I mention railways, for to have raised either prosaic subject would have inflicted a mortal wound on the night.

During this period of cruising and boozing a conditioning of mind took place that came to regard Saturday night out as inviolable. Whilst such peremptory thinking is not original amongst young men, the die thus cast would prove so adamantine that any displacement of Saturday night pleasures by work or other commitment would always be accompanied by grim avowal to make up for the forfeiture. Another concept heled into the psyche at this early stage was a statement by a drinking companion, a statement which was as ungrammatical as it was sententious, but one which is nevertheless repeated verbatim: "Work hard, play hard, that's us!" We all had full-time jobs, but would find additional work in evenings or at weekends to supplement our income, only then to go out and promptly drink away the extra cash. Even so, to put in enough extra hours so that one is free to spend as much as one may care to spend on pleasure still strikes me as a not unsound approach, though writing at a much later stage in life I would have to temper it with the hope that such waste be within limits of reasonableness. Young men free from financial constraints of a steady girlfriend, or even greater restraints of marriage, mortgage and children, spent surplus cash on the only two materialistic outlets presenting themselves: automobiles and alcohol.

As spirited young men tearing around Yorkshire in newly purchased motor cars out to enjoy life to the full, my companions and I were slow to learn the snares of mixing alcohol and driving. On one occasion I was passenger in a mini car *en route* to a village public house when the driver took too fast a left-hand bend that was followed by a hump-backed bridge resulting in our being air-borne over the bridge and landing on the wrong side of the road. Had there been a vehicle travelling in the opposite direction a disastrous head-on collision would have occurred. Once the small vehicle slammed back onto the macadam, the driver quickly swerved back to the proper side of the road and continued driving as if nothing had happened.

Shaken, I said, "Took that a bit too fast, didn't you?"

"Just a little bit, just a little bit," said the driver unruffled.

Stories circulated of another mini car approaching a fork in the road over which a railway bridge passed. The driver had a last minute change of mind regarding which route to take, failed to take either and smashed into the abutment between both routes virtually destroying the automobile. A mechanic who saw mangled remains of the car was shocked to learn all four occupants survived suffering only minor injuries. It was said the men's extremely relaxed state through advanced drunkenness saved them from greater harm. Another story tells of one man's heavy drinking that incapacitated him to the extent he could no longer stand at the bar, only kneel. When asked by friends later in the evening if he would be all right driving his car home, he replied "Drive it, I can't even see it!" When recounting the night's events at a later date, the man concerned was purported to have said: "It's terrible, you know, when you open your eyes and you can't see anything." Though at one stage literally blind drunk, somehow he had been able to drive home safely.

The worst experience I had was driving home in thick fog after drinking excessively, when combined impediments of alcohol and atrocious visibility caused me to drive in the wrong direction several miles before realizing the mistake. Even though I was eventually able to turn round and reach home without further incident, to relate the story now makes me groan in despair at my own irresponsibility.

I do not write these accounts of Dionysian mix of pleasure and pain to panegyrize driving under the influence, but to place on record what would prove to be only a brief period of recklessness amongst teenagers. In the mid-1960s, ownership of cars amongst large numbers of young people was relatively new, it previously having been a privilege of other than the working class. Multitudinous inebriated youthful drivers was a new phenomenon. But since any respectable person would be indoors during late evening, we were more or less alone on country roads so that any danger would principally be to ourselves, as has been illustrated above. As time passed, with roads becoming more crowded and the incidence of drunken driving increasing, laws were inevitably and properly enacted to counter the menace. Legislation apart, somewhere between impetuous youth and staid maturity comes realization that the only answer to drinking and driving is to eschew it completely.

Whilst excessive drinking might actually increase tolerance for alcohol, an evening's indulgence at a well-known East Coast holiday camp taught there will always be a limit to enjoyment of beer. An evening of drinking took place in a large hall, the tone of which was set by two songstresses periodically serenading us from a suspended cradle that moved slowly around the ceiling, the ladies' sequin-covered legs dangling above the fuddling rabble leering at them from below. Four of us were drinking at a pace far too fast for two of us. One man left. Just as I was thinking of doing the same, one of the other two fell over backwards in his chair, demolished the chair in the process, then playfully hit the other man over the head with a broken chair leg. The buffoon-like behaviour was enough to convince me it would be better to leave the large, crowded, bawdy premises and return to the chalet that was our home for a fortnight.

Whilst crossing a wide footpath between the bar and rows of chalets, something smashed into my face. I fell to the ground. Utterly bewildered, I clambered to my feet, dusted myself off and continued walking. I had gone but a few paces when exactly the same thing happened again. Thanks to over-consumption of alcohol, all I wanted to do was to get back to the chalet and go to bed, so was not too troubled by the misfortune. After being smacked in the face and dragging myself off the ground for a third time, I began to wonder who or what was inflicting the blows, but was still too drunk to care, and eventually staggered back to the chalet to collapse into deep sleep. Whether it was a day, a week or a month later, I cannot remember, but explanation of the triple attack eventually dawned on me. No thing or no one was striking me, I was simply falling over head first blind drunk, the blunt object hitting my face was the ground on impact.

CHAPTER SIX

To leave behind for now intemperate adventures, another momentous discovery during late teens will give some idea of this young man's level of sophistication. It is difficult to comprehend how any person could become excited over something as dull as filing systems, but in the first year or so in public service, that is exactly what happened. I acquired a passion for the manner in which governmental files were numbered. In any department, files were divided into major categories by prefixing them with letters. All files for, let us say, dog licences might be marked DL, sewerage S, highways H and so on. Within that nomenclature, individual files and sub-files were numbered creating typical file numbers of DL.43, S.89/228 and H.12/14/e, a system that was neither ingenious nor original, yet one that appeared fascinatingly labyrinthine when first met. An office drama illustrated the degree to which I became obsessed with filing systems.

    A departmental head needed to overhaul his filing system and was visiting different offices to see how paper records were kept. The senior clerk in the office in which I worked went through cabinets showing the visitor how files were arranged, and detailed the sub-divisions, which were particularly complicated in this instance. I listened intently. At one stage, I thought the senior clerk had overlooked an important issue, a major omission that could not go uncorrected. Flushed with *elan*, I leapt to my feet, interrupted the senior clerk, and said impertinently, "And there's the files that we use for [so-and-so] that were subdivided alphabetically, but because we ended up with sub-files AA, BB and so on, we should have subdivided them numerically."

    As the visitor listened to the uninvited outburst with startled politeness, a typist in the corner sprang up and down in her chair frantically waving her hands in a mute attempt at getting me to sit down and shut up. I finished what I thought ought to have been a much appreciated contribution to the exposition. The senior clerk turned to glare at me icily. On conclusion of the unpardonably rude interruption, he allowed a brief pause as parties reeled from shock, then said with commendable restraint, "You carry on with that typing that you're doing Mitchell, and we'll continue looking at the filing system. We got along quite well before you came along, and we can get along quite well now, thank you."

The senior clerk's upbraiding for the unforgivable breach of office etiquette struck swiftly. I dropped back into the office chair like a bird knocked out of the sky, buried my face in my chest and began hammering as hard as I could on typewriter keys hoping everyone would forget the indiscretion as quickly as possible.

Despite this regrettable episode, boundless enthusiasm led to setting up a personal filing system at home. A handful of files quickly grew into many, with some copying governmental practice of multiple sub-divisions. After a few years, the foolishness of having to give over so much space to files became apparent, and they were thinned out. Several files opened and numbered in the 1960s are still with me today, and the domestic system has seen periods of rapid re-expansion, though care has been taken to avoid the original excesses.

Yet a fascination with filing systems did not prove strong enough inducement to remain in public service. A secure position may have been envied by some, but I did not view the future so favourably, seeing instead the remainder of working life, some forty-five years, incarcerated in a collection of small offices connected by a corridor, promotion being rewarded by moving up the corridor one office at a time every ten years or so. Others doubtless cherished a lifetime career involving very little moving around. I felt entombed and wanted to move on. Days in public service were numbered, and time might have been opportune to think about becoming a signalman, but as the railway network was being butchered at the time, the idea of embarking on a career on British Railways would have been of utmost folly.

CHAPTER SEVEN

In the summer of 1966, I would leave home, leave Yorkshire for good. I would never, ever, regret growing up amongst green pastures, buff cornfields, hawthorn hedgerows and narrow lanes of the North Riding, but that same idyllic countryside that had provided an ideal playground for imaginative children and that had later furnished an Arcadian backdrop to a brief period of touring public houses had few careers to offer, so I looked elsewhere. I would be leaving behind a unique place in Bickle signal box and a unique person in Dan Patterson.

Sombre resignation weighted the air on the occasion of the last visit, by which time the solitary freight train had gone, and the axe of Dr. Richard Beeching, the man appointed to streamline British Railways, hung over the whole rural line. "What are you going to do if they close the line?" I asked Dan Patterson on this last day.

"Take redundancy," he replied with neither hesitation nor emotion.

"Wouldn't they offer you a job in another signal box somewhere else?"

"Yeh, they have to, but I wouldn't take it," said the signalman flatly.

I was disappointed that he wished to end his railway career so abruptly, but his mind was obviously made up; doubtless sound arguments prompted his decision to retire early. On hearing my plans to move from the area, Dan Patterson's cheery face fell, but he recognized that an adult is free to wander, free to wander more than just the few miles up and down the trackside as I had done as a child. We chatted for a short while, delaying the sad moment when we would have to say goodbye, possibly for the last time, thereby breaking an eleven-year old bond. I am an optimist, or, more accurately, I despise contemplating the worst. Moreover, I contemn melodrama, so on that last day in Bickle signal box, I suppressed thoughts that I may never see it nor its guardian again. When Dan Patterson and I parted, it was with little emotion. I finally got up from the now very much battered and worn wooden bench, no coat of paint having been applied since I was a boy, and paused in the middle of the operating floor to take one last look at the still brightly coloured lever frame, at the once-enigmatic block instruments and at the pellucid signalling diagram. Determined to preserve an evenness of colloquy that had prevailed throughout adult visits to the signal box, I played down the awfulness of the occasion, and did not address my old friend squarely in the face (who had now risen to his feet also) but stood sideways.

I turned my head slowly to say, "Well, Dan, might see you sometime."

"Yer never know. You take care, Mitch," he replied.

Our friendship was too close for the formality of shaking hands. I turned fully away from the man, and with head down exited both inner and outer cabin doors to negotiate those wooden stairs for what in fact would be the very last time. I never again saw Dan Patterson, nor Bickle signal box, nor its signals, its trains, its railway tracks. Deliberate suppression of the senses had allowed me to breeze through that sad, last Saturday afternoon without having to face the truth that the box and its steam engine trains had been the most influential events to have occurred in childhood, that the place was still a powerful draw as an adult, and that there was a strong and dreadful likelihood all would be swept away when the line closed, leaving only memories. Even if I had chosen to dwell on the finality, I could not have foreseen that boyhood memories of steam and signals would acquire in the future an eminence even greater than that which had already been attributed to them by the time of the last visit in 1966.

A certain uprooting would take place in the near future, one that would transplant the author to surroundings altogether different from those known so far, surroundings so rich in experiences he would be swept up and away with them to the extent that memories of one small signal box in rural Yorkshire would be buried amongst countless other matters no longer pertinent to a new way of life. When removed from the county of birth, I did hear of the final closure of the line that ran through Bickle, and dwelt briefly on the unhappy loss, then got on with life. I am now indebted to a fellow signalling enthusiast for supplying precise details as to how the end came, details which I had neither the inclination nor the tools to retrieve at the time.

In March 1967 the line closed to traffic, but signal boxes, signals and all other infrastructure remained *in situ* but out of use: in a word, mothballed. May 1968 saw the final, official abolition of signal boxes with which I had had any connection, that is, Bickle, Kewlby and Pellerby North; doubtless soon after that date the structures were demolished and railway tracks themselves lifted. Beyond Pellerby North trains occasionally still ran from a southerly direction to a facility known as Pellerby South, about five miles from Bickle. Pellerby South had at one time been a signal box whose existence had been wrapped in mystery: as a boy I never knew it was there and only found out about it many years later. Sidings at Pellerby South clung on till October 1969 when they too were closed, and with that action the last remnant of a railway line that was and is a crucial part of one's life disappeared.

In the 2000s there is little room in East Coast Main Line schedules to add passenger trains to meet growing demand for rail travel. Network Rail, custodians of infrastructure, now contemplate parallel routes to augment existing main lines. No doubt authorities wish they could have back as an alternative route the line I used to know, but apart from the astronomical cost of reinstatement, houses now stand on what used to be trackbed in Bickle, and an over-bridge has been filled in at Grington, a mile further south. However, I am told the monolithic station wall at Bickle still stands, a monument to lost splendour.

CHAPTER EIGHT

Two final, powerful recollections from the North Riding of Yorkshire remain: they concern steam engines.

By 1966, steam locomotives throughout Britain were being permanently withdrawn in vast numbers, only to sit forlornly in sidings awaiting dispatch to scrap yards and the cutter's torch. Withdrawal of engines was not a uniform drawing down of numbers across the country, but a patchy closure of steam sheds one by one, with steam traction ending abruptly at certain locations but continuing to be a major source of motive power at others. The railway enthusiasts' press covered fully the demise of steam by listing which sheds were to close and which were to remain open for the time being. Those who did not study their reports, including the author at the time preoccupied with worldly diversions previously detailed, were ignorant of where and when to find the last steam engines. This ignorance brought two surprises. For the first, we must go back a little while, probably to the year 1965.

Trips on the bicycle often took me close to the East Coast Main Line that ran through the heart of Yorkshire. One day whilst cycling along a road parallel to the main line, I sensed a dark object out of the corner of the left eye. I turned, and was astonished to see the unmistakable streamlined outline of a Class A4 steam locomotive hauling a parcels train. In shock, I wobbled and nearly fell off the bicycle.

The A4s had four wheels on the front bogie, six driving wheels, and two wheels on the rear bogie - a 4-6-2 wheel arrangement classifying them as a Pacific locomotive. First introduced in 1935 to the designs of London & North Eastern Railway's Chief Mechanical Engineer Sir Nigel Gresley, the A4s are considered one of the most successful steam engines ever, an accolade justified by one of the class, 4468 *Mallard*, establishing a still unbroken world speed record for steam of 126 miles per hour on 4 July 1938. *Mallard* is one of six A4s that have been preserved. Until ousted by diesel traction in the early 1960s, the A4s ruled the East Coast Main Line with panache, but by the middle of the decade had been relegated to lesser duties, such as the train of parcels coaches now slowly rolling northwards being watched by someone on a bicycle.

I was able to keep abreast of the A4, a feat not as demanding as it may seem, for distance reduced the engine's apparent speed. The train slowed down, perhaps for a signal stop or for a diverting move. A quarter-mile or so between the high-stepping A4 and me placed the machine at perfect distance to adore elegant lines of the streamline casing, to admire synchronized great circles of six-feet-eight-inches driving wheels so close together they seemed to touch, to weaken at the knees (already tired through pedalling) at slow sensuous undulations of the Walschaerts valve gear, to salivate over the deep rich colour of Brunswick green livery just discernible beneath a coating of soot and grime. Barely able to control the bicycle through disbelief, I soaked up as much of the spectacle as I could before the magnificent engine, noiseless in deceleration, drifted out of sight behind a building to continue its journey without audience. Unfortunately the locomotive was too far away, or too dirty, or both, to identify by either name or number.

At this point mention must be made of the book *British Railway Steam Locomotives 1948-1968* by Hugh Longworth. Hereon, several references are made to the volume. I must acknowledge the tremendous help it has been in making sense of patchy recollections and scant notes from the final days of steam. Concerning the A4s, the book reveals that at the beginning of 1965 only eleven of the original thirty-four were still in service, that by the end of the year only six remained, and that by September 1966 all had been withdrawn. If the sighting was in 1965, then it was close to the end of active service for this class of locomotive.

A second recollection from Yorkshire dates from the period after I had left home, but on an occasion when I had returned for the weekend to see family. I do not know the date, but it was probably when driving back to work one Sunday evening in the late summer of 1967. As I approached a bridge that crossed the East Coast Main Line on a skew, I was astonished to hear the distinctive rhythmic thunder of a steam engine close by. I slowed down to see smoke first billowing into the air to the right, then, as the train passed under the bridge, to the left. I pulled into the side of the road, and scampered to the railway boundary fence just in time to behold the spellbinding sight of a work-worn Class WD locomotive (wheel arrangement 2-8-0) clanking its way southwards on the Up Slow line with a train of mixed freight. As usual, the WD executed its duties in a reliable business-like manner; it mattered not that a shocked and goggle-eyed individual watched from a bridge above.

The WDs' striking simplicity of line and indisputable capacity to pull had struck awe in me as a boy, and for that reason had become my favourite engine. That boyish awe returned on a day in the late 1960s as I stood at a wooden fence watching the locomotive doggedly haul its lengthy train on long straight tracks of the East Coast Main Line. Somehow knowing that this train would be the last normal steam working I would see in Yorkshire, I stayed to watch the train first dwindle to a dot, then to vanish. The sighting was difficult to believe because, thanks to ignoring the railway press, I thought steam operations had ceased in the area. In fact steam operation in north-east England came to an end in autumn 1967. Hugh Longworth's book tells us that out of a total of 934 built, only thirty-four WDs survived by the beginning of July 1967, of which ten were withdrawn later that month, the balance finally leaving British Railways' service in September of that year. Again, I was witnessing a final fling of an important class of British locomotives. It is possible that the engine's journey southwards was its very last in revenue-earning service, its ultimate destination being Draper's scrap yard in Hull, but this is pure conjecture.

When, for me, the curtain finally fell on steam in Yorkshire, it was fitting that it came down on a Class WD, the very locomotive I had adored as a child.

CHAPTER NINE

Uncomfortable rituals of the first day in a new job - those of learning one's way round a mazy building, of endeavouring to remember names, of grinning foolishly as clammy hands engaged in polite greetings that both parties wished would be over as quickly as possible - were out of the way and my employer released me for the remainder of the day to move into lodgings they had obligingly arranged. I emerged into warm July afternoon air to take a close look at the centre of Birmingham which, at that time, was part warren of sparkling new shops, part massive craters where more new shops would be built and part traditional high street department stores spared redevelopment. As road traffic impatiently whizzed about this patchwork of old and new, I strolled around in quiet contentment at the prospect of having a few hours to do whatever I wanted to do before work started in earnest tomorrow.

Hunger gnawed at the stomach. Drawn to one of several recently completed shopping complexes dotted about the city centre like children's sandcastles on a beach, I found a restaurant and sat down at one of many empty tables. A smiling, smartly turned-out waitress quickly appeared. Seeing no menu, I asked, "What do you have?"

"Salad?" She answered my question by asking another, whilst at the same time lifting her face to even brighter aspect.

"Er...I wanted something a bit more like a meal. What else do you have?" I asked.

"We only have salad this time of day," replied the waitress, her smile ebbing somewhat. "Lunch is finished."

I ate salad. A lack of straightforwardness struck me here. A proper answer to my first question would have been the answer I had to winkle out of her by asking a second question. If the waitress had been asked to explain her scandalous behaviour, she probably would have said in pitiful defence that she was only doing her best to keep the customer happy in less than satisfactory circumstances of having no proper menu to offer. Had I been more compliant, a disappointment would of course have been avoided. Memory of the waitress vignette persists because it was one of the first experiences in a new setting, and because it marked the beginning of a long, slow, sometimes painful process learning that Yorkshire bluntness, as useful as it may be in cutting through superfluous verbiage, was generally considered gauche in the city where obliqueness is a preferred form of conversation.

For the first six months of what would be a twelve-month stay in the West Midlands the postman would find me in a suburb sprouting from one of numerous arterial roads radiating from Birmingham city centre, in a short street where nothing seemed to stir but where in contrast a couple of hundred yards away the hustle and bustle of commuter traffic daily pumped workers back and forth to pursue their employment. I would be one of those workers. The Ford Anglia was left behind in favour of joining the throng using city buses, to experience the tension of mixing with complete strangers, to enjoy the not necessarily incompatible sensations of gregariousness and anonymity - of joining in yet staying apart. As we waited impatiently at a bus stop, we would look down the long straight road at platoons of blue and cream double-decked Corporation buses supposedly heading towards us but which, owing to the attenuating effect of perspective, seemed to be making no progress at all. At last a bus would arrive, when we would all scramble aboard to be whisked off as fast as the driver could safely convey us to conduct our business in the centre of Birmingham. (Great Barr route buses were apparently so heavily used in the morning some passengers resorted to riding to the outlying terminus in order to secure a seat for the inbound journey.)

Despite a preference many had for public transport, private cars far outnumbered buses in rush hour traffic, which is not surprising since the automobile dominated Birmingham's economy. At that time, car factory rates of pay were the highest in Britain for blue-collar workers, enabling single young men to buy such luxury cars as Jaguars, disgracing my humble Ford Anglia. Birmingham's wealth, courtesy of the automobile industry, was never more conspicuous than in its city centre department stores where well-dressed shoppers filled the aisles to browse over quality merchandise piled high for their benefit. Supreme confidence of the city as a whole shone through in the new Bull Ring shopping centre and in the freshly-built, much lauded Ringway, a fast highway encircling the whole city centre elevating the motor car to the status of deity, relegating the pedestrian to the status of nuisance. Time would prove adulation of the automobile mistaken, but in 1966 Birmingham was exceedingly proud of its city centre, the redevelopment being much admired throughout the country. This glossy, glassy, classy setting gave one young man his first taste of city life.

CHAPTER TEN

Though pleased with urban life, I went back to rural Yorkshire once a month to visit family. On returning from one such trip, I stowed my bicycle – a bicycle which had taken me across much of the North and West Ridings of Yorkshire – in the boot of the Ford Anglia. Hankering after green fields and hedgerows, at first opportunity back in Birmingham I mounted the old steed and pedalled furiously straight out of the city. Like many principal cities, Birmingham is built in a basin: any way out is uphill, and though a gradient is of little consequence to motorized transport a cyclist feels every slight change of profile. After about thirty minutes of arduous pedalling I broke out of the city to enjoy the rolling Warwickshire countryside. Several trips into rural areas of both Warwickshire and Worcestershire followed, but in due course I grew tired of a long city haul just to glimpse a few miles of agricultural land. An idea of taking the bicycle in the boot of the car to the city boundary, parking, then cycling the rest of the way was dismissed as indolence.

I made no further attempt to flee Birmingham but took to exploring on two wheels quiet residential neighbourhoods, the backstreets, the capillaries that fed the main arterial roads. Those a mile or two from the city centre, as opposed to the affluent outer suburbs, exuded an air of secrecy, a suggestion they were holding something back. To liken them to The Casbah in the 1938 film *Algiers* would be going too far. But the silent backwaters were indeed holding something back, they were attempting to protect privacy of residents from foreign interlopers on a bicycle, for inhabitants of the West Midlands were very private people. In time, uneasiness about expeditions into secluded quarters brought them to a close, so I looked to maps for further inspiration.

The first Ordnance Survey map purchased about 1960 covered that part of the North Riding of Yorkshire in which I used to live. The amount of information exploding before the eyes as a map is unfolded was yet another momentous discovery of teen years. By the time I moved to Birmingham I had accumulated many Ordnance Survey maps of the one inch = one mile Seventh Series, all purchased for cycling trips. Sheet 131 covering Birmingham was soon added to the collection. A good part of the map was found, with little surprise, to be an extensive mass of grey-coloured built-up area.

In expeditions in and around Birmingham I had so far come across not one single railway line, but Sheet 131 revealed a mass of railway lines converging on the city centre. I set about finding them. One cycling trip took me to the Small Heath district where I encountered a wide tract of railway still signalled, astonishingly, with semaphore signals. The forest of semaphores stretching as far as the eye could see told of Great Western Railway origin, as arms moved to the lower quadrant for the proceed aspect. I could make no sense of them; I had no diagram to show how many tracks were signalled, which of the red-armed signals were homes and which were startings, and neither did I know which signal box controlled them. The delightful if baffling array of railway signals gave no prescience of another surprise in store.

To my right a plume of fluffy white smoke appeared above roof tops. After what seemed an agonizingly long time watching the smoke ball grow and grow, a steam hauled train of mixed freight finally came into view. The locomotive, now without any noticeable exhaust, slowed down its train to pass on a track separated from me by a number of sidings. It came to a stand some two hundred yards away. In a state of shock equal to that experienced upon seeing the A4 and the WD in Yorkshire (and for the same reason of encountering a steam engine when least expecting it) I remained transfixed as the medium-sized locomotive gently simmered at a distance. I contemplated cycling round streets to get a closer look, but was afraid the train might move off meantime. I did not know if a signal was holding it for another train to pass, or if it was waiting to change crew, or whether it had reached the end of its journey. After about thirty minutes I gave up hope of further action and left to explore elsewhere.

In 1966 numerous manual signal boxes were extant in the West Midlands, but having no knowledge of them and their not being marked on the one inch to one mile Ordnance Survey maps, I came across very few. Of those I did see, most were inaccessible. Only one held out hope of a close look, that was Lifford Junction on the Camp Hill route from Kings Norton to the centre of Birmingham, but after cycling round its elevated position several times, I had to conclude it, too, would keep its secrets. It appeared somewhat derelict and may have been out of use at the time.

CHAPTER ELEVEN

Between Birmingham's northern and western boundaries and Wolverhampton stretched a cluster of contiguous towns known collectively as the Black Country. In addition to Wolverhampton, names of many, oddly, began with the letter W: Walsall, Wednesbury, West Bromwich, Willenhall. My home for the second six months of the year-long stay in the West Midlands would be not in a W-town, but in Dudley. The name Black Country had been attached to the area at some point in history owing to its prevailing smokiness (though by the late 1960s many factory chimneys had ceased to belch smoke) but was misleading in that it suggested a general bleakness of character, which I found not to be the case. On the contrary, the physical geography of the area and the man-made structures placed thereon combined to provide a visual feast, contrasting sharply with the settled radial symmetry, the quiet homogeneity of Birmingham. In the Black Country each town centre, each road junction, each factory was unique. Highways corrugated by mining subsidence threaded their way across the area, not in a predictable cobweb pattern of the neighbouring big city, but in an angular, haphazard manner attempting to link every town with every town.

In the Black Country the turn of every corner and the conquering of every hill - and there were plenty of both - opened up a new vista. In this heaving, rippling, tumbling landscape a route might rise high over a wooded ridge only to plunge into a sea of council-built houses and estate roads. Look here! a massive, gaunt steelworks perches on a high plateau dominating the skyline. Look there! a dark heap of industrial spoil in which rain has carved deep gullies sits sullen and brooding. Look over there at sombre still waters of a canal making off in a straight line with overgrown towpath following obediently alongside.

Encouraged by the highly industrialized and densely populated nature of the area, railway lines of the Great Western Railway and of the London and North Western Railway strode, wriggled and burrowed there way across this riot of infrastructure. Only the latter's main line between

Birmingham and Wolverhampton paid little attention to contours as it bravely sought the straightest route between two centres, incorporating a long high embankment upon which sat Dudley Port station. Other routes appeared to have the opposite policy, following anguine alignments to avoid obstructions at all costs, by digging deep to pass under highways, by curving sharply round factories and by rising and falling like choppy sea to follow lie of the land. Particularly endearing in their weaving about were the Great Western Railway main line at Swan Village, near West Bromwich, and the London and North Western Railway route from Wednesbury to Dudley via Great Bridge and Dudley Port Low Level.

At Dudley station major reconstruction was under way during 1967. The old track layout required much reversal of trains, so was being torn out, to be replaced by a simple double junction, one line heading for Wolverhampton, the other diving under the A4037 road towards Great Bridge. A feature of the new arrangement was a new lower quadrant starting signal about half a mile north of the junction, the excessive distance being necessary to permit installation of a set of points within that half mile to serve a banana siding. Most surprisingly to me, this extensive civil engineering works required construction of a brand new mechanical signal box. Had I had more foresight, more drive, more time and more gall, I would have asked those building the signal box if I could have a closer look, but did not. It was another missed opportunity. It was another case where I was trying to do too many different things, and was unable to pay attention to something which I now feel was of great importance, the commissioning of a new mechanical signal box.

When exploring railways I usually left the Ford Anglia at lodgings and rode the bicycle because it would fit into tight corners a motor car would not. Many lineside locations offered no place to park a vehicle whereas a bicycle conveniently leant against a boundary fence. It was whilst on one such ride that I met a fellow-railway enthusiast who, too, roamed the area on bicycle, but who was specifically hunting for steam engines. To meet someone who shared an affection for railways was a refreshing change from the company I normally kept, that of colleagues from work whose lives primarily revolved around work and secondarily around boozing and womanizing. The new-found friend and I agreed to team up on joint expeditions. By this time, my ear had become attuned to the West Midlands way of speaking, so I had no difficulty understanding this local man.

To digress briefly, the West Midland dialect was most readily identified by the diphthongal change of the *ie* sound to *oi* transforming ice into oice, and by a sing-song way of speaking. It had in common with Yorkshire dialect pronunciation of the letter *u* in the word cup as a deep sound, as in bush, never the *ah* sound uttered by people from the South. The location of Birmingham was close to the southern limit of the deep *u* vowel pronunciation, if not the actual limit, a fact that placed the West Midlands dialectally in the North of England. Speakers in the Black Country differed from neighbours in Birmingham in their use of a special all-purpose pronoun-cum-verb, a word which I think would be written as um. An example of its usage would be in an exchange between two friends:

"Where um going?"

"Um going shopping."

In that instance the meanings of um were clear, but more than once I had to ask people to whom they were referring by um, which irritated them because they never had misunderstandings amongst themselves.

To return to cycling expeditions, the young man recently met told me steam engines could still be found at a certain time of day in Wolverhampton, so we agreed to meet one evening and cycle there. On arrival at the former Great Western Railway station of Wolverhampton Low Level we found, as predicted, a steam locomotive quietly simmering on one of the tracks. It was probably the station pilot, that is to say, it remained in the vicinity of the station throughout the day solely for the purpose of shunting vehicles about the platform area. It was a Class 5MT (power rating 5 mixed traffic) 4-6-0 designed by Sir William Stanier of the London, Midland and Scottish Railway. Well liked by footplate crews, the locomotives were known affectionately amongst railway enthusiasts as Black Fives.

From a distance we gazed at the engine for quite some time, but despite our unspoken wishes for it to move it remained motionless. Like naturalists in the bush watching wild game, we leant against our bicycles amidst central Wolverhampton's mix of architecture, eyes glued on the slumbering beast a distance away. But as the bright daylight gleam of urban sky gave way to vespertine shades, we reluctantly concluded the locomotive was staying put. Not wishing to make our way home in complete darkness, we had to leave the Black Five to its solitary ruminations, and dash. My friend and I made one or two more journeys by bicycle, but as my stay in the Black Country was limited, in due course I lost touch with him.

CHAPTER TWELVE

Earliest months in the West Midlands were dominated by, work aside, pleasures the conurbation had to offer. One of the first to catch the eye was Birmingham's ice rink. Since I had never skated in my life, the place allowed me to correct that character defect, but not without first having to suffer indignity of staggering about like a new-born foal whilst six-year old children sailed by with the grace of an accomplished ballerina. After about ten sessions I could complete a couple of circuits at fair speed without falling over, but never mastered what appeared to be the physically impossible feat of skating backwards.

Only a few weeks passed before the ice rink itself led to a new venture. When leaving the rink at about 21:00 hours, I began noticing exceedingly well-dressed women making their way in the opposite direction. At first I thought they were heading for a late session at the ice rink, ignoring the facts tight skirts would render skating not only problematical but foolhardy and heavy make-up would be inappropriate for hurtling round on skates. One evening I hung around to see where the women went and discovered they headed to a different part of the ice rink complex to be devoured by a small door.

To investigate the phenomenon, I forsook the ice rink one evening, dressed smartly and left lodgings by car at about 20:30 hours. On arrival at the complex, I waited till a group of apparent fashion models went by on their way to the mysterious door. I decided to walk a short distance behind them, not too close to alarm them, but close enough to give the illusion to anyone who might be interested that I was in the same party. On arrival at the voracious portal, I narrowed the gap to stand immediately behind the gaggle of young women. The fearsome door opened to illuminate pretty faces with a flood of red light. After a few words I did not hear, the women trooped inside. I shuffled ahead to the doorway to be met by a man dressed in black suit and bow tie whose demeanour, or lack of it, whose coldness and whose massive craggy appearance suggested he had been hewn from a very large block of granite. His duty was to guard the doorway; he looked down at me, a very long way down. I looked up, smiled, then turned forwards and boldly followed the women in. Granite man looked me up and down as I walked by, but did not return a smile because granite cannot smile. Neither did his rocky countenance betray thoughts (because granite cannot express emotion either) about insolence of a person who had just passed before him, an ingress Jane Austin might have described as having been gained with borrowed feathers. But granite man did let me in.

Once again I stood behind the group of young women whose progress had now been halted at a small window where money to gain entry changed hands, in one respect an encouraging sign in that it narrowed possibilities as to the character of the establishment. But it was also a disquieting development in that I had not anticipated an expensive evening. Having paid the necessary fee, which may have been ten shillings (I cannot remember) I walked along a tantalizingly long corridor whose floor, walls and ceiling were covered in thick red carpeting. The peregrination brought to mind Alice following the White Rabbit down a rabbit hole. The corridor eventually opened out into a shining, luxuriously furnished room dispensing alcoholic drinks. It was filled with women whose colourful blouses and pencil skirts revealed forms that curved in and out in the right places and did so in agreeable proportions. Some women danced in an area set aside for that. A handful of men stood around admiring the bevy of gorgeous women.

The greatest shock on entering this den of delight, the exact nature of which was yet to be revealed, was the loud thumping music that pounded incessantly against the ear-drums. The music was a form of American popular music I did not know, but more on that in due course. As time passed I would come to associate the music with ever-presence of desirable women. I would learn they were not models after all, but perfume counter sales assistants, secretaries, machinists, rubber stamp mounters and any type of woman who had the bone structure, dress sense and wherewithal to wear fashionable attire. Truth eventually materialized that the establishment now presenting such wondrous sights and sounds was my first discotheque. It would not be the last. I soaked up every moment of the new experience, until about 01:00 hours when thought of work the next day brought celebrations to a close.

On the subject of work, new friendships were forged amongst colleagues, young men in business suits, men about the age of twenty. We were afflicted with a special kind of enthusiasm and self-confidence peculiar to that age that compelled us to believe we were right on all matters and everyone else was wrong. We all had two other things in common: none were native to the West Midlands, and every one of us liked beer. The two shared characteristics converged on our feelings about local brews: some beers were superior to others; flavour of the latter group, we concluded, must have been an inexplicably acquired local taste. As part of gallivanting, one or two of us visited discotheques, but did so independently.

At the age of twenty, a man has discarded an adolescent belief that myriads of young women are waiting patiently for him to select one to be his own, and has learnt the opposite is generally true, choice is invariably made by the woman. But he still remains victim of his own male conceit by substituting an equally fatuous notion that desire of any young woman for him will always be no less than his desire for her. The fervour with which this philosophy was pursued was matched only by its failure to produce results.

In conversation at work I told a colleague of meeting a young woman in one of the city discotheques where the evening had seemed to progress satisfactorily to the extent of a date having been arranged to meet at a certain well-known landmark. (The story would be more vividly told if I could remember site of the intended tryst, but I cannot bring it to mind; it may have been in Edgbaston.)

"We'd arranged to meet at 8 o'clock, so I got there early to be safe, about twenty to eight," I told my colleague. "I waited there, but she never turned up. I waited till about twenty to nine before giving up and going home."

My colleague's visage had grown progressively more serious as the story unfolded. "What was she like?" he asked.

"Oh, not very tall. Slim, quite pretty really, with long brown crinkly hair," I replied.

"I know her. She did the same to me," said my colleague grimly.

Two men in the same work place suffering identical fate suggested the young lady habitually arranged dates at a monument only to gloatingly stand up each of her would-be beaus. For all I knew, the siren could have asked another man to meet her on the same night she was supposed to see me, and we both had been encircling the – whatever it was - in the dark looking for her, each unaware of the other. One only hopes that when this woman did finally meet someone she genuinely liked, she remembered to turn up at the notorious place to seal the friendship.

Another conversation with a colleague at work went along the following lines:

"Hey, I met a couple of really classy girls at this club on Saturday night," I gushed.

My interlocutor, a man who had lived in cities longer than I had, looked at me sourly beneath a furrowed brow, and commented with acerbity, "The number of times I've heard that said...." He was implying any man who formed such an elevated opinion of women would soon be proved wrong. On reflection, my colleague was right in that the aloofness perceived in two women had been no more than flat indifference towards the person earnestly pursuing them.

Birth of what at the time appeared to be a most promising entanglement took place in another discotheque. The evening proceeded with stunning smoothness and was encouragingly rounded off by the young lady accepting my offer of a lift home. At her front door, following a long, eager goodnight kiss and with arms still locked around each other, the object of my now blazing affection told me with disconcerting candour: "I'll have to go in now, 'cause my boyfriend lives next door and I don't want him to see us." The wound inflicted by this doorstep disclosure was so deep it peremptorily extinguished all hope of romance. Crestfallen, I released her. On seeing a bright countenance fade before her eyes, the young woman administered a mollifying peck on the cheek and smiled, but then opened the front door, melted into the dark security of her home and left me standing. Quietly but resolutely the door closed in my face.

For days I pondered the improbable circumstances of boyfriend and girlfriend living next door to one another, ultimately concluding the woman's feelings were obviously sufficiently strong to spend most of the evening with me and to share a clingy embrace at the end of it, but she clearly did not wish to see me again, her story about a boyfriend next door being merely a fib to bring an abrupt end to the dalliance.

Despite inevitable naïve misjudgements made by a citied country boy, the vast number of women available in the conurbation ensured at least one friendship did take root, but those roots proved too shallow for a sturdy romance to take hold.

The Midlands interlude, then, plunged this young man into a heady sea of sensations as he embarked on a new career, as he sampled new forms of leisure activities and as he found himself amongst great numbers of the opposite sex, the likes of which he had never before experienced. Regrettably, little time was given over to railways. Human nature tends to steer a person away from the unpleasant, so that given the choice of seeing the very last steam engine that might operate out of Wolverhampton Low Level station or spending an evening drinking with colleagues, I tended to go for the merry-making rather than the melancholy.

Thus a battle raged between on one side inviting, brightly-lit public houses and sparkling but deafening discotheques, both harbouring steel-bodied women with flawless make-up applied on already flawless complexions, and on the other side unknown, unget-at-able signal boxes that jealously guarded secrets of their intricate track layouts and complex methods of working, and the area's last steam engines making cameo appearances or huddling together in doomed engine sheds awaiting the last call. Parties on the first side won the battle in the West Midlands. But the battle would be fought again over a longer period in a new theatre where those same forces would in turn rise and fall in pre-eminence. The West Midlands was just a rehearsal. The new theatre would be Liverpool.

CHAPTER THIRTEEN

Amongst superb architecture that adorned Liverpool and proclaimed its position not only as a major port but also as England's third largest city stood a structure in French Renaissance style known as the former North Western Hotel. Behind and adjoining this building was Lime Street station. As the terminus of a direct line to London, Lime Street was the most important of three city centre stations. But from another point of view Lime Street station was no more than part of a sprawling wheel of railway lines centered on the suburb of Edge Hill. Between Lime Street station and Edge Hill four tracks ran for about one-and-a-half miles through tunnels and under bridges. From Edge Hill the main line to London Euston curved off southwards. The line to Manchester via Chat Moss carried straight on eastwards. Another spoke from Edge Hill dug a two-mile long tunnel through sandstone to emerge at the dockside station of Riverside where boat trains met ocean-going vessels. Interlaced with passenger lines were numerous freight-only tracks, including the Circular Goods Line that traced a horse-shoe shape at the eastern end of Edge Hill, and the Bootle branch that made off northwards to reach Liverpool docks.

When I took up residence in Liverpool, a move precipitated by work, little time was lost in purchasing Ordnance Survey sheet 100 which instantly revealed this complicated knot of railway in the city's geographical centre (the commercial centre being on the waterfront). From rented accommodation in the suburb of Walton, I set about exploring Liverpool's railways.

The choice between comfort of a car or hard work of a bicycle for railway expeditions – or for any other expedition for that matter – would not, for most people, be a difficult choice, but Dorothy L. Sayers enlivens the debate by having Lord Peter Wimsey say:

"Nothing is so virtuous as a bicycle."

Such lofty thoughts never consciously crossed my mind when I chose the bicycle, though I may have gone so far as to admit that sacrifice is preferable to indulgence. The bicycle was obviously more economical, but its flexibility and care-free nature weighed equally in the unwavering decision to use it. So, glowing with virtue, I pedalled off in search of railway.

I headed for the thoroughfare of Rathbone Road, which skirted the Edge Hill complex. An unmarked minor lane off Rathbone Road would, it would be revealed, place the explorer in the best position to see the whole area. A grassy bank rose from the minor lane; on top of the bank ran railway tracks. I climbed a path up the bank, a path that had been worn by countless bodies scrambling up and down. On a fine summer day in the middle of the week (my work pattern allowed such days off) the bank top presented a demi-panoramic view of railway tracks running mainly east and west but occasionally crossed by tracks in other directions, like an uncombed head of hair. Though no trains were moving, encouraging wisps of smoke here and there confirmed that for which I had hoped: steam engines were still active in Liverpool.

A soaring dome of intoxicating stillness settled on the whole area. As commerce enjoyed an afternoon nap, my feet froze to the spot whilst I sampled with relish the opium of demulcent silence.

Then, SSHHWHHHOOOMPH. The unmistakable bark of a steam engine starting up broke the spell. Again, SSHHWHHHOOOMPH. The explosions, about half a mile away, resounded throughout the area, and were accompanied by writhing balls of white smoke shooting into the atmosphere. The initial beats and matching expulsions of exhaust were vigorously repeated as a train began moving its load. In which direction I could not tell. As the locomotive accelerated, volcanic orbs of smoke rocketed into the air; exhaust beats echoed like rapid cannon fire around Edge Hill's man-made valley of a biscuit factory on one flank and railway infrastructure on the other. The commotion remained a mystery until I saw swiftly approaching a guard's van. I deduced the steam engine generating so much noise and pyrotechnics was pushing a freight train up a steep gradient towards me. With deafening *staccato* exhaust, the locomotive's ferocious assault impelled thirty assorted freight wagons as if they were some monstrous battering ram. In little time the guard's van shot by in front of me, with the guard positioned on the rear verandah. Then, as goods wagons rattled by, the train driver eased off the regulator to reduce the locomotive's output. The climb was nearing its end. Finally the steam engine itself rumbled by with exhaust smoke now faded to a wisp, the exhaust beat softened to a whisper. It was a member of the rugged Class 8F 2-8-0 freight locomotives, another highly successful London, Midland and Scottish Railway design from the office of Sir William Stanier. The 8F completed its propelling move by depositing its train in sidings east of

Rathbone Road, sidings reached by an over-bridge. Shortly afterwards the 8F, now uncoupled from its train, drifted by to pass right in front of me on its way down gradient. The ground shook under such massive weight.

I luckily witnessed several times this magnificent spectacle of steam locomotives storming the grade at Edge Hill. Most engines were 8Fs, but an occasional Black Five was seen. Though not immediately apparent, the elevated position taken up was in the middle of a marshalling yard where trains were brought to have their wagons sorted into different destinations. In modern marshalling yards trains are slowly pushed over a hump, individual wagons uncoupled and allowed to drift by gravity into sidings that will eventually make up complete new trains. Progress is checked by retarders, that is, power-operated beams that bear against wagon wheels to slow them down thereby avoiding vehicles crashing into one another at speed. Edge Hill marshalling yard was an older type of yard where wagons were slowed in their descent by manually applying the vehicles' hand-brakes. The yard was known as Edge Hill Gridiron because its layout resembled that utensil.

Not long after the 8F locomotive had passed by, the train it had just delivered began to move engine-less slowly downhill under control of shunters. It was the shunters' job to break down the train by releasing wagons one at a time to roll by gravity into sidings further down the Gridiron. One of the men chalked a number on the wagon end signifying into which siding it should go. Hand-operated points were set by another to direct the vehicle into that siding. Each wagon was detached using a long shunter's pole to unhook the chain coupling. As a freewheeling wagon went by, another shunter would run alongside, grasp the horizontal brake handle, press it downwards to apply the right amount of brake pressure and pin it in position, an operation demanding great balance and a high degree of agility and co-ordination. The footpath along which the shunter ran had to be tended scrupulously to prevent falls, much in the manner a batsman fusses over turf near his crease to prevent it unpredictably deflecting a bowler's ball.

Sidings into which wagons rolled would eventually become outbound trains. I recall an occasion when the shunter was unable to sufficiently slow a wagon's progress in time for another man to throw the right points. As a result, the wagon ended up in the wrong siding. Since the locomotive that had brought the train in had left, no means existed to retrieve the errant wagon and to place it in the right siding, the consignment would now be going to, say, Manchester instead of Carlisle; it would have to be re-sorted at Manchester. The shunter, long-chinned, lean and wiry, was a conscientious person and was genuinely upset by his gaffe. He flopped his arms by his side and tilted his head in despair as weight of the consequences came down hard on him.

In addition to being a fascinating place to watch train movements, Edge Hill had much to offer a student of signalling. Edge Hill power signal box, a modern electronic establishment as opposed to a lever frame, was in charge of the London main line between Lime Street station signal box and Allerton Junction signal box, a relatively new manual box in Liverpool's southern suburbs. Olive Mount Junction took charge of the line towards Manchester whilst a number of other mechanical boxes oversaw the network of goods lines running through Edge Hill. The only signal box in any way accessible was Pighue Lane Junction close to the lane off Rathbone Road where I had first gained access to the Gridiron. (Presumably the name of that lane was Pighue Lane).

Pighue Lane was a simple but busy two-way junction. More than once I was fortunate to witness a run-round movement. Trains first arrived from the direction of Exhibition Junction signal box, which was to the west, then proceeded through a tunnel to Olive Mount Junction signal box where the steam engine would detach and run round its train by travelling back through the tunnel on the opposite track to be re-coupled at Pighue Lane. Trains then took the right fork at Pighue Lane to head northwards for Liverpool Docks via the Bootle branch. Exhibition Junction box controlled an apparently extensive layout, but was infuriatingly out of reach to a non-trespassing train watcher.

After visiting Edge Hill a few times, anxious to miss nothing, I studied Ordnance Survey Sheet 100 for further concentrations of railway hoping to catch more steam in action. The map showed several lines meeting at Bidston on that bolus of land sandwiched between the River Mersey and the Dee estuary, the Wirral Peninsula, an area containing small seaside resorts, dormitory communities and Birkenhead's shipbuilding industry. The Mersey Ferry that plied between Liverpool's Pier Head and Birkenhead's Woodside landing stages took me and my bicycle to the Wirral. I made for Bidston via the A553 road. Close to my goal, I had to stop suddenly, for I saw a steam engine in the distance.

I had never seen a 9F. When seeing one for the first time, the eye is immediately drawn to a large space through which daylight may be seen between five pairs of driving wheels and the running plate, the running plate being a ledge running the entire length of the boiler. But it is the vast smoke deflector plates at the front end and the elongated boiler barrel that bestow such dignity, such authority, on this highly successful, immensely powerful freight engine. Introduced in 1954 to much fanfare, the Class 9F 2-10-0 was the last type of steam engine to be built in Britain, its design being credited to the British Railways Board's R.A. Riddles. In newsreels of the 1950s, building the 9Fs was described as the "end of steam", but the 1960s' sight of the 9F now slowly but sure-footedly beginning to leave Bidston with a heavy load, gave no hint of finality. As I propped myself against the bicycle on a rise overlooking the complicated railway junctions at Bidston, I had to be content with a distant view of the 9F, because I could not get close enough fast enough before the train disappeared.

I had just witnessed a shipment of iron ore beginning its journey from Bidston Docks to Shotton steelworks in North Wales. Try as I might, I could never again catch a 9F ore working at Bidston. The workings were, in the first place, dependent on there being an iron ore ship in Bidston Docks, in the second place one would have to know someone privy to the time of day trains were running in order to be sure of seeing one. The only other time I saw a 9F in live steam was a glimpse of one drifting round a triangular track formation in Walton, Liverpool.

In 1967 the abundance of steam traction around Liverpool clouded the fact that the number of steam engines on the whole British Railways network was rapidly shrinking. My attitude towards the looming demise of steam remained half-hearted. Of course I lamented passing of the steam engine, but the numbers of locomotives working locally deflected the mind away from the awful prospect that some day there would be none, thus prompting a foolish but understandable self-deception that allowed one to pretend steam traction was still going strong rather than in its final throes. The immense joy in watching steam trains go by and their sheer numbers at the time temporarily washed out anxiety about the future.

CHAPTER FOURTEEN

For several months, life drifted by in a haze of happy-go-lucky wanderings hunting for steam engines as time permitted, work being the only regimen that imposed any sort of order. Such an *insouciant* approach was not to last. I cannot now remember what eventually gripped the collar and shook sense into me that unless I moved very quickly, I would never again see a steam locomotive at work on British Railways. An article in the *Liverpool Echo* or conversation with a friend may have finally brought home the message. The looming demise of steam was not just a once-in-a-lifetime event, not even a once-in-a-millennium event, but a once-in-the-whole-history-of-civilization event where the machine that had risen to supremacy in the nineteenth century, that had literally been the engine of the industrial revolution, was now being irreversibly eliminated from Britain's national railway system. Almost in a state of panic, I began racing round to find the last steam engines. The story that follows is not a comprehensive account of the end of steam, merely what I saw of of it.

Lime Street station, but three miles from lodgings, was first stop in a frenzied search for live steam. A visit found what at one time would have been described as a ubiquitous Black Five simmering at a stand with chimney towards the buffer stops. Behind it stood a rake of empty passenger carriages the engine had presumably brought in. A small crowd of railway enthusiasts of various ages, making notes and discussing the finer points of locomotive design, gathered round the no longer commonplace engine. The driver leant from the fireman's side window (the six-foot side) for it was that side that faced the platform. His countenance was that of a middle-aged man, one of settled disposition. His squarely-structured face evinced he had balance and depth of character necessary to absorb rules and regulations, to remember gradients and speed limits, to understand signalling systems, and to be able to combine all this knowledge with the complex task of driving a steam locomotive.

The driver watched expressionless as glum enthusiasts shook their heads in sorrow. Cognizant of the need for nostalgia to give way to modernization, the driver remained emotionally neutral, his serene eyes showing neither disdain for their emotions nor sympathy for their loss. Thousands of railway enthusiasts would be grief-stricken at the loss of steam traction, but the driver's professionalism accepted the unstoppable eclipse of Victorian technology by motive power of the twentieth century. After a time, most of the despondent enthusiasts drifted away. When only a couple remained, I took a deep breath, walked up to the driver and asked, "Where did this engine come from?"

"Stafford," he replied politely, quietly, accurately.

I nodded, but that was not the answer I was looking for. I did not get the answer I was looking for because I had asked the wrong question. I had wanted to know in which engine shed the locomotive was based, not from which shed it had been transferred. Thinking back, it was obvious the engine was based at Edge Hill, so obvious the driver did not consider anyone would ask such a banal question.

I had never been a train spotter standing on platforms solely for the purpose of noting engine numbers as they passed by, but since time was fast approaching when there would be no more steam engines to spot, now seemed an appropriate moment to change that position. My notes show that a Black Five 44877 was in Lime Street Station on 5th April 1968. Whilst I cannot be absolutely certain, it seems highly likely that this notation and the vivid recollection described above refer to the same occasion. *British Railway Steam Locomotives 1948-1968* informs us that engine number 44877 was withdrawn from service in August 1968 and scrapped.

Vowing to see Edge Hill shed, I studied the Ordnance Survey map, then cycled round and round Edge Hill trying to get close to the premises, but without success. In early May 1968, Edge Hill engine shed closed, along with its neighbour Speke Junction shed. Edge Hill, the premier steam depot in Liverpool, one time home of mighty London, Midland and Scottish Railway Pacific express passenger locomotives, one of the most important sheds left in Britain and right on my own doorstep, had closed without my ever being near. Clearly, days of steam engines savagely attacking the gradient at Edge Hill Gridiron were over. The Gridiron itself was an outmoded means of marshalling traffic; it, too, was to disappear. (Some forty years later, a college stands on the site.)

The last I saw of Liverpool's fleet of steam engines was an elegiac, forlorn row of 9Fs at the otherwise deserted Speke Junction engine shed on the southern tip of the city. Stripped of their motion, these once mechanical masterpieces now stood cold, lifeless and rusting, of no further economic value other than to be cut by oxyacetylene torch into small pieces to be melted down to make – we will never know what.

CHAPTER FIFTEEN

By 1968 I was regularly if belatedly purchasing copies of railway enthusiasts' magazines. They reported that steam's defiant last stand would be acted out in three locations little known to the world at large, all in Lancashire. Taking on the aura of holy shrines to which pilgrimages must be made before they closed, names of the last three sheds will be forever engraved on the hearts of all who loved steam: Carnforth, Rose Grove and Lostock Hall. I would visit each one.

Carnforth station might be known to some as setting for the film *Brief Encounter*. The engine shed at Carnforth would eventually pass in its entirety into private ownership to become Steamtown, a celebrated haven of preserved steam, but at the time in question it was being used both by preservationists and by British Railways. I visited this town at the northern extremities of Lancashire several times before and after the steam shed changed hands. Memories of those visits blur together so I am afraid I cannot clearly remember the individual day I went there to see the final days of British Railways steam. For that reason I give no account here. My notebook does, however, record seeing Black Fives 44950 and 45305 at Preston on 4th May 1968, which seems to be the likely date of visiting Carnforth, being on my way through Preston to get there.

No cloudiness of memory surrounds the two remaining sheds, for visiting a place (or meeting certain people) only once in a lifetime is so perfectly unique it imprints on the brain an indelible image. Thus my trips to Rose Grove and Lostock Hall needed no camera to record the event. In one case though there remained an obstacle: I had not the faintest idea where Rose Grove was; I could not find it on any of my collection of Ordnance Survey maps. Fortunately, a friend far more knowledgeable than I was told me the shed was in the vicinity of Burnley, which my maps did not cover.

Accordingly I drove from Liverpool to Burnley in search of the elusive steam shed, but took with me a young woman who was my friend at the time. Fears preyed on the mind that the whole day would be spent touring round Burnley searching for the shed, but those fears proved to be ill-founded. Whilst approaching Burnley from the west, I kept glancing over to the left where railway tracks ran parallel to the main road, in case the engine shed was there. A poorly maintained building held out hope, but not expecting to find the shed so early in the expedition, I was driving too fast to stop. We therefore continued towards the centre of Burnley until a convenient turn permitted access to several side streets that eventually brought the Ford Anglia to the entrance of a steam shed. We had found Rose Grove. We sat in the car gazing at the fuliginous smoking edifice for a few moments, its frowning, restricted entrance doing little to encourage visitors.

"What do you think of it?" I asked my companion.

Now, this young woman's enthusiasm for railways had been zero before we met. After we had met it had risen to a level that could be expressed as zero + 1 Angstrom unit, the infinitesimally small increase entirely owing to a need to listen to railway explanations why I could not see her on this day and that.

"S'dirty," was all she could say in reply to the question.

"I'm going to take a look round," I said.

Leaving my friend sitting in the Ford Anglia, I stepped over the threshold dividing public from private property and, peering into the tenebrous engine shed, saw near the entrance a work-dirtied 8F simmering at rest, its tender piled high with lumpy coal, its fire moderately built in readiness for the next turn of duty. Even though the locomotive was stationary with no crew at the controls, a low but substantial roar of thousands of gallons of water close to boiling point pervaded the murk. Fires were kept lit on engines between trips to reduce time in getting up steam and to avoid excessive expansion and contraction so detrimental to the machines' structure when fires were dropped. The engine's driving wheels, at four feet eight-and-a-half inches, seemed small, but it was that very reduced wheel diameter that gave the 8F its pulling power. Two impediments halted further exploration of Rose Grove shed. First, knowledge that any steps, even the handful I had already taken, were trespass. The shed was too dingy to gauge how many more illegal steps would have to be taken to walk the length of the building: six steps were forgivable, six hundred not. Second, brown leather shoes were unsuitable for the viscous mixture of grease, ash, cinders, soot and water covering the shed floor.

I stood for a while absorbing as much of the smoky, sulphurous atmosphere as possible until the sound of a moving steam engine turned my head. Outside the shed, another 8F was making to and fro movements across pointwork, only to disappear from view behind the building. I waited a while longer, but the engine disappointingly did not re-appear, so I rejoined my grim-faced companion in the car.

"There's an engine moving about over there. I just want to see if it's coming in the shed," I said, lifting my voice as much as possible, without actually singing, in the hope of firing some interest in my companion. The unction was to no avail. She sat stony-faced and speechless. A few more minutes elapsed before it became apparent the locomotive would not be obliging with a further appearance. On reflection, presence of a work-ready engine at the end of the shed I had just inspected and disappearance of an apparently inbound engine suggested that new arrivals were attended to at and entered into the far end of the elongated shed, from which point they gradually moved up until their next turn of duty.

I would have happily stayed there an hour or two in the hope of more action, but the young woman was desperately bored and adjured that we tarry no longer. Bowing to the young woman's wishes, we left Rose Grove, a charming appellation for a place that failed to charm either in the field of aesthetics or in the opportunities to enjoy steam's last fling. We returned to Liverpool.

The last engine shed of the trio, Lostock Hall, was, I was told, next to a station. It was found on Ordnance Survey sheet 94 to be not far from Preston. A train journey would be appropriate, one I would make on my own. On arrival at Preston station, I approached a porter, a short man with broad shoulders but otherwise of spare frame, for advice.

"Could you tell me please where I can get a train to Lostock Hall steam shed?" I asked.

The man glared at me as if I had just mouthed the foulest vituperation imaginable. He squared himself, glared, tensed his muscles and snapped, "Lostock Hall! I wish they'd blow the bloody place up."

He swivelled his torso in an incipient motion to take off without answering, thought better of it, and turned to address me again. "Platform nine," he snarled, swiping the air in the direction of that platform.

I fled the man who was fed up with steam lovers asking how to get to Lostock Hall, purchased a ticket, and boarded a diesel multiple unit on platform nine. After a short journey, I alighted at the simple urban halt of Lostock Hall, walked to the end of the platform and down the platform ramp to stand at the entrance to Lostock Hall engine shed. A far more modest facility than either Carnforth or Rose Grove, it was as wide as it was deep. Sunshine poured into the shed's yawning entrance lending it a cheery, friendly air, which seemed to legitimize unofficial visits. As puddles of dirty water were the only obstruction to a visitor on foot, I felt no trepidation in passing through the welcoming rictus and entering the shed.

To my surprise, most of the twenty-two engines there had been cleaned, or partially cleaned. I would learn at a later date that a band of enthusiasts called, enigmatically, either the Merchant Neverers or the Master Neverers, went round cleaning steam engines in these final days. Such an act would have been unthinkable at any other time, in part because cleaners were once employed to do just that, in part because trespassers clambering about steam locomotives would not have been tolerated. It seemed authorities looked the other way as the end of steam drew close, which may be explained by some of those in charge being railway enthusiasts themselves and by those who were not perhaps feeling sorry for steam fans who were about to see the object of their affections wiped out.

Notes show that at Lostock Hall on 14th June 1968 were Black Fives 44713, 44806, 44816, 44950, 44971, 45149, 45212, 45388 and 45407 plus 8Fs 48115, 48253, 48293, 48294, 48323, 48335 and 48546. Additionally, Black Fives 45305 and 45436 were cold – or dead, to use railway terminology - and may have been at the end of their lives. Also at Lostock Hall were three dead Class 4MT 2-6-0s to the designs of H.G. Ivatt, a successor to Sir William Stanier, numbered 43019, 43027 and 43106. Number 43106, tucked away at the back of the shed, was rubbed and burnished to a brilliance unseen in an engine; the locomotive must have had a special place in someone's heart. Also seen at Preston on the way to and from Lostock Hall were Black Fives 44897 and 45353 plus 8F 48723.

As I wandered up and down rows of locomotives at Lostock Hall feeling the heat radiating from those still in active service, noting the coldness of those not, I yearned for some kind of light engine movement as assurance steam was still alive and well, albeit near the end of its existence. But it was not to be, all engines stood motionless and unattended. Once I had taken in all there was to take in, there seemed little point in lingering. And as the passenger train timetable left few options for the journey home, I left. So many locomotives destined for oblivion in two month's time yet still in fine external condition - all crammed into a small shed - evoked the emotion of an animal lover visiting a home for stray cats and dogs coming away with a feeling of heart-breaking helplessness at being unable to do anything about their ultimate fate.

CHAPTER SIXTEEN

It was said that withdrawal of steam traction from British Railways was too hasty, that many engines had decades of useful life in them. Indeed, the standard classes, that is, those such as the 9Fs designed by British Railways, could not have been older than British Railways itself, which came into being in 1948. Additionally, many Black Fives were built after nationalization. The official response appears to have been that strong financial arguments existed for rapidly doing away with steam. Perhaps another factor was that British Railways wanted to change its image. Whatever the justification for the decision, the last three weeks of British Railways steam in 1968 were a far cry from times I knew as a lad in the 1950s when we enjoyed a cavalcade of steam trains at the bottom of the garden - or at least across the field from the bottom of the garden. Our family was not unique in that privilege. A railway network far more extensive than it is now employing mostly steam traction ensured my siblings and I were not the only children living close to railway lines, not the only children spellbound by the magic of steam. Now, as the steam era drew to a close, many of those who had adored steam as children and who now wanted to savour its final moments had to travel great distances to north-west England. I was lucky in that work had taken me to Liverpool, close to the steam engine's final stronghold, but even I had to travel many miles to see the last workings.

Visits to the last three steam sheds had seen plenty of locomotives, but just about all were stationary. In order to see steam at work, I pored over Ordnance Survey maps and selected an open location near Lancaster on the West Coast Main Line that looked promising. Driving there on a perfect summer's day, I waited an hour, but no steam engines appeared. Then, as if from nowhere, the familiar smoke-box door design of a Stanier engine rumbled into view. It was but a light engine, an 8F travelling in the Up (southwards) direction. As it drew nearer, I leant over the boundary fence as if in a sub-conscious effort to reach out and touch the machine. As I gazed at the locomotive passing in a shallow cutting below, my heart sank and my face saddened at a spectacle that was about to disappear. The driver beckoned the fireman over to his side to see the figure now watching their progress. They returned my gaze. Footplate crews of course had no part to play in the accountancy dictum that steam must come to an end. Formerly seeing their role as essential but unsung components of British Railways, footplate crews now found themselves focus of eyes that revered their status as final custodians of beloved machines, of eyes that mourned passage of motive power whose controls they skillfully operated, of eyes that desperately besought the men not to abandon their charges. On seeing my dejection, the traincrew became downcast too. As with all passing steam engines, the moment came and went too quickly, with the locomotive and sympathetic crew trundling off into the distance to exit from view as quickly as they had entered.

Any more steam engines at this location seemed unlikely, so I drove to Lancaster station in the early evening hoping for more activity. On Lancaster's Down platform, I joined three other railway enthusiasts, including a boy of about twelve years, where we would be blessed with a rapid succession of steam movements. First, a lengthy express freight stormed by on the Up Main handled with ease by a Black Five. What greater final tribute to the power of steam could there be than a fiery Black Five roaring by at fifty miles per hour hustling a long fitted freight? Next, an 8F-hauled mixed freight approached from the south. It diverted off the main line, took the Down platform line and slowly passed right in front of us. We could not believe out luck! With brakes grinding, the engine came to a gentle halt in a bower of softly swirling steam in front of a red colour light signal at the platform end. The locomotive now stood a short distance from the band of steam lovers. Oddly, not one of us approached the footplate crew to ask their destination, their home shed, or reason for their quiescence. Perhaps if only one of us had been there, an approach might have been made, but in the presence of others we exercised restraint. No one wished to appear juvenile - not even the juvenile. Neither did we talk to one another. Self-consciousness, insularity or diffidence may have impeded conversation. A more likely explanation is that such discourse would have been communal appreciation, which does not come easy, for the love of steam (like love for a woman) is intensely personal.

An explosion of steam on the Down Fast announced a northbound express freight. In little time the steam engine tore by, but we saw only a narrow slice between stationary freight wagons in front of us; only one short blast of steam found its way between the gap as the locomotive flew by. All too soon the speeding freight with guard's van swaying in the rear was gone. It left four people standing on the platform stunned by the speed at which the locomotive swept its urgent, rattling train through Lancaster. It left them frustrated at being deprived of a better view and saddened by the thought they would soon never, ever again be able to enjoy the exhilarating, breath-taking, unstoppable charge of a steam-hauled express freight train. Why did it all have to end?

After a short while, the colour light signal at the platform end changed from red to yellow revealing that the train in front of us had been sidetracked in favour of one that had just torn through. Seconds later, a small audience enjoyed the rare privilege of witnessing close-at-hand the incomparable drama of a steam engine starting from dead stop. With the driver's first tug on the regulator, a deafening bark from the 8F's chimney was followed by another, then another, then another, each blast of wriggling grey smoke coming quicker than the one before. Four besotted spectators admired the smoothly gyrating system of rods, glistening with grease, attached to the driving wheels that controlled steam intake to the cylinders, the Walschaerts valve gear. The goods train triumphantly snaked out onto the main line and accelerated. Under a reddening northern sky, the twilight of steam slogged resolutely into the twilight of the day. With no more steam traction in sight on this pleasant July evening, I left Lancaster station for home.

Despite obscuration of the Down express freight, I and my compeers had been treated to a glorious procession of machines we had journeyed to Lancaster to see. But the glory had lacked proper appreciation of it; only four spectators had watched, and then in absolute silence. The show had deserved a football stadium-sized crowd to rise to their feet and roar deliriously as the Up express freight tore through like a winning goal, to groan in despair as view of the Down express freight was withheld like a missed penalty, to join in the beat of the 8F starting up as if chanting ecstatically the home team's name. But no. The glorious show had to make do with four reserved Englishmen keeping to themselves the absolute delight in all they had just seen.

The end was nigh. Regularly scheduled steam motive power would cease on British Railways on Saturday 3rd August 1968. It seemed likely that on Monday 29th July the local Independent Television station, Granada Television, would include in a news broadcast an item on steam's demise. The guess would prove correct. I wanted to see the broadcast but since conflicting disciplines of frugality (avoiding spending money if at all possible) and hedonism (squandering whatever was left after being frugal) forbade ownership of a television set, I asked my companion of the time if I could watch the news at her house. She agreed.

It was Monday evening in the last week of steam. In one of thousands of modest dwellings that, in contrast with architectural gems elsewhere, spread anodyne uniformity across Liverpool to give the city its homogeneous character, a young lady, her elder brother who had happened by, and I sat on a sofa in front of a television set patiently waiting. The Granada Television newsreader, a man of smart appearance aged about thirty, after disposing of other news items, turned to the report we were waiting for. In introducing the filmed report, he said all remaining steam locomotives in Britain would be withdrawn from regular service at the end of the week.

The film would prove to be as evocative as any on the subject of steam traction. The camera crew had found a highway that ran parallel to railway tracks, and had somehow ascertained when a steam-hauled train would be due, or perhaps they had just waited. The subject of the film in other circumstances would not have been considered noteworthy, for it would be nothing more than an 8F 2-8-0 doing what it had been doing for the last twenty years hauling a goods train. But this goods train would be one of the very last on British Railways to be hauled by a steam engine.

The television crew's van kept pace with the train, keeping squarely in picture a full-length broadside shot of the locomotive, which was neither fighting hard against a grade nor coasting downhill, but simply progressing with constant and moderate effort. A continuous side-on view itself is a rarity in filming trains. A narrative ran for a short while, of which I have no recollection. Then, displaying immense sensitivity to the allure of steam, the commentary ceased, to hand over airwaves to the lone voice of the steam engine. The film now not only showed rotations and swayings of the Walschaerts side motion and a banner of dusky smoke billowing from the chimney, but also allowed the audience to hear without interruption the pronounced rhythmic drumming beat of the locomotive's exhaust. The film captured exquisitely all in steam that enchants its followers. But the newsreel went a stage further: by keeping pace with the train, it was able to hold in suspension, to extend that otherwise oh so brief but spectacular crescendo of a steam engine passing right in front of the observer. Emotional impact of the broadcast was heightened by the fact that any film, still or moving, edits out all extraneous material above, below and to the side of the subject matter, and focuses attention on a rectangle, in this case the screen of a black and white television set.

For a minute or two the film gloriously gave the viewer one of the best views ever of a steam engine at work, but the record could not go on for ever. The television crew kept abreast of the locomotive until it was no longer possible to do so, until the highway on which their vehicle travelled veered away from the railway track alignment. At that juncture, the steam engine and its train slowly curved away to steadily increase the distance between it and its observer, eventually to dwindle into the distance. It was a parting of the ways, metaphorically and in reality, with the steam freight train going down the line to extinction and the television van and crew continuing into the future with the rest of civilization.

At this final, crushing view, when all I wanted to do was to reach into the television set and pull the steam engine back, the throat arched, muscles under the chin tightened and moisture in the eyes almost closed them. On a living room sofa three viewers remained momentarily silent as the film ended. My friend and her brother looked at me then at each another. On seeing how irretrievably upset I was, the young woman got up from the sofa and walked out of the room in disgust at such a shameful display of unmanliness. Her brother coloured somewhat and squirmed in his seat, unable to comprehend how a railway train could almost reduce a man to tears.

The television station handed its airwaves back to humans in the form of the Granada newsreader who had introduced the item. He was now moist-eyed with down-turned mouth; he appeared somewhat shaken. Uneasily, he moved on to the next piece of news. It was clear he was not a railway fan, for had he been so, he would have been unable to speak; he would have crumpled into a blubbering heap at the attempt. The report had moved him. Perhaps, like most men, he had liked trains when a boy, but had forgotten their appeal and had left them behind in childhood. The film clip may have reminded him how much he used to enjoy watching steam engines, then only to tell him there would be no more. Or the man may simply have not realized how moving a steam engine at work really was.

CHAPTER SEVENTEEN

Footage broadcast by Granada Television was the last normal steam working I would ever see, as all such rostered activity came to an end on Saturday 3rd August 1968. *The Railway Magazine* documented the very last steam goods train on that date to be the Heysham to Carnforth box van train, code number 6P52, hauled by Standard Class 4MT 4-6-0 number 75019. However, a total of four locomotives that began their shift on Saturday worked on minor duties through till Sunday, the very last one being Black Five 45212 seen at dawn shunting the 23:45 Euston sleeper train at Preston.

British Railways were however to allow two special additional days of steam traction. On Sunday 4th August enthusiasts' groups were allowed to charter their own last steam specials. The following Sunday, the 11th, British Railways ran its own special.

After studying itineraries for the 4th August excursions and after studying Ordnance Survey maps, a location was found in Lancashire (one that I am now unable to pinpoint) where three steam specials would go by. I inculcated upon my woman friend the significance of this date, that such a show would never, ever be seen again. She querulously agreed to go along.

Blessed with good weather, we positioned the Ford Anglia at the roadside and joined about fifty other railway enthusiasts in a field bordering a curved embankment along which trains would pass. After about half-an-hour's wait, all were rewarded by the spectacle of two excursions sweeping regally by about twenty minutes apart, one of which was double-headed. All engines had been immaculately cleaned, doubtless by the Merchant Neverers, and appeared to be in excellent running order. Heads poking from carriage windows looked down upon a host of camera lenses looking back up, like reflections in a pool. Fifty cameras clicked, clicked and clicked again to record steam's swan song. This peasant took no photographs, but simply stood and watched. If anyone had asked why I took no pictures, I would have answered that it was far better to absorb every last detail of the pageant with one's eyes rather than to bury one's head in the technicalities of photography and miss actually seeing the trains go by. (The argument paid no regard to the necessity of recording on film this never-to-be-repeated event, and camouflaged the parsimony of the individual making it.) On that day we could have stayed longer to see a third steam excursion, but my non-enthusiast companion was becoming increasingly restless, so we left.

On Sunday 11th August, for fifteen guineas one could join British Railways' very last steam train. It was out of my pocket, and also beyond the financial reach of many who would have liked to have ridden the train. Black Five 45110 took the train from Liverpool to Manchester, Standard Class Pacific 7MT 4-6-2 number 70013 *Oliver Cromwell* took over from Manchester to Carlisle via Blackburn and Hellifield, Black Fives 44871 and 44781 double-headed the return to Manchester along the same route where 45110 once again took charge for the final leg back to Liverpool. Thus all ended at Liverpool Lime Street station, just three miles from home. On that otherwise pleasant afternoon, I made my way down town to the concourse of Lime Street station to join a crowd of enthusiasts, pressmen and television crews awaiting steam's final hour. The advertised arrival time passed, but twenty minutes later heightened activity amongst the crowd heralded the incoming train. Stanier Black Five 45110 glided smoothly into the station coming to a gentle, sizzling halt a short distance from the buffers amid a hail of camera flashes.

To some the Black Five was the antithesis of the kind of locomotive that should have been used on this grand if solemn occasion, a named Stanier Pacific 4-6-2 of either the Princess Royal Class or the Duchess Class would have been more appropriate. The engine chosen did not even have a name, just a serial number. Despite misgivings by some, it was upon a humble Black Five, a mixed traffic locomotive of well-balanced if unremarkable, even nondescript appearance, that the honour befell. Perhaps like evolution, the highly specialized may enjoy limited success, but the all-purpose survive.

A crowd swarmed round the cab of locomotive 45110 to talk to the driver, an overnight celebrity, who bowed his head to speak to them on the platform below, and perhaps to sign autographs. Questions can be imagined. "What was your top speed?" "How old is this locomotive?" "Will you miss steam engines?" The arched body of the driver became submerged in the gathering as he responded to enquiries as best he could. No questions were fired at the fireman who stood bolt upright behind the driver. With sweat reducing his hair to tangled seaweed and more sweat pouring down his temples, the fireman silently surveyed the clamouring throng beneath him as he vigorously rubbed his streaming face, neck and upper torso with a rough towel. Doubtless the fireman had worked furiously to maintain a good head of steam as the crew tried to make up lost time. The last couple of miles into Lime Street station were downhill which would have allowed the man to recuperate, but now that the locomotive was at a stand without a cooling draught, ever-present heat radiating from the boiler toasted the already baked fireman.

I could not get close to number 45110 for admirers (or mourners) still milling round. The driver continued to entertain the crowd whilst the drenched fireman looked on. As a few spectators began to drift away, I gazed upon the last steam engine and pondered how long to stay. A part of me said make the most of the day and wait until the locomotive moves off into the gloomy depths of Lime Street tunnels, whilst a part of me said to linger to the bitter end would only prolong what was a devastatingly sad occasion. Events of the preceding weeks had wrung out all solicitousness, all regrets, all melancholy about the end of steam, such emotions having been replaced by resignation about its inevitability, by acceptance of the hopelessness of wanting otherwise, by recognition that life must go on after steam. Even so, examination of the subconscious penetralia would probably have revealed an underlying feeling that a great wrong had been perpetrated.

I decided I had had enough of the funereal event, and left for the street, pausing at the edge of the concourse to steal one last glance. Number 45110, once an anonymous general purpose locomotive now propelled to fame as Britain's last steam engine, still simmered as a modest crowd clung to the relic of what was imminently to become a bygone age. "No more," I said to myself, and fled the station to return home to Liverpool's suburbs.

Endings are frequently not the clean guillotine-cut they are perceived to be. To a casual observer engine number 45110, still emitting a gentle roar at the buffer stops in Lime Street station, marked the end of the line for steam traction, figuratively and in actuality. Such an observer would not have realized that once empty carriages had been drawn away, the locomotive would have had to reverse out of the station under its own power. In fact later that day engine 45110 travelled back to its home depot of Lostock Hall. Even that was not the very last British Railways steam operation.

The Standard Class 4-6-2, also known as the Britannia Class, with clean lines, high riding plate and prominent smoke deflectors, must be a strong contender for the title of most beautifully proportioned locomotive ever built. Number 70013 *Oliver Cromwell*, the last working representative of the class, after participating in the special train on 11th August was destined for preservation in East Anglia. Unannounced, it travelled overnight under its own steam from Lancashire to reach Norwich on Monday, 12th August. (One wonders how many crew changes were necessary to move a steam engine across such a lengthy cross-country route.) It is understood Black

Five 44871, which also participated in the 11th August special, was also in steam on the 12th.

Details of these minor moves after the main journey serve no useful purpose other than to clarify for the pedant exactly when steam did end. But no discussion about hours and minutes can alter the fact that at some point in the year 1968 fires were dropped for the very last time on main line British Railways steam. Though the factitious fifteen guinea special of 11th August 1968 is the accepted last day, for me the death of steam took place in front of a television set on 29th July 1968. The broadcast brought to a close adoration of steam engines that began with Class A3-hauled Pullman passenger trains, Classes WD and J27 goods trains and Class J21 pick-up trains parading through Bickle, that continued with opportune sightings in Yorkshire and the West Midlands, that was rejuvenated by Edge Hill's exhilarating 8Fs and Black Fives, and that neared its end with a desperate race to catch as many steam engines as possible in the final weeks.

Even those who had but a passing interest surely could not fail to be moved by events of August 1968. But it was of course the seasoned enthusiast who suffered most. The steam engine that had infused into countless followers a love of its power, its majesty, its aroma, its gallery of movement, its orchestra of sound, was now a love lost to those followers of steam. A nation mourned.

CHAPTER EIGHTEEN

We remember well events in life that transported us to ecstasy briefly or that plunged us into despair, perhaps not so briefly, and we might even remember circumstances that brought about only a moderate elevation of mood or those that we found only mildly disconcerting. But recollections rarely dip into periods of life where nothing of any significance occurred, where daily comings and goings were marked neither by exhilaration nor scabrousness (but which, paradoxically, we might look upon as good times when the sword of adversity strikes). One of those bland periods of existence followed the end of steam.

By the time the final, final steam engine ran on British Railways in August 1968, most emotions about the loss had been disembogued and replaced by a period of reasoning that, in order to be at peace with the steam ban, took sides with British Railways. I told myself sentimentality had no place in the modern world, even in a state-owned enterprise such as British Railways. Railways throughout the world could not cling to a high-maintenance, Victorian mode of power requiring two people on the footplate at all times when other forms of propulsion, diesel and electric, enjoyed lower costs and could get by with only one man at the controls. There were a couple of areas where steam enjoyed superiority over diesel, notably the relative ease with which a crawl speed could be maintained, and better braking through greater weight, but in arguing these minor advantages, I was only trifling with my own logic since there was not the remotest chance British Railways would reverse their perspicuous decision and bring back steam engines into general traffic.

The above mental peregrinations that allowed life to proceed after steam were lubricated in their task by dosages of Walker's Bitter, a delicious beer with a nutty flavour and slightly soapy texture that made the job of consuming it less than onerous. Close proximity of a public house to a new place of employment proved a temptation too great. I would frequently adjourn to the premises after work to consume enthusiastically several pints of nectar, to unsteadily catch a bus home, but then only to flop onto the bed incapable of anything. Wastefulness of the routine quickly became apparent, after which a more measured approach to quaffing prevailed. Another distraction of the time that ironically, and even disrespectfully, coincided with the nadir of steam was the zenith of fashion hemlines. Heart-racing fleshy exhibitionism diverted a man's mind from anything he was thinking about whenever a wearer of the exiguous garment was close by. The apparel was so short it was pronounced a hazard to passing motorists. With two powerful and worldly forces of assuagement at work, the dispossession of steam engines was left behind to pursue brighter matters elsewhere.

But weeks of carefree living were numbered. Thoughts kept returning to Class A3 locomotives gliding effortlessly through Bickle with Pullman trains, to Class WDs pounding through the same station with their distinctive clanking motion, to more recent experiences of Class 8Fs blasting up Edge Hill Gridiron propelling heavy loads. But it was the final hours of regularly scheduled steam traction on 3rd August 1968 that haunted me most. On that date steam locomotives were at work as if it were just another day, the next they were all gone. Absoluteness of the steam ban became unbearable, how could the end be so final? How could something that had brought delight to millions cruelly come to an abrupt n again? It was like a bad dream.

I hate parting with anything. Some losses are irretrievable, such as bereavement or a relationship that has run its course. Otherwise I cling like a limpet to things that go back a long time, such as a long-standing friendship, an old reference book, behaving in a reasonable manner. It was this long-held view that anything of value should be cherished, should be retained at almost any cost, that eventually expelled acceptance of the ban and brought me round to questioning the finality of steam on British Railways.

In an agonizing period of questioning my own questioning, I vacillated between on the one hand dismissing the idea of seeing main line steam again as dream fodder and on the other hand of vowing not to rest until I had done something – anything - that stood a chance of reversing the steam ban. Silent conversations with myself distilled into the notion that steam engines were an essential part of British tradition. For them to be missing was almost as great a hiatus as, say, the letter K missing from the alphabet. The language could get by without the letter K, but is it not far more preferable to keep the letter when it is already in place? So it was with steam.

Over the course of several weeks, the concern progressively occupied more and more of one's thoughts, until nothing else mattered but the emancipation of steam.

CHAPTER NINETEEN

The next year or two would prove to be if not the most important period in the life of the author, the most celebrated. Regrettably, I no longer have records of what took place, so what is now told must rely purely on memory. I think 1969 was the key year.

The British Railways ban on steam locomotives would be a formidable obstacle to overcome as they owned the rails and could do whatever they pleased with tracks. Any one individual, particularly a person of no great standing, would obviously be foolhardy to take on such a monolithic structure as a state industry, therefore contact would have to be made with other parties. To explain steps taken in that direction, a disclosure must now be made concerning the narrative covering the end of steam.

The country did not suffer complete annihilation of steam engines in August 1968. One survivor was British Railways' Vale of Rheidol line where narrow gauge steam locomotives continued to operate. Another was preserved *ex*-London & North Eastern Railway Pacific A3 locomotive *Flying Scotsman* whose existing contract permitted it to run on main lines for some time after the summer of 1968. But of far greater significance were scores of steam engines saved from destruction by preservation societies who bought them from British Railways at scrap value. This information was not revealed in preceding chapters, for, to have mentioned preservation whilst describing British Railways' final withdrawal of steam traction would have enervated an account of the devastatingly mournful nature of that withdrawal.

To elaborate on the preservation movement, many years prior to 1968, even when steam was still going strong, fans of the steam railway with enough foresight and enough drive had begun raising funds to purchase redundant equipment from British Railways in order to preserve that which they loved. In some cases whole branch lines were purchased. In other cases societies were set up solely for the purpose of buying and restoring to running order one particular steam locomotive. The two were often intertwined, so that one group operating a branch line would utilize motive power owned by another group, some individuals having an interest in both entities. Such proliferation of preservation schemes inevitably resulted in setting up a body to co-ordinate efforts. It was that very organization of railway preservation societies which I thought would be my best hope and to which I would write outlining a case for challenging British Railways' steam ban.

Many hours were expended - hours spent riding the bus to work, watching laundry revolve in the launderette, laying awake at night, standing in a bar drinking Walker's Bitter – mentally draughting out what would eventually be a very long letter. Thinking whilst drinking accounted for most of the time spent ruminating, and may well have been the most productive. I have little recollection of the contents of the missive (which is surprising considering its length) that was eventually dispatched, but its main suggestion was the setting-up of a committee (which all good bureaucrats will agree is the first step in dealing with any problem) that would attempt persuading British Railways to allow carefully managed steam specials over main lines. Arguments were put forward that such specials would be an additional form of income using resources that would otherwise be lying idle at weekends. In an ill-founded belief that the longer a committee's name the more authoritative it would sound and therefore the greater chance of success it would have, I suggested a title of National Steam Locomotive Owners Joint Negotiating Committee. I offered to act as secretary.

Posting the letter brought immense relief. The vexatious problem of what to do about the steam ban, though by no means solved, had at least been placed on the road to solution. Or so I hoped. More importantly, the quandary was no longer unhealthily imprisoned in me, where it disturbed sleep and interfered with more frivolous pursuits, but was disseminated amongst other parties. It was not a case of dumping the problem on others, but of seeking help in finding a solution. Having volunteered to take care of paperwork and hoping people could be found to sit on the committee, I patiently awaited a reply.

CHAPTER TWENTY

After a lapse of time an envelope arrived in the post bearing the preservationist organization's insignia instantly revealing the sender, which envelope I nervously and impatiently ripped apart to reach its contents. The letter extended an invitation to attend a gathering of the aforementioned body of preservationists, which I duly accepted.

A few weeks later I was at that meeting. As business got under way, about one hundred enthusiasts listened to debates concerning different railway preservation schemes up and down the country. Here were men who could argue the validity of using tractive effort to measure a steam locomotive's merit, men from all walks of life who would don overalls and be covered in filth to care for the loves of their lives, men who were in charge of a sweep of semaphore signals as appealing as any landscape planted by Capability Brown. A small number of women shared these attributes. Later in the meeting the subject arose of a certain letter received.

The chairman of the assembly, sartorially confident and with beaming countenance, spoke with a well-educated, resounding voice. "We received a letter," he began, "a very long letter, I should add," his voice lowering and hurrying over this middle part of the sentence, "suggesting we should set up a committee to try to get BR to overturn their ban on steam. The letter is from..." The chairman broke off his address, donned a pair of round-rimmed spectacles, bowed his head, and hastily grubbed amongst papers in front of him for the writer's name. Not finding it, he spoke in low voice to someone beside him, "What's his name?" Between them, the two men at last found a letter, and the chairman resumed his booming oratory.

"The letter is from a Mr. M. Deaver of Liverpool. Stand up Mr. Deaver."

Not used to public prominence, I was already fidgeting at the proclamation so far. When asked to rise, embarrassment painted the face. Nevertheless, I rose, raised my hand, and grinned. The chairman stared briefly at the awkward sight ten rows in front of him, then said, "Mr. Deaver will be secretary of the committee. Thank you Mr. Deaver."

Numb with shock at already being appointed committee secretary, I clumsily sat down.

The chairman continued on the matter of steam returning to the main lines. "This is an absolutely super idea," he said, piling copious emphasis on the syllables *ab* and *sup* in a manner of speaking found amongst educated people from the southern half of England. Such manner of speaking would be largely supplanted in later times by Estuary English. "We think a total ban on steam by British Railways," said the chairman, "is completely unreasonable, especially when they could be making money out of us. So we've got to do what we can to make them change their mind."

The chairman looked towards the ceiling for inspiration, twirling his spectacles in his right hand whilst doing so. On deciding nothing more could be added at this juncture, he looked at me and said, "See me after the meeting, Mr. Deaver." He then moved on to the next item on the agenda. It is possible some of those present representing preserved lines were antipathetic to main line steam as such excursions might draw crowds away from their own operations. If there were such objections, none were voiced.

The symposiarch, though maintaining a polite and business-like manner, ploughed through the agenda with formidable directness and enthusiasm. After the meeting, I delayed approaching him because I knew there would be many with whom he would wish to speak. Whilst mingling with the crowd, I overheard one of the organization's officers talking about my letter. "When we got this letter," said the man, "we thought it was from someone like a retired army colonel. Then this young fellah stands up..."

I was startled at hearing this, and moved off to another part of the large, crowded room lest the interlocutor spot me, which would have been an embarrassment for both of us. I had no idea my expatiation would come over in such fashion; there had been no intention to be overtly authoritative. I had spent endless hours thinking about the right words to use, and had drawn on several years' training in public service to put together an impassioned plea. This combination of official language and passion had apparently been interpreted as authority. Concerning the description of young fellah, in 1969 I was twenty-three years old. I suppose I was relatively young compared to the majority at the meeting.

In another part of the room an opportunity presented itself to meet the chairman. "Ah, Mr. Deaver," said the chairman as he outstretched his arm to beckon me closer. "Splendid idea. Now, what I'm going to do is get together some people I know who'd be good men to have on the committee. And I have an idea for someone who'll be an excellent chairman. I'll let you know everyone's names, then we can get together. It'll be the Return to Steam Committee, the name you suggested was too long-winded. We want something snappy, something that says what we're doing. I'll be in touch."

As the chairman swung round to dive into another intensive conversation with a man patiently waiting, the grandiose name I had struggled to put together over pints of Walker's, the National Steam Locomotive Owners Joint Negotiating Committee, shattered into tiny fragments like a clay pigeon. Return to Steam Committee was indeed punchier, and was the name that would carry.

CHAPTER TWENTY-ONE

In due course the chairman sent names and addresses of four men who, in addition to the chairman himself, would make up the Return to Steam Committee. Information then came to hand that the first meeting would take place at one of the member's residence in the Home Counties. Following directions, I drove the Ford Anglia from Liverpool to the address given. As I travelled further south in beautiful spring weather, contours softened, vegetation grew more lush and trees embraced country seats with greater eagerness. At these homes shrubs, grasses and informal flowerbeds melted into bricks and mortar as if all were cast from the same mould. The last few miles of country lanes saw laden boughs and luxuriant grasses spilling onto asphalt surfaces.

Directions had been faultless, I drove straight to the given address. As I parked in a driveway, our host appeared and directed me to the back lawn. There, with introductions out of the way, six men in open-necked shirts and rolled-up sleeves lolled in various postures on a rich turf to bask in sunshine without *impedimenta* (save the secretary's notepad and pen laying at the ready). Cautiously but amicably they eyed up those not previously met. I was a stranger to all except the organization chairman.

First member of the Return to Steam Committee was linked to a group preserving one of the biggest and most powerful steam locomotives ever to run in Britain. This giant of steam was currently trapped on a very short length of track leaving no room for the machine to flex its very considerable muscles, never mind to run at speed. The man was from the West Midlands, and typified men from the country's heartland in having broad shoulders, a strong neck, and bulldog determination to succeed. He was a health care professional, and spoke with the kind of soothing self-confidence one needed to hear when being looked after. As with all men of position, his life was full; he would wonder how I found time to be the committee's secretary.

The locomotive with which the second committee member was associated was also marooned on a short stretch of track, so he, too, had a vested interest in easing the ban on main line steam. This tall, athletically-built man with an impressive head of black wavy hair had been a keen sportsman when younger and continued his interest in football by fervently supporting a nearby First Division football club. A northerner employed in commerce, this man's down-to-earth approach would prove to be a valuable asset. Aware not only of our homologous membership of the committee as northerners but also of my relatively junior status, he tended to watch over me.

The career of the third committee member brought him in contact with the British Railways Board thus securing a priceless conduit to the opposition. He was a tall man, his impressive stature being matched only by his boundless intellect. Despite his towering over most people in both height and mental capability, he retained the mildest of manners, had a ready smile, and always spoke in soft but cultured tones. Lambent eyes revealed great depth of thought accompanying each utterance.

The fourth member was the chairman of the preservationist body, the man who had first appointed me as committee secretary. His key position in the movement required perception, even-handedness and a clarity of thought necessary to deal with preservation schemes that often stirred up a maelstrom of emotions. An authority on military affairs, he prided himself in being a manager of men. His diplomatic skills were a vital ingredient in the committee mix. His effervescent self-confidence and irrepressible enthusiasm inspired all who met him. In civil service parlance, his position on the committee was that of *ex-officio* member.

The committee was honoured to have as its chairman an international figure from the world of the arts. Again a tall man, his chairmanship lent to the committee not only his household name but exuberance, charisma and an unshakable belief that the campaign could and would succeed. As with all other members, his motivation was an inextinguishable passion for steam engines. The warm, open manner in which he addressed everyone he met belied the celebrity status of a man whose work was admired by millions.

Phillumenist, philogynist, the sixth member of the committee acted as its secretary, and worked very hard at his place of employment shuffling around pieces of paper. Neither tall nor broad, the impact this man had on the world at large could best be described as negligible. Achievements included winning a bag of flour at a church raffle in Thirkleby and being able to instantly recognize an excellent pint of Walker's Bitter when he tasted one. He boasted winning a dancing competition in Kingstanding doing The Twist, but this was said to be all torque.

Its secretary aside, the Return to Steam Committee brought together some of the most important and some of the most influential people in the British steam preservation movement. In their effusive personalities, in their social standing, in their sheer physical presence they towered over me. Though a garden shed compared to these pillars of society, I felt neither unworthiness nor inadequacy in their company, only awkwardness. However, this was no time for introspection. A vow to serve the committee with faithfulness and alacrity, to execute their orders to the best of my ability overrode any ill-at-ease. With a determined Midlander, a solid Northerner, a contact in high places, a seasoned diplomat, a charismatic chairman and a tenacious secretary, how could the Return to Steam Committee not succeed?

The meeting got under way untidily (as the secretary had not, to his disgrace, circulated an agenda) but enthusiastically, with some general discussion on the daunting task of persuading the British Railways Board to change its mind about steam. After a period, I asked the man who enjoyed close contact with the Board, "What's the latest from BR?"

The rangy man opened his mouth to say something, but momentarily held his breath as he carefully scrutinized words he was about to speak. "There's no crack in the ice yet, but the blowlamps are going hard," he said slowly and quietly, concluding the sentence with a boyish smile.

After further discussion amongst members, the same man made a suggestion. "I think the first thing we need to do is send out a questionnaire to all preservation societies and locomotive owners asking which, if any, of their engines they would like to run on BR, if we get permission. That way, we have something to go to the Board with."

The committee unanimously adopted the resolution. After tea and biscuits, we thanked our host for his hospitality, and left in the warm evening sunshine to return to four corners of England.

CHAPTER TWENTY- TWO

Fired with success of the Return to Steam Committee's first meeting, I was eager to get started, but did not have the knowledge to put together a questionnaire as instructed, so had to ask help of others. Exchange of several letters produced the necessary questionnaire and supplied a list of names and addresses to whom the form should be posted. The typed questionnaire bore at its head the title of the umbrella organization in whose name the exercise was being conducted. Underneath were the words Return to Steam Committee, underneath those headings was my home address. At the time I was in lodgings in a neighbourhood of east Liverpool where several streets bore names associated with Russia, names presumably given at a time when Britain enjoyed at least neutral relations with that country, rather than being in a state of Cold War, which was the case in the 1970s. Thus my home address had a Soviet flavour. Underneath the address, there followed a short explanatory paragraph which I signed as Secretary to the Committee. The lower part of the form contained the questionnaire proper, and included enquiries about the mechanical state of locomotives, whether they had a current boiler certificate, and so on.

In those days, office technology for producing printed material in quantity involved disengaging the typewriter ribbon and typing on a wax-coated stencil, making corrections as needed with correcting fluid that had a mildly intoxicating bouquet. One had to hammer on the typewriter keys with sufficient force to ensure characters cut right through the wax coating. The stencil was then attached to the drum of a duplicating machine and the required number run off on duplicating paper. For some long-forgotten reason, I chose blue duplicating paper. Forms were then individually addressed and posted to about fifty organizations across Britain.

Whatever recipients thought of news about the Return to Steam campaign reaching them in a blue duplicated letter from a Soviet-sounding address was of no consequence, because replies soon started pouring in. The whole exercise was of course a bureaucrat's dream, thoroughly enjoyable and not at all burdensome as the West Midlands committee member feared.

My domestic filing system, still ridiculously over-complicated at this time, was expanded to embrace Return to Steam Committee business. The questionnaire carried one of the new file numbers: P.4/1/B(3).

It is testimony to the good name of the organization whose name I used and on whose behalf I was acting that, ultimately, only one questionnaire was never returned, and that was owing to a dispute over precise ownership of the locomotive.

I delayed compiling results of the survey till almost all replies were in. The committee had expected only a limited number of preservation societies to nominate their locomotives, but, to everyone's surprise, nearly all said they wanted to see their charges running on the main lines again, even if some of the engines were not yet up to required standards of maintenance. A list had to be drawn up of all engines put forward, but in what order should they be catalogued: numerical? alphabetical? by age? The conundrum had to be solved diplomatically because the list could not be seen to bestow superiority of any one locomotive over another. I did not know what to do, and again had to consult others. Excellent advice resulted in locomotives being listed by weight, with the heaviest first, tonnages being found in the popular handbook published by Ian Allan *British Rail Locomotives and Other Motive Power*. The completed list would be presented to the committee.

The Return to Steam Committee met in full on one other occasion when its members converged on a railway preservation site that clung to the foothills of the Pennines like a corrie to a mountainside. It was the preservation site with which the man from the North was associated. Full committee paraphernalia accompanied the gathering this time, including a photograph album acting as minute book in which minutes of the previous meeting were glued. At the beginning of proceedings I placed the pasted minutes in front of our illustrious chairman to sign. He did so, but with a questioning smile that said "Do I really have to do this?" Artists are not normally burdened with such punctilios; bureaucrats, by contrast, would be distraught if the inveterate procedure were not followed.

I am afraid I have no recollection of the business conducted, but it probably included receiving the list of nominated locomotives for main line running. After the meeting closed, each member was thrilled with a ride on the principal steam engine at the site. To round off a thoroughly enjoyable day, the member from the North invited everyone to his home for an evening meal. His hard-pressed wife had to quickly supplement what was to have been only a family meal. After we had finished, I said to his frazzled wife, "That was really good, thanks very much."

Her tall husband leant over me and said quietly, "I could tell that was from the heart, the way you said it." It was indeed from the heart. As a bachelor living alone, I seldom cooked a proper dinner. A well-balanced meal was a rarity and much appreciated.

The next major exercise, as far as I can remember, involved writing a progress report on behalf of the committee chairman. The committee's work was not inordinately complex, neither were there delicate issues that begged judicious choice of words, so the task of draughting a report ought to have been relatively easy, which it proved to be, until the last sentence or two where I could not think how to round it off. I would lay down scribbled notes for a day or two, come back to them, but still be unable to complete the task. Impatient with my own ineptitude, taking pen and paper I repaired to a favourite haunt in Church Street in the centre of Liverpool to see if the usual remedy for intractable problems would work. The first two pints of Walker's Bitter achieved nothing but quench a thirst. The third pint succeeded in switching over the mind to a condition that sieved all thoughts, allowed small, incidental, irrelevant notions to drop out, and that retained only matters of substance upon which to concentrate. Such an intoxicated state of mind is not recommended for driving in traffic nor for balancing a set of accounts, but is very useful for dealing with simple yet stubborn problems. For a brief period I was able to focus intently on what had already been written in the report, then the last two sentences came to me in a flash. Regrettably, memory lets me down at this point. I have no idea what the penultimate sentence was, but the final sentence comprised just one word, "Onward!" Lest they escaped into the alcoholic atmosphere that created them, I scrawled down the words as quickly and as legibly as three pints of beer would permit, then celebrated with a fourth.

When a tavern's call for last orders drew near, I usually had to make a decision whether or not to complete the evening with another pint, but in this case I probably compromised by buying only a half-pint, in view of the bus ride home. The next day I typed the complete report and with immense satisfaction dispatched it for approval.

The committee met briefly on one more occasion, though not all members were able to attend. Thereafter, business was conducted more informally. However, around this time, another memorable event took place. A ball was held in Clapham Museum, home to numerous locomotives that had been retired, cosmetically restored and placed on permanent exhibition. I received an invitation for two to attend, so took along my girlfriend of the time. During the course of the ball, we strolled round exhibits, dined on beef stroganoff, and said hello to the handful of people I knew. Then, I saw some distance away, the chairman of the Return to Steam Committee talking to a group that included another celebrity: a young actress who had become famous through her role in a certain well-known railway story. In such close proximity to famous people my friend and I fidgeted nervously. At one stage, the chairman looked in my direction and may have been gauging whether or not to beckon me and my companion over. But he probably sensed our discomfort and decided against it, instead resuming a conversation with the young star and her chaperon. Despite this missed opportunity, the evening was a spectacular occasion, a resounding success, and another high point in an exciting but brief period of the author's life.

CHAPTER TWENTY-THREE

If this book were a work of fiction, the story of the Return to Steam Committee would now advance in one of two directions. One account would feature a happy ending with the committee eventually persuading British Railways to change their minds, and amid much popping of champagne corks and palmy celebration, a Return to Steam special train would victoriously storm out of one or other of the capital's stations carrying as its guests of honour the elated six-member committee who had succeeded in their crusade. The other version would reproduce a crushing letter from British Railways which would begin: "I am directed by the British Railways Board to refer to your recent communication concerning the operation of steam traction..." The letter would be only one page long and would end: "...having regard to all circumstances, the Board considers arguments for reviewing the ban on steam locomotives are without merit, and they must therefore decline your request.

I am, Sir, your obedient servant..."

But this book is not a work of fiction. Real life is not so tidy. The truth is the Return to Steam Committee neither succeeded nor failed in its mission. Steam did return, but not through the direct efforts of the Committee.

After the brief meetings referred to above nothing happened for a time. An uncomfortable feeling overtook me that the whole project had been put on hold, because letters I dispatched enquiring after progress went unanswered. The effervescent enthusiasm and unrestrained eagerness of committee members that had so impressed their young scribe in the preceding twelve months now appeared to have evaporated into thin air. Had I done something wrong? I began to repine, felt I was being snubbed and was completely at a loss to understand why all the time and effort put into the Return to Steam campaign now seemed to have been without purpose.

From the nascent idea of doing something rather than nothing, through the incipient formation of the committee, its subsequent meetings and papers that followed, steady progress from one stage to the next ensured its secretary kept busy and remained enthusiastic. Now the Return to Steam Committee itself appeared to have run out of steam. I did not attempt to reach by telephone any of the five committee members, for to do so, I thought, would be an impertinence. Several dispiriting weeks of perplexed isolation passed, with doses of Walker's Bitter only marginally ameliorating the condition.

Then in October 1971 news broke: the British Railways' fortress-like barricade had been breached. A renowned beverage maker in the West of England had succeeded in obtaining permission to run a steam engine and carriages they owned over British Railways' metals: private industry had succeeded where the Return to Steam Committee had not. The bittersweet news briefly stunned me. I felt bitter because no invitation had been extended to the Return to Steam Committee – at least not to its secretary – to be involved in vital negotiations which must have taken place before the West Country steam run was made. But the news was sweet in that the principal aim of the committee, and my own personal dream, had been fulfilled, regardless of who had been instrumental in that fulfillment.

No hint had been given talks were under way. Looking back, I had no grounds to feel slighted because meetings between company executives and British Railways mandarins would have been out of my depth. I had never felt completely at ease in the presence of the five just men from whom I took instructions. If I had been called in to act as minute-taker in the negotiations between the beverage maker and British Railways, as industrious and as meticulous as I may have been, endeavours would have been hampered by poor knowledge of protocol, social ineptness and searing self-consciousness. No, I had no place at the negotiation table. Such crucial talks were best left to those who grew up in, who were educated in and who currently moved around in that stratum of society where matters of national interest were confronted on a daily basis.

A brief period of seesawing emotions – of wounded pride at being left out, of elation at the return of steam to the national network – soon gave way to halcyon days of contentment: aims of the Return to Steam Committee had been realized, even if the committee itself could not take credit. British Railways' concession to steam traction would in due course be extended beyond one isolated trip. News reached the ears that permission would be granted for a limited number of other steam locomotives to operate over secondary routes, mainly in the north-western part of the country. Profound serenity settled on one like a warm snug blanket.

A surprise communication came through the post. The famed West Country beverage maker who had broken the steam ban was organizing a celebratory dinner on their private train, and I was invited to attend. Accordingly, I journeyed to that part of England to find myself one day climbing aboard an exquisitely outshopped dining car to take a numbered place at a table for two laid with fine linen and sparkling silver cutlery. The rake of preserved carriages would not move beyond the company's private sidings on this occasion. I would dine on caviar.

All seats appeared to be taken in the dining car, except one opposite me. Then, about half-way through the meal, an impeccably groomed man of distinguished appearance approached, smiled, and asked if he could join me, a request to which I had no objections whatsoever. After making himself comfortable, the man introduced himself as a senior executive with the company that owned the steam engine and train on which I was now enjoying lavish hospitality. As a steam engine owner, the company had been included on the Return to Steam Committee list of potential operators. The man sitting opposite had been the person to whom I had addressed correspondence. Though somewhat taken aback by this intelligence, I was able to hold a conversation, albeit one that lacked depth, but which included thanking the executive for inviting me to the celebration. An opportunity presented itself to enquire how the company had succeeded in changing the mind of British Railways, but to broach the subject would, I felt, have been unduly forward. There was also risk of betraying disappointment that the private company had stolen a march on the Return to Steam Committee.

The man smiled gently as we ate and as we indulged in polite conversation. As much as anything, I think he was amused to be face to face with the source of a one-time stencilled letter on inexplicably blue paper bearing a Russian address. The source did not see his way to offer an explanation for cheapness of the communication, nor its colour, nor the unintended allusion to the Cold War. After we had finished eating, the executive, still maintaining the smiling good nature that had radiated throughout our tete-a-tete, asked to be excused, got up, bade me good afternoon and departed for more pressing business elsewhere. His quondam correspondent was left to ruminate on the surprise meeting.

In time the Return to Steam Committee suffered the fate of being an entity without a purpose, as the task it had been set up to accomplish had been transferred to and executed by others. In different circumstances the correct procedure would have been to call one last meeting to pass a resolution that the committee disband itself. But it was plain to see parties would be too preoccupied with lining up their locomotives for possible main line running to worry about such a petty bureaucratic formality. So the Return to Steam Committee was never officially dissolved but simply ceased to meet, and in such fashion the author's original idea simply faded into obscurity.

The last contact I had with any of the committee members was after a meeting of the umbrella organization under whose banner the committee had been set up, when I was able to speak to the chairman of the assembly. As we approached one another, the chairman was very much aware that, a year or so ago, he had had to withhold from me information about the impending relaxation of the steam ban. An ephemeral moment of eye contact was all that was needed to transmit a message from him to me of sincere regret at having to do so. A similar momentary look in the eye was all that was needed to convey from me to him that I understood, that I accepted such sensitive matters were preserve of a few. After some mundane exchanges, I explained future plans. "Well, I'm going to drop out of the picture now," I said to him. "There's no woman in my life at the moment, so that's the number one priority now!"

The military man smiled his usual beaming smile and nodded. Warmth of his manner and expressiveness in his countenance conveyed a message of deep gratitude for my constancy as secretary of the Return to Steam Committee.

"You'll be back," he said. "You'll be back."

We shook hands. I left the gathering bringing to an end the story of the Return to Steam Committee which, if nothing else, illustrated how passion might compel a person to rise above his station in order to reach a goal towards which that passion was driving him, even if he might fall back to anonymity afterwards. I had had my fifteen months of fame and would never again on such scale rub shoulders with people of influence and position. Bustling city life and smoky bar rooms now beckoned. I would withdraw, drink Walker's Bitter and contemplate other pursuits.

CHAPTER TWENTY-FOUR

In retrospection, a major problem in 1968 was that several owners of preserved locomotives were in a hopeless position of having nowhere to run their engines. Even if value of the Return to Steam Committee were questioned, the campaign was at least doing something rather than nothing. It filled a vacuum. At least it let the world know we were serious, and arguably that may be the best that can be said for the exercise. It is possible private discussions were taking place with British Railways in other circles during the entire period the Return to Steam Committee existed, in which case the committee could at least have been playing a minor role in presenting an organized and official position.

To turn to circumstances of the steam ban actually being lifted, I do not know if any member of the Return to Steam Committee played a role in talks between the beverage maker and British Railways. If any member did take part, the most likely man would have been the chairman of the preservationist group (rather than the chairman of the Return to Steam Committee who was in much demand elsewhere). If the first-named chairman did not sit in on negotiations, it is reasonable to extrapolate he was privy to their being under way.

During the same period, a railway event occurred completely outside the world of the enthusiast, yet one which may have influenced a decision about steam. In June 1971 it was announced that the Chairman of the British Railways Board would retire in September of the same year. Since the steam ban was lifted in October 1971, the question is asked whether the concession sprang from the new Chairman being more favourably inclined towards steam, or at least less vehemently opposed to it.

But wait, the period from June to September 1971 corresponds to a period described in Chapter Twenty-three when I was puzzled and frustrated through lack of progress in the Return to Steam campaign. At that time, I could not understand why committee members appeared to be avoiding contact. Suppose the incoming British Railways Chairman were more sympathetic to steam, it is possible at least some of the committee members were aware of that fact, and it is possible they had inside knowledge that a change in chairmanship of British Railways was likely to see a change in policy. They could not, of course, divulge such privileged information to all and sundry, especially someone as sundry as the committee secretary.

Given the sequence of events, it seems likely that, despite the Return to Steam Committee's efforts and the efforts of all others, more than anything else it was a change in chairmanship of the British Railways Board that facilitated a return to steam.

Many years after the Return to Steam Committee had passed into history, I recall enjoying a trip to Stratford-on-Avon and back hauled by *ex*-Southern Railway Merchant Navy Class Pacific 35028 *Clan Line*. Travelling at modest speed through London's suburbs on the return journey we passed a London Underground surface-level station about eight tracks over. A man aged about forty, waiting for the tube, was astonished at our train's passing. His face shone as if illuminated from within, his eyes widened with child-like amazement, his mouth broke into the broadest of grins. Quite possibly this man loved trains when he was a boy but had lost interest when steam engines disappeared. He probably had no inkling steam trains were running again. I imagined his dashing home to tell his wife and children of the unexpected and wonderful sight of a steam engine hurtling through London loaded with happy passengers. The Return to Steam Committee secretaryship was a labour of love, but if any value could be attached to it, the explosion of joy in this man's face as he watched the steam train go by reimbursed me one thousand-fold.

Lovers of steam in later times have been able to enjoy the object of their affection as never before. Preserved branch lines offer the enthusiast the chance to take a round trip behind his favourite engine, and then to stay at the lineside to watch it go by as many times as daylight permits. Furthermore, all these joys may be experienced in a setting that has been painstakingly restored to an earlier period, complemented by refreshment rooms, souvenir shops, car parks and other convenient facilities that engender an atmosphere of intimacy making for delightful family outings. As time goes by and funds permit, more emphasis is being placed on equipping preserved lines with full signalling that, in many cases, strictly adheres to rules in force during the period to which the line has been restored.

Since the early 1970s the number of main line steam specials has steadily risen to reach a figure that is typically twenty a month. Some specials run regularly, notably on the Fort William to Mallaig line. An impressive catalogue of express steam locomotives haul main line trains over most of Britain, sometimes beginning their journeys from principal termini, including those in London. The engines include not only the standard classes built by British Railways, but classes of engines built by each of the four companies that existed prior to nationalization in 1948: Great Western Railway; London, Midland and Scottish Railway; London & North Eastern Railway and Southern Railway. Perhaps one of the most sensational steam excursions commemorated the fifteen guinea special of 11th August 1968. On 10th August 2008 a special train re-traced the original route of Liverpool, Manchester, Blackburn, Hellified to Carlisle and back. Number 70013 *Oliver Cromwell* re-enacted its original performance on the Manchester to Carlisle section, the locomotive's first main line outing since its identical trip forty year's previous! Who would have thought in 1968 such an event would ever take place.

Attractions of a preserved branch line and main line steam are now able to be combined, with trains running through from one to the other. Steam engine drivers from preserved railways may take their trains onto Network Rail, the successor to British Railways.

To turn to individual preserved locomotives, we now know that grim final weeks in the summer of 1968 when scores of splendid machines looked destined for scrap now look not quite so grim. Of the 842 members of the London, Midland & Scottish Railway Class 5MT Black Fives, no less than eighteen have been preserved, an astonishing two per cent of the entire stock! Of the same company's Class 8F 2-8-0s, no less than seven were rescued. The following engines seen at Lostock Hall in June 1968, which at the time were thought to be doomed were, I am delighted to report, saved: Class 4MT 43106, Black Fives 44806, 45212, 45407 and 45305. Of the same class, number 45110 that hauled what was considered to be the last steam train on 11th August 1968 was also preserved.

What better expression can there be of the love of steam than the decision to build from scratch a brand new engine. No member of the London & North Eastern Railway Class A1 Pacific had been saved from scrap, so, at a cost of three million pounds, a brand new engine to that design was built in 2008. It was numbered 60163 and named *Tornado*.

Nothing in the preservation movement could have been achieved without, in the first instance, an irrepressible passion for the beauty and excitement of a steam engine railway. To transform dreams into reality, to purchase a huge tract of real estate that would one day become a heritage railway line or to buy a discarded, rusting piece of machinery for restoration to a proud steam engine demands single-minded strong-willed dedication and organizational skill found only in a few individuals. But that is only the beginning. Once purchase is made, restoring motive power and infrastructure to first class condition is a lengthy undertaking and one that is never really complete. In particular, the unglamorous task of re-tubing a steam engine boiler requires special skills and dedication. One can see a driving force behind steam engine restoration: it is an accomplishment denied elsewhere, the bringing back to life of something that was dead. The resurgence of steam motive power owes much to a huge army of volunteers who have given their time to renovate railway lines and locomotives for the rest of us to enjoy. We will be for ever indebted to the original men of vision, to those who have given countless hours of free time to convert that vision into reality, and to all those who, by patronizing preserved railways and main line excursions, ensure the steam railway will be around for many generations. Long live steam!

CHAPTER TWENTY-FIVE

Mention Liverpool and, for many, only one topic springs to mind, football, which is hardly surprising since the city boasts two Premier Division football teams, Liverpool and Everton. The teams enjoy long histories of success in both the Football League and the Football Association Cup. To some, the name Liverpool has only one connotation, the Royal Liverpool Philharmonic Orchestra, which, in the 1970s, was under the masterful baton of Sir Charles Groves. Others might say the Liverpool dialect is its most striking feature. The dialect, by the way, offers two different pronunciations of the word *there*, the first of which is thur. The second employs an odd vowel that generates a pronunciation half way between *thee* and *there*. But it could be said the most unchanging and unchangeable feature of the city of Liverpool is the humour endemic amongst its people who, almost without exception, were sharp, verbally inventive and very funny. In some parts of the country a witticism might be dispensed with much fanfare, but in Liverpool quips were so common they were played down. In any case, coruscant wit is funnier when delivered in subdued tones.

Spontaneity flourished. A bus conductor climbing to the upper deck slipped on a step, stamped on the troublesome thing and shouted at it "Stay still!" When a works canteen tea lady accidentally dropped a cup that predictably shattered into innumerable pieces on the linoleum floor, a workman, without lifting his head from a newspaper, muttered, "It's down there on the floor somewhere, Mary." I had just alighted from a bus with arms full of shopping when one wag, seeing I was ill-equipped to defend myself, approached with feigned menace saying, "Whaddya mean…!" I need not have been alarmed, for the man stopped some distance away and broke into laughter. If I had seen the joke quickly enough, I could have responded with encumbered and equally false bravado saying: "Wanna make something of it, then!"

Humour of the inhabitants of Liverpool – who, incidentally, were often referred to as Liverpudlians, sometimes as Scousers owing to a one-time partiality for a mutton dish called scouse - could strike with painful acuity. A young lady might tell a young man she would like to take him home to meet her family: "Then we can all have a laugh!"

Much humour was based on missing the point. On a winter's day a citizen of Liverpool might say, "It's cold enough for two pairs of bootlaces." The supposed logic being pursued here is that as temperatures dropped, people would begin to put on two of everything: shirts, sweaters, coats, etcetera. If the weather became even colder, they would continue doubling-up until the only item of apparel left to duplicate were bootlaces. (Choice of the word bootlaces rather than shoelaces gives some idea of the saying's antiquity.) The point being missed in this joke is that an extra pair of bootlaces would do absolutely nothing to fend of cold, and the absurdity of trying to thread two laces through eyelets meant only for one embellishes the *bon mot*.

In a crowded smoky bar I could not help but overhear the scintillating banter of two men in front as they drank beer, each line they uttered as original as it was funny. Regrettably, but not unsurprisingly since I was myself enthusiastically drinking beer, I cannot remember a single word they said. I smiled at first, then broke into laughter as each man bounced enough jokes off the other to fill ten television situation comedy shows. After a while I feared intruding on their privacy, and reluctantly moved away. An ability to draw on a seemingly bottomless well of fresh jokes spawned numerous professional comedians, Arthur Askey and Ted Ray are the earliest I remember. Scores of stand-up comedians followed.

I had always enjoyed inventive humour, such as BBC Radio's "The Goon Show" from the 1950s, and Anthony Newley's later television programme "The Strange World of Gurney Slade", so welcomed in the late 1960s a humour that specialized in inserting the absurd into the everyday, the humour of television's "Monty Python's Flying Circus". Each day after the BBC show aired, offices and factories throughout the country buzzed with workers' re-enacting the latest outrageous scripts, sometimes word for word. I missed many episodes through not owning a television set. The Monty Python team, who made fashionable the word *silly*, became universally popular and in Liverpool augmented the indigenous wit.

A drinking partner of the time and I would stand in public houses dreaming up our own Pythonesque sketches. Most would not pass the test of sobriety, but one worth mentioning (a subjective opinion admittedly) is the idea of an all-night cricket match for the benefit of fans who worked during the day, the entire game taking place in total darkness. We concluded the game would progress no further than the first ball of the night. Since no one would know that the bowler had actually bowled, and if they did, they could not see where the ball went, players would spend the rest of the night doing absolutely nothing but standing around in the gloom.

My friend and I also had a catch phrase. If one of us experienced a *déjà vu*, or even if there were a slightest hint of the phenomenon, one would point at the other and look him in the eye, which would be a signal for both of us to say in unison, "That's funny, have you ever had that feeling of *déjà vu?*" Then, after a suitable pause, we would both shake our heads dismissively and say "No." Occurrences of a *déjà vu* are normally infrequent, but when habitually and repetitively drinking beer, the chances of duplicate action were high, and awareness of it heightened by eagerness to say our lines. An example of saloon bar repetition would be a beer-mat sticking to the bottom of a pint glass and falling off when the glass were lifted. When we described our *divertissement* to friends, it was met with disbelief.

CHAPTER TWENTY-SIX

To return to earliest days in Liverpool, the first impression in the late 1960s was of wide, bus-soaked main roads that seemed more aptly than anywhere else to match a metaphor of being the city's arteries. The city seemed to draw life from these bustling thoroughfares lined with inviting shops, cosy public houses, aromatic fish and chip shops and brightly-lit launderettes. Side streets were largely quiet, dimly lit and devoid of activity. The area known as the Pier Head, where the splendid Royal Liver Building gazed across the ferry landing stage and River Mersey, could in some respects be considered the city centre. From there the city's green double-decked buses raced to outer suburbs, turned round, and hurried back again, crocheting together an inner ring of former grand residences now sadly neglected and either let out as rented accommodation or boarded up, Le Corbusier high-rise flats that cleft the sky like gigantic silver-spangled dominoes, swaths of warm red brick Victorian terraces that were the heart of Liverpool, vast council estates whose roads wove and turned about binding the houses together into one mass, affluent suburbs with shady trees and carefully tended gardens and finally another ring of council estates that added bulbous projections to the city purlieus. Bus drivers, whose distinguished mature features crowned with silver hair always reminded me of politicians, were assisted at that time by conductors, usually younger men, as one-man operation had yet to be introduced.

Buses crammed people together, and as in Birmingham, this lively mixing with the rest of the population encouraged using buses rather than the motor car. Furthermore, there had always been a love-hate relationship with my Ford Anglia. The mobility it provided was ideal for a philandering way of life, but I despised the vehicle's wastefulness, any motor car's wastefulness. I eventually came round to thinking expenses of running a motor car outweighed its usefulness in spooning. It was sold in May 1969.

When I first moved to Liverpool in 1967, there was no conscious decision to make it my permanent or semi-permanent home because, as usual, I had no grand plan. Whilst a state of bachelorhood did not in itself tie a man to any city, events would prove that a single man without encumbrances would find residence in Liverpool by no means unpleasant. In rural Yorkshire, girls were not easy to meet owing to their natural paucity and through an insularity common to all inhabitants of that county. In the West Midlands, only a few unattached women were about during the evening (apart from discotheques) as if a stigma were attached to being single - either that or they disappeared down manholes or up drainpipes whenever a potential beau appeared.

Not so the women of Liverpool. They filled the buses, they thronged the streets, they piled into and spilled out of public houses and night clubs in droves. When walking with a friend one day I was so taken by a young woman on the opposite side of the street, I did not see a pillar-box and walked straight into it, a glorious moment of slapstick had it been caught on film. Not only were there vast numbers of women, but their disposition to be outgoing, friendly and funny was the opposite of those met in other parts of the country. Their high spirits were justified.

A *joie de vivre* had always been present in Liverpool, but the population's mood and the status of the city as a whole had been elevated by the phenomenal success of four young musicians whom the world came to know as The Beatles. By 1967, the group enjoyed international fame and no longer performed in their city of birth, yet the tidal wave of euphoria driven by The Beatles' fame still rolled vigorously and engendered a tremendous feeling of pride amongst all. For years I would ride the crest of this wave and share in the joyful gregariousness that bubbled through not only the city's younger generations but through people of all ages and in all walks of life.

CHAPTER TWENTY-SEVEN

Night clubs celebrated Liverpool's new-found fame. By the late 1960s I had found several clubs, but newer and more stimulating haunts had yet to evolve. Clubs had always featured live music, the type of act varying with the character of the club. A trio comprising pianist, double-bass player and guitarist would suit a club catering for older people. A popular music group, usually referred to then as a pop group but later as a rock band, would cater for a younger set. A change would soon be under way.

In the late 1960s pop groups would play a couple of sessions during the course of the night, the breaks in between being filled by disc jockeys playing records. Whilst records played dance floors were full of young people enjoying the music, but when the band played most dancers would drift away to bars leaving only a handful of people to appreciate a performance. Apathy towards live music did not go unnoticed amongst club owners. As time passed clubs ceased to hire groups, much to the chagrin of musicians, and gave over the entire evening to recorded music resulting in dance floors being packed from start to finish. These clubs were true discotheques, but the term or the abbreviation disco was hardly ever used by people who went there, probably because it cheapened or trivialized or even mocked the places that were like shrines to them. If patrons did wish to talk about establishments they frequented, the word club would be used – knowing full well the interlocutor would be aware he or she was not referring to a Rotary Club, Tall Story Club, working men's club, gardening club or model railway club. I recall asking a companion to describe a club I had never visited. Abashed, he replied in a stutter, "Well, yer know, it's like – like – it's a disco 'n all that. You know whadda mean." He could scarcely utter the word disco because he loathed it.

The certain type of American music heard in discotheques had first struck me as being oddly restrained, as if artists were not singing at the top of their voices, but presence of fine women wherever it was played had not escaped notice during visits to Birmingham's establishments. Whether through sub-consciously linking the sound with the opposite sex or through a conscious turn-round in musical taste, I grew to like the music, though it is not to everyone's taste. It was the popular music performed primarily but not exclusively by black Americans.

The music is sometimes referred to as R&B, but since the alphabetism originally stood for rhythm and blues, the description is not accurate. Discotheque music had its roots in gospel music, the spiritual music of American churches. It could be said lineage then progressed through what was called doo-wop music (because backing vocalists often repeated the words doo-wop as accompaniment) through recordings by such groups as The Platters and The Drifters (the latter group enjoying enormous popularity in Liverpool) to become soul music. Marvin Gaye was perhaps the greatest executant of soul music. About 1970 some soul recordings acquired a hypnotic, thumping base line to become infectious dance music that would be referred to as disco. Most disco records were by black American artists, but a principal exception was the British–based white group the Bee Gees.

Whilst conversion of most of Liverpool's night clubs to discotheques was slowly but inexorably under way, live performances of popular music could still be enjoyed in the Empire Theatre which welcomed a host of international entertainers including American soul groups. The Jackson Five featured the puzzling Michael Jackson when he was still a boy. Pin-point choreography of The Temptations was the most visually stunning live performance I have ever seen, though by the mid-1970s only two of the original five famous members remained. One new night club reversed the decline of live entertainment by dividing the establishment into two parts, a cabaret area and a smaller section given over to a discotheque. A singer who had left The Temptations, David Ruffin, appeared solo there, but at the time the name meant nothing to me, so I did not go. I could not understand why a woman friend (not a girlfriend, but one of a number of young ladies I unsuccessfully wooed) told me: "That was the most fantastic night ever!" That David Ruffin was the name of the lead singer in many of The Temptations' hit records, such as "My Girl", was one of countless pieces of information that never came my way owing to having no firm roots and therefore being unconnected to much that went on. Other examples of being out of touch were missing episodes of "Monty Python's Flying Circus" through owning no television and ignorance of the rapid run down of steam traction in 1968 by not keeping abreast of railway news. Though no man is an island, he can have a jolly good go at being a peninsula - which creates a moat that keeps at a distance anything he does not want to be associated with. The danger in peninsulating himself though is missing connections that could readily improve his lot.

Fashion played a vital role in the life of a single person. Liverpool demanded conformity of dress amongst unattached people, with choices remaining limited until fashion became a free-for-all in the late 1970s. Through the earlier part of the 1970s the well-dressed young man had to wear cigarette-style trousers, colloquially referred to as parallels, the trouser bottoms being eighteen inches wide, not half an inch more nor half an inch less. The style may have been peculiar to Liverpool. At some point the interloper of flared trousers became fashionable, but their popularity lasted only about a year before the parallel style once again regained supremacy. For many years shirts had to be of the button-down collar type – the brand name Ben Sherman being dominant – but one year cheesecloth-style shirts were in vogue. Around 1970 most clubs insisted men wear jacket, shirt and tie. At that time mohair suits were the rage, a friend and I had versions sky-blue in colour. As time passed, strict conditions of entry melted away as many night clubs allowed more informal attire. Even so, men's fashions remained locked into a very narrow field of that which was acceptable, whilst women's fashions changed year to year, which only serves to highlight the inordinate lengths to which the human race will go to seek out a partner.

CHAPTER TWENTY-EIGHT

As the 1970s got under way new friendships inspired greater confidence which in turn opened doors to night clubs never before visited. Evenings began either by meeting friends in one of numerous public houses in Liverpool city centre, or by meeting inside a club. In the latter case I would find a hostelry to down four pints in an hour whilst contemplating the night ahead, which young lady might be there, which young lady might not be there. Tapsters were quick to assess customers. I recall one stealing a glance then adjusting the dispensing nozzle to make the beer frothier, as he had judged (accurately) a preference for beer with a good head. Young people drank standing up as it afforded a better view of others and, particularly in the case of young men, permitted consumption of greater volumes of alcohol by keeping the digestive system vertical and free; sitting down placed a kink in it. Public houses favoured by club-goers generally stood on prominent sites within the eastern end of the main shopping area. Not far away several night clubs were located in, by contrast, dingy, grubby, back-street former warehouses or light industrial premises. Their exterior inelegance, as will be seen, belied extravagance within. Entrance was through small doors guarded by security personnel wearing black suits, bow ties and grim faces whose task it was to scrutinize clientele. We called the guardsmen bouncers, though the preferred term is door supervisor. In clubs that I went to people were generally in their late teens and early twenties who had put behind them their first major romance and who were looking for another.

Enjoyment of Liverpool's discotheques peaked for me in about 1974. As I look back through the frosted glass of several decades to recall scenes that took place in an alcoholic blur, facts are difficult to retrieve, almost impossible. Even so, the ghost of a memory exists of one exceptional evening in 1974, which I will endeavour to interpret.

The evening began in a certain club with a friend and I enjoying the first round of beer in a ground floor bar. Whilst drinking we occasionally glanced round to see which women were there whom we knew and which women were there whom we would like to know. Care was taken not to appear too eager. Being cool is an overworked expression but one which accurately summed up our approach at this early stage of the evening. We may well have broken into conversation with one or two women and agreed to see them on the dance floor later.

From 23:00 to midnight this bar area was packed as revellers primed themselves with alcohol prior to going upstairs to the dance floor. Women would generally go before men. No one looked at their watches to time this progression as it was done on instinct, each party knowing the proper moment to move.

When we eventually did go upstairs, my friend and I joined other chiselled-featured men (I carried no extra pounds at that time) congregated along one side of the dance floor. We all wore shirts opened wide at the collar to reveal some form of medallion, the value of which depended on the individual's pecuniary circumstances; my medallion was made of tin. At this stage in the evening the dance floor was occupied mostly by women, typically long and lean, a look made famous by a well-known Liverpool songstress in the 1960s. Fashion at the time decreed women wear trousers that fit the hips snugly, in some cases so snugly the woman could not sit down. Deafening bass-dominated disco music that filled the brightly lit area could not fail to animate all but the most wooden individuals. The music of Barry White was hugely popular. The song "Rock the Boat" by The Hues Corporation, was a particularly happy tune. What is it in the combination of voice and musical instrument that makes a song more uplifting than others? Is the key in which a tune is written a factor?

Dance steps were ridiculously simple. All one had to do was keep feet a little apart, and with them facing slightly outwards, move first one foot then the other forwards and backwards a few inches in time with the music. The simple form of dance was almost universal, and is still widespread at the time of writing. Dancers who most readily caught the eye were those women who tempered movement to a minimum, who augmented it with subtle shifting of hips and shoulders and whose bone structure was such that hips and shoulders were the same distance across. Their dance looked like a well-lubricated mechanized parallelogram.

Bolder or more inebriated men, such as my friend and I, joined women on the dance floor, chiefly done by walking up to two women and touching their elbows gently with the hand as a signal to split them temporarily. If we were acceptable to them, they turned to dance with us. For the duration of the record we mirrored faithfully steps of our partners. However, there would be nothing stopping a man prancing around backwards and waving his arms like a windmill, but chances the woman would ever again dance with him in her whole life were slender. (Liverpool men *never* danced separately from women, as I have seen in other parts of the country.)

Conversation was possible above the loud music only by talking in short spurts, by limiting sentences to a handful of words, and by delivering them in a forward bobbing motion in time with the music to hurl them straight into the woman's ear. "Come here often?" would be a good example of this form of short, sharp communication, but the line was so hackneyed it was probably never used.

    I had been visiting this club regularly. In the previous two weeks I had danced with a young woman when conversation had progressed particularly well, so well in fact that if I asked her for a date, I felt confident she would agree. She was there again that night so, with my companion, I carefully positioned myself about the dance floor to guarantee a dance with her; my friend would dance with her friend. When time came, exchanges with the delightful young woman sparkled brightly. I learnt she would not be staying late at the club. In view of that I had no hesitation in asking if I could see her again in a few days' hence. She agreed. We parted joyfully on that understanding.

    The above arrangements were made during a session of up-tempo dancing. Whilst my companion and I had no qualms about striding onto the dance floor to join females, most men were more inhibited and waited around the periphery until slower records played. The first batch of what were called slowies was probably played about 00:30 hours (though nobody took note of the time) and was heralded by dimming lights and opening bars of a current slow ballad. This was the signal for testosterone-driven hoards to invade the dance floor. As with faster music, pairs of men approached pairs of women. Each man would wrap arms round that soft and inviting curve between a woman's waist and hips, and the couple would dance in a slow shuffle tracing small circles on the dance floor for the duration of the record. No men were condemned for predatory behaviour, no women were accused of being acquiescent, for if they felt unhappy about such roles they would not have been in the place. The young woman with whom I had made a date had left, but bursting with self-confidence over the upcoming tryst, I now joined other women on the dance floor in that sociable human conjunction referred to as smooching.

    Suspended revolving globes covered in tiny glass mirrors dappled the entire dance floor and occupants with showers of moving light. Extremities of the room faded into darkness. The disc jockey looked down helplessly from his cubicle on the soiree instigated by romantic records he played. Most couples locked into a lips-to-lips embrace while dancing even though they were complete strangers. I was not excluded from such treats. Intoxication brought on by the combined effects of the woman's perfume, of alcohol, of the crescendo in Al Wilson's "Show and Tell" - surely one of the best slow records of all time - and of the unadulterated pleasure of such close corporeal contact with the opposite sex created a wave of sizzling emotion that suffused irresistibly through the body from the feet upwards to reach the head with such dizzying force I almost passed out with pleasure. Care had to be taken not to fall over. When a record ended, most couples released each other like cats bored with a toy mouse, and, emboldened by the feast of favours, moved on to the next complete stranger for another bout of indiscriminate intimacy.

Amidst this frenzy a few couples did not part when records changed, but remained locked in one another's arms continuing to revolve slowly in time with the music. The man gazed straight into the woman's eyes speaking words of little substance but which nevertheless singled her out as the person he most wanted to be with, his facial features thrusting towards her to amplify the message. In response to this declaration of feelings the woman, eyes wide and bright, smiled broadly as amorous waves crashed against her glowing countenance. She returned small talk confirming emotions were mutual. From such shallow beginnings many a meaningful relationship sprang. As for myself, I was more than content with the young woman previously spoken of, and resisted temptation to be greedy.

Amongst young people of Liverpool, successfully meeting someone of the opposite sex was referred to as copping off. Precisely, copping off described having made a date to meet again in a few day's time or described the action of simply leaving the premises in company of a partner - even if they only walked together to the end of the street and never saw one another again.

The passionate and capricious exchanges described above would worry some who would say such tender moments should be reserved for true love, but it has to be understood that in these exclusive pockets of time and space emotions were so inflated that facial contact was regarded as little more than playful embellishment. Compare this frittering away of affection with classical writing where a single action is perceived so torrid it sets the page aflame, as in Thomas Hardy's *Far from the Madding Crowd* when Sergeant Troy takes advantage of Bathsheba Everdene:

> He had kissed her.

CHAPTER TWENTY-NINE

The steamy session whilst slow records played, the musical chairs of passionate embraces described in the previous chapter - in greater detail than some would care to hear I dare say - was the only such occasion I remember. Such Bacchanalian behaviour was routine for some I am sure.

Despite amatory fireworks, it was not a promise of titillating togetherness that kept calling me back to clubs. It was the thrill that each night just might be the night to meet that special person, someone with whom a deep, expansive, mutually agreeable and at least semi-permanent relationship could be forged. Most club-goers were of the same disposition in hoping for a once-in-a-while fruitful chance encounter. Only a minority of men and an even smaller number of women looked upon clubs as arenas for sexual conquest. The whimsical and haphazard conditions under which boy met girl not surprisingly resulted in only a handful of couples achieving the principal aim of the exercise: the majority returned home in the same unattached mode they were in when they entered the club. It is a sobering thought that if the coming together of large and equal numbers of the sexes *did* guarantee most would pair off, night clubs would soon be out of business.

Despite continuing exposure to hedonism rampant in the night clubs of Liverpool and despite numerous encounters brief and otherwise, throughout the 1970s I remained a bachelor, which begs the question why were there not an instance when chemistry was just so irresistibly right: why did I not marry? (The closest I came to a wedding ceremony was being called in, virtually off the street, to witness a young couple's hasty nuptials, at the conclusion of which I impertinently kissed the unknown bride.) The process of meeting the right person is extremely complicated for which no rules are written. The laying bare of affections described previously should ensure, one would have thought, that given enough exposure most participants would pair off. But it did not happen.

If the king of hearts were taken from a deck of cards and the pack shuffled, the chances of then drawing the queen of hearts to join the king would be one in fifty-one. Goodness knows what true statistics were of finding a good match in a night club, but odds of fifty to one of two well-matched people being in the same club on the same night and actually making contact seems about right. To begin, the alcoholic hurly-burly prevailing in discotheques dulled physiognomical ability to judge character and therefore hampered finding the right person. Even so, eye contact could still be relied upon to determine whether a chance meeting had any hope of bearing fruit. Even after drinking to saturation, eyes can no more hide truth from a beholder than a beholder can fool himself or herself that what he or she is seeing in a person's eyes is other than that which is plainly obvious. There is no mistaking a startled dilation of the pupil, a sympathetic sag of the eyelid, a surprised raising of the eyebrow or a bored lifeless gaze. When a man is pursuing a woman, a dry icy stare tells him not to move any closer because she is not interested. Warm, moist, laughing, illuminated eyes crimped at the corner tell the man she likes him. What ought to be a fail-safe method of assessing a woman's feelings unfortunately breaks down because men, through sheer ego, often ignore explicit ocular clues and persist in wooing an unresponsive female till rebuffed at a late stage.

Nevertheless, even when parties correctly read a promising look in the other's eyes, mistakes can happen.

"Hi there!" said the tall slim woman with flowing auburn locks who was obviously pleased to see me.

"Hi there!" I replied recognizing her from a few night's ago.

"Lively in here tonight," she said.

"Yeh, I had a heck of a job getting to the bar," I said.

"Lot more people here than there were last week," she said.

"Yer right," I said.

Stony silence then displaced conversation. The young woman loured and said, "You were with Dave the other night, right?"

"No, I was with Jimmy,"

"You're name's Eddie, right?"

"No, Mitch."

With that, we both realized the horror of each mistaking the other for someone else. The woman said no more, took an awkward step back, turned round and stomped off.

Mistakes can also be made in choosing words to open a conversation. Three women were dancing together, one of whom particularly appealed. I planned to barge into the threesome with the intent of singling out one, a tactic that sometimes failed embarrassingly if the intrusion were resented. I deliberated for some time on words that would ease the operation. The process of breaking into the group of three, I thought, would be similar to the action of separating one segment of a fruit from the remainder prior to eating. Whilst waiting for the next record I mulled over a metaphor. With this fruity mental image locked in place and with effervescent confidence that the woman would be impressed with its originality, at the beginning of the next dance I strode straight up to her and said magnificently, "Can I peel you off?" A second or two elapsed before the woman's mixed expression of disgust, perplexity and annoyance annihilated the broad smile that had been beaming in her face. "I meant...I meant...could I dance with you," I stuttered as the gravity of the *faux pas* sank in. The woman glared warily but benevolently condescended not to completely turn her back, but to continue dancing for the remainder of the number, half facing her friends, half facing the buffoon who had just accosted her. When the record ended I sped from the dance floor in disgrace and headed straight to the bar.

Simply through encountering huge numbers of women, pairing off was bound to happen from time to time. The previous chapter described how, during an exceptional night out, a date had been agreed with a delightful young woman. We had arranged to meet at a well-known hostelry in Liverpool's outer suburbs. Nervousness had always been a problem, but was usually cured by a pint or two of favourite medicine, so soon after we had sat down at a table I began tackling the first pint. About half its contents disappeared quickly. Then, a careless motion of the hand accidentally knocked over the glass spilling the remainder down the front of a smart, tan-coloured suit I was wearing. The very treatment that ought to have ensured the evening went smoothly turned the night into a disaster. Chances of a bright future with the young woman had just been irreversibly ruined. I sat there for a brief time, speechless, hoping that what had just happened had not happened, that the *contretemps* was just a horrible apparition, but the large damp patch embarrassingly staining the front of my suit was irrefutable evidence to the contrary. The young woman, faced with a mortified, soggy, silent man opposite her, a man who obstinately refused to face up to the predicament, took the initiative and suggested we should call it a night and go home, which we did. She saw little in the episode to advance the relationship. I was devastated. At a later stage in life when taking an interest in astrology (a phase single people often go through) an astrologer friend told me if a door opens and one does not go through, it will never open again. In this case the door fell off its hinges rendering it impassable.

Some dismiss astrology as twaddle; others allow it to rule their lives. A companion and I strode onto a dance floor one evening to join two young women for an up-tempo record, which was done in the usual manner of gently touching elbows to let them know our intent. As the young lady and I turned face to face there occurred that heart-stopping moment of stillness beloved by film-makers when two strangers meet, when all around vanishes into oblivion leaving the couple standing in misty solitude to gaze into one another's eyes and ostensibly to fall in love. We managed to stumble through a few dance steps and exchange banalities before the woman snapped out of the trance to ask abruptly, "What star sign are you?" I told her. My reply immediately broke the spell causing the women to recoil, stagger momentarily and relinquish all warmth from her face. Though she politely continued to dance till the end of the record, clearly she had no further interest. A few weeks later whilst walking down Parker Street in Liverpool city centre at lunch time, the same woman and I passed one another on the pavement. She glared at me with such piercing hatred it felt like having one's skull split open by a meat cleaver - all because I was the wrong astrological sign.

Abundant astrological coincidences compel one to at least keep an open mind on the subject. Curiously, however, a marriage most likely to last is one between two certain star signs that are deemed incompatible by astrologers. Perhaps in that case a constant craving for re-assurance on the part of the woman demands the sensitive man give constant attention thereby locking the pair permanently together, even though they may not be completely happy. Numerology is another tool single people may use in their quest for the right person and again one which they should not scorn too hastily. The railway signalling code for Obstruction Danger was arbitrarily chosen as six beats on the bell: numerologists have it that the number six has devilish connections.

To return to the mating game, if I had to pick one single reason why I never settled down in Liverpool it would be the phenomenon of women who bewilderingly behaved like flibbertigibbets. An essential ingredient of discotheques, such women were not genuine flibbertigibbets, at least I am reasonably confident most of them were not, but behaved so as a defence mechanism. Like Atalanta chasing after golden apples, these women would be attracted to a man on impulse. They acted and prated foolishly in his company. Masking true intent, the behaviour allowed a woman to privately assess whether the prospective boyfriend met her standards by testing him in conversation. If at some point in the evening the loquacious woman discovered the man not to be of the substance she hoped for, exercising a woman's prerogative to be mysterious, she would exit just as crazily as she had arrived without feelings being hurt. Probably owing to remnants of Yorkshire dourness, I was never able to conduct a conversation with a woman who acted in this apparently imbecilic way.

I said earlier that no rules existed in the complex process of meeting the right person. That is undoubtedly true from the man's point of view in that he sets no prerequisites, at least none that can be succinctly written down. That is not the case for some women who divided men into two clear groups, those who were worthy of consideration and those who were not, the qualifying factor being possession of a car. Through most bachelor days I did not own a motor car.

CHAPTER THIRTY

Liverpool romances ranged from those that never progressed beyond a dismissive first date to those that journeyed across that plateau of contentment usually referred to as going steady where the principal focus in life is the partner almost to the exclusion of all else. Such journeys must end with the relationship either becoming permanent or disintegrating. Mine disintegrated. Throughout the 1970s I lived alone, never finding anyone with whom I could happily live under the same roof. *The Sunday Times* of 20th September 2007 published statistics showing two per cent of the population lived alone in 1973; in 2007 more than ten per cent of people aged between twenty-two and forty-four years lived by themselves.

In the late 1970s, tired of relationships that stood no hope of lasting, I made a deliberate attempt to look for someone special, but as always when one tries too hard, success absconds. Discouraged, I found myself stepping into the background to make way for men more likely to be enamoured by tinny chatter of pseudo-flibbertigibbets, men with tighter jaws and more luxuriant heads of hair, down-to-earth men who held blue-collar jobs whom women seemed to prefer, men who had the exuberance and nerve I had had years earlier, for it required a lot of nerve to lock into a passionate embrace with a complete stranger.

What is often called the club scene was in a constant if slow state of metamorphosis. When new clubs opened, or old premises were refurbished, the element of newness would be a major draw propelling the discotheque to immense popularity at the expense of older clubs that consequently saw a drop in numbers. But that new club's pre-eminence would only last until it, too, was ousted by another. So it was that one wave of club-goers would pronounce such-and-such a club *the* place to be, and a year or two later when they had settled down to steady relationships, the next wave looking for partners would have a different opinion on the best place to go.

Most did not succeed in meeting someone during first discotheque visits; some persistently missed opportunities. Those men who for whatever reason were left behind might find themselves, cloyed by over-exposure, leaning against a bar in a former hot spot gazing across a dance area that a year or two earlier was so tightly packed no floor was visible but which was now thinly populated with not quite so young women who, too, had chosen not to pair off. A woman's continuing state of spinsterhood would probably be explained by either over-fastidiousness or defiant independence.

People of the opposite sex have to meet somewhere. Clubs described, despite their heady swirl of sensations, were nothing more than present-day versions of dance halls, which themselves superseded gatherings on a village green, if one went far enough back. Discotheques' esoteric dalliances were preserve of those who knew the places actually existed, of those who had enough money, of those who had the self-confidence, and, in the case of men, who had the dash to take advantage of coquetry on offer. Though superficially indistinguishable from discotheques of a later period, Liverpool's in the 1970s differed in two important aspects. First, any deviation from the idea that night clubs were places to meet the *opposite* sex would have been incomprehensible. Second, discotheques were free from the scourge of AIDS which may be transmitted through kissing.

It is conceivable many young people of Liverpool knew nothing of the pleasure-based world within their city. Others who might have known perhaps would have no truck with such decadence. However, the secret escaped in 1977 when the film *Saturday Night Fever* revealed all and irreparably shattered the mystique and exclusiveness of discotheques.

When spirits were low at some point in the late 1970s I began doing voluntary work one evening a week. This pairing of gloomy mood and gushing charity has to cast doubt on proper motivation. It is said people undertake voluntary work because it makes them feel good, but that surely is not the best reason, though it is better than no motivation at all. Disappointment at not having met the right woman and yet feeling very fortunate in otherwise enjoying a care-free life - a collocation of self-pity and smugness - were probably factors in the decision, but they alone ought not to have been the reasons for helping others.

I assisted, in a minor way, with reform of petty criminals. There may have been buried deeply in the subconscious a notion of saving souls. A feeling of civic duty may have come into play, but that is surely mere perfunctoriness. Genuine philanthropy is the only valid argument for helping others and whilst there may have been a measure, it was certainly not my main reason. It is not easy to disentangle the muddle of motivations that prompted voluntary work, and the basic question remains unanswered: was it done through genuine concern for others or did I do it just to satisfy myself? Milton, referring to mankind and to mankind's constitution, provides the answer:

> ...within them as a guide... umpire Conscience,

Nevertheless, I persevered but achieved little because I took no initiative in judging what I was capable of and what I was not capable of, in turn owing to lack of experience in social work. A minor incident underlined how little progress had been made and contributed to ending the experiment. I had been able to forge something approaching a friendship with one young offender to the extent that he had invited me home to meet his wife and children after we had been out for a drink. He must have felt secure in my company for, on the way home, he said in a low voice, "See that shed over there," pointing to a dilapidated outbuilding faintly visible in the darkness, "I'm gonna do that place one night!" He quickly realized his *insouciance* in taking into confidence someone trying to persuade him to lead an honest life, and became instantly silent. For the remainder of the walk home, I held my head down and said nothing.

CHAPTER THIRTY-ONE

Numerous references so far to drinking beer are not meant to encourage others. It should be noted our consumption of alcohol in Liverpool was limited by not having the resources to drink excessively just for the sake of it (binge drinking as it is sometimes referred to) and by a need to retain some semblance of good behaviour if one were to hope of success with the opposite sex. Nevertheless, a description of leisure life in public houses and night clubs raises two major questions, the first being whether consuming so much alcohol was too much. Condemning alcohol just to condemn alcohol is suspect. Still, some will rise quickly to their feet declaring that drinking vast quantities is indicative of a condition requiring treatment, but I will stand up just as quickly to say that the principal issue is whether drinking beer, regardless of quantity, causes harm. In the case of a bachelor there is no risk to family, and I was never foolish enough nor thirsty enough to drink so much I ran into debt. It is said a person's predisposition to drink shows at work and will often result in the toper losing his job, but I drank only every other night and, furthermore, on the day after drinking, the mind was much clearer and work proceeded much smother than on days when I had not drunk the previous evening. Those who rose to their feet before will now rise again to point out a dependency, to which criticism I have no answer.

Many gifted people are able to sail through demanding careers without resort to stimulant or lenitive, but many of us needed help in coping, whether the prop was tangible, such as cigarettes, alcohol or Valium, or was of behaviour, such as arrant ill-manners or petulance. Of these aids surely alcohol consumption, the leveller of men, when undertaken outside work is least objectionable and least harmful.

Alcohol is a useful catalyst in social life, but drinking beer without restraint is not to be recommended because it is injurious to the alimentary canal, even though one would have thought regular flushing out would be naught but beneficial. We are also informed alcohol over time destroys brain cells, though so far I have not noticed any effect, or maybe there is an effect I have not noticed, or maybe I only think I have not noticed - oh, I don't really know whether I have been affected or not. Anyway, as unhealthy as immoderate drinking was, the fog of cigarette smoke that used to hang like murky chandeliers in taverns was likely far more damaging. Of greatest concern might be missed opportunities. One might ask what alternative path could life have taken had drinking been eschewed in favour of greater achievement? I regret to say it is an avenue not worth exploring since (most) normal healthy single males consume alcohol to fill the vacuum of no female company.

A second major question asked is what place does a treatise on Liverpool mating habits have in a book expressly about railways? A short answer is that I feel I owe an explanation, or perhaps an excuse, why very little happened concerning railways during the 1970s. A long answer is that it is necessary to grasp what went on and what did not go on in Liverpool's night clubs to understand how those events affected the role railways would play in future life, though a complete revelation is beyond the scope of this book. To delve into why affairs of the heart and railways were irretrievably entwined, I will shortly need to draw an analogy with something from the world of science. Railways have always been my main interest, but that has not precluded a passing interest in scientific developments.

Life would eventually become tedious were it not for momentous changes that periodically descend upon it. For example, marriage alters spouses' outlooks and commands them to make new plans. For those who attend university, innumerable opportunities open up, opportunities that would not exist had the student not risen to high scholastic standard. We are drawn to certain vicissitudes by their appeal, or through custom or sometimes through factors beyond our control, and we take advantage of that which calls us forth, then, enlightened, emboldened, enriched, empowered, take off in an entirely new direction. Does this not sound like a modern scientific marvel? Does it not sound like the exploration of space where a probe swings by one planet to change course on its way to another? It seems to me life's journey is indeed like an inter-planetary mission.

Similarity between peripeteia and inter-planetary travel lies in the manner in which space probes exploring outer reaches of the solar system use planets to alter trajectories and to boost momentum. A spacecraft's course is projected to pass close to a planet where the planet's gravitational field will first accelerate the craft towards it, but where the probe's original trajectory is sufficiently clear of the planet's orbit to prevent the spacecraft from plunging into it. The probe cannot resist entirely the pull of gravity so its course is bent and, with accelerated speed, it curves round the planet to take off in a new direction. Is this not like life-changing events that attract us from time to time and from which we emerge to advance along new paths? In my case Liverpool's discotheques and heavenly bodies therein were a powerful draw and remained so for many years, but as the year 1980 came round, the gravitational pull these pavilions of pleasure exerted began to lose its strength and the year would see life take off in a new direction. The train of events that launched a new venture is described below.

Crest of the gleeful wave generated by The Beatles ridden in earlier times had, by 1980, collapsed to a trickle, and I was paying the price of all who missed opportunities to settle down, the price of loneliness. The final blow was an encounter which initially held out hope of a promising relationship but which devastatingly somersaulted to reveal that the woman concerned was already permanently attached to another, a chance meeting having taken place whilst that permanent attachment was temporarily severed. The discovery brought on a state of dejection of no less magnitude than the state of elation when the woman was first met. It seemed fate determined I was not to meet the right woman in Liverpool. A further blow to social life on Merseyside had been the taking over of Walker's Brewery in Warrington by a national company. General despondency was compounded by events at work taking an unsatisfactory turn.

During most of the Liverpool stay I worked for a small firm of wholesale and manufacturing stationers. Originally employed, vaguely, in an "administrative capacity", I was promoted to Invoicing Manager when the previous incumbent left. The job involved overseeing eight females who prepared, typed and checked invoices before dispatch. I ran a tight ship and used to take great delight in being able to locate the price of more obscure items of stationery, or being able to recall where a certain customer was located in the credit control system – which was very surprising for someone with poor memory. Perhaps the key to memory is whether one is really interested in the fact, or maybe I am better at recalling exceptions rather than rules. In this pre-digital age the firm's credit control system was based on thousands of Addressograph-Multigraph embossed metal plates used to print labels. If we had an address plate for a customer, then the customer had an account. It was far more complicated than that of course, and it was those complications that took up most time.

In the mid-1970s I was promoted to take charge of sales in a specially-made-to-order section of the company. Within a short time, the department enjoyed a boost in sales. That fillip occurred not through a flair for selling but through meticulous attention to detail in preparing factory work orders. Hard work was rewarded by repeat orders. The job was hectic requiring frequent visits to other departments. So frequent were comings and goings, I had to place on the corner of my desk a small cardboard box lettered and coloured on three sides with department names. Each time I left the office the box had to be turned to indicate where I was.

A frantic pace of work left little room for levity, but I recall an occasion when the managing director's secretary called in to give to me a small piece of office equipment – I cannot remember what – that had been a gift from a Japanese supplier. "Here, you can have this, Mitchell. It needs putting together, though. You'll be able to do that," said the woman. With that, she left the office briskly.

I examined the packet of components. I could see, whatever it was, would take some time to assemble, but knew printed instructions would speed up the process. I tore into the package to recover the instructions. They were in Japanese. "These bloody instructions are in Japanese!" I cried out in exaggerated distress. "How the hell am I supposed to put it together when it's written in Japanese?" I glanced over my shoulder at the young man and woman who worked for me in the same office. Both were desperately trying to conceal hysterical laughter at the unnecessarily theatrical but nevertheless comical outcry just given out by their supervisor. The managing director's secretary had played a minor joke by presenting me with an unsolvable puzzle. In turn I entertained my two assistants by pretending to take the jape seriously.

It has been said that whilst captains of industry may be at the helm, it is youth and energy of junior and middle managers in their twenties and thirties that actually drive the economy. I certainly fell into that age bracket. But despite constant hard work and a steady rise in sales, the section's initial leap in turnover was not repeated. An unfavourable economy dampened efforts. In 1980 company statistics suddenly revealed that whilst I had kept well-oiled the wheels of one particular light industry, the financial results were unspectacular. Somewhat like the Return to Steam Committee, full marks were awarded for diligence, but no shining trophy in recognition. I began to think about a change in career, even if upheaval showed rank ingratitude to an employer who had financed my rakish existence for the last twelve years, a paternal employer who had guaranteed employment and showed every promise of continuing to do so. The employer might even have gone so far as attempting to broker a marriage for a junior manager who would certainly have been better off with stability in his life. I speculate that an attempted match failed owing to my lack of interest in tennis, which was to have facilitated an introduction.

With life in the doldrums I was at a loss to know what to do, not for the first time finding myself without direction. In the event, railways came to the rescue.

CHAPTER THIRTY-TWO

Enthusiasm for railways is never lost. Once acquired it becomes part of the individual, like manner of speech or slope of the shoulders. A love for railways can expand to the point of shutting out more deserving claims on time, or can be squeezed into a small corner, shrivelled and neglected, but it will never go away, even when mauled by an exacting career or worldly excesses.

During dark ages of dissipation I had still found time for occasional bicycle rides to look at the post-steam railway network, though much of Liverpool's infrastructure was now run down. Rides to see the complex of lines and sidings around Warrington were always rewarding. Occasional trips on electric trains to the seaside resorts of Southport, New Brighton and West Kirby took the rider past numerous lineside buildings which could hastily be described as signal boxes but which technically were not necessarily so. During journeys the structures' glistening windows and light-coloured paintwork flashed by like ghosts in the night giving no clues to their purpose, their names impossible to read at speed. Even more fugacious, innumerable slender white signal posts shot by tantalizingly withholding their message from the traveller, semaphore arms largely being visible only to the train driver. Signals and signal boxes alike teased the enthusiast by making him yearn for more yet pertinaciously remained out of reach. Only a handful of identifications were possible, such as New Brighton, where signals in the station area were clearly worked by its one box. All other installations and trackside paraphernalia were a fuzzy string of signalling equipment without name or number.

This deplorable nescience remained uncorrected for some thirty years till the Merseyside Railway History Group published parts one and two of *The Last Merseyrail Signal Boxes* describing signalling on the electrified lines radiating from Liverpool. The books at last cleared up for me mysteries of seaside signalling and recorded for posterity details of signal boxes, all of which have now gone. What appear to be signal boxes may be divided into two categories. First, true signal boxes that signal trains to one another. Second, gate boxes which are installations purely to supervise level crossings, installations that receive information on the whereabouts of trains second hand by various electrical means. Differentiating between the two is complicated by many signal boxes also overseeing level crossings.

The signalling system in force in Merseyrail signal boxes was Absolute Block, the same Absolute Block I knew at Bickle. Even when dealing with a rapid succession of commuter trains, the same three-stage routine of Line Clear, Train on Line and Line Blocked (or Normal) was followed as boxes belled trains to one another using inveterate bell signals of two beats for Train entering Section, 2-1 for Train out of Section, etcetera. Of particular interest was Bidston East where the signalman had to continually throw his junction first one way then the other as passenger trains ran alternately to West Kirby and New Brighton, no mean feat when trains ran closely together in rush hours. It was said to be the second busiest mechanical signal box in Britain, beaten only by one in Wimbledon, London.

Sadly, all signal boxes and gate boxes were swept away by newer technology, the last of them closing on 17th September 1994, their work being taken over by Merseyrail integrated electronic control centre - though administratively so, modern signal boxes are no longer called signal boxes. Meanwhile, through the 1970s presence of so much mechanical signalling around Liverpool kept alive an interest in the subject, but it was another branch of the hobby that would ultimately engineer change.

By 1978 the path taken to catch a bus for work took me past a model railway shop where each morning, provided a bus was not in sight, I would pause to gaze at the display of model steam engines, rolling stock and allied equipment. Night life, such as it was, still consumed most of my surplus cash, so there was little to spare. I would stare at the merchandise on display like a hungry orphan. I eventually succumbed and bought an ancient motor-less "00" gauge Britannia Class Pacific, a lifeless husk I still possess today. I pushed the powerless machine up and down a short length of track marvelling at the reproduction Walschaerts valve gear, a simple amusement but one which whetted the appetite. Steadily, more time and money was diverted away from nocturnal indulgences towards building a basic model railway, which in turn sparked interest in the model railway press.

An article in one of these periodicals made passing mention of a group of enthusiasts who studied signalling. Up till that point I thought I was the only one on earth who loved signals, so by courtesy of the magazine made contact with that group. This reaching out to like-minded individuals fired a renewed passion for real signalling, rather than just models, leading to officially sanctioned visits to signal boxes. Intensively worked signal boxes on Merseyside's busy urban railways once again threw a spotlight on the joy of ringing out bell codes on telegraph instruments, the delight of heaving on a serried row of brightly coloured levers, the thrill of watching trains go by, all of which saw re-birth of the boyhood notion of becoming a signalman. It was however by no means certain a position could be obtained locally. Nevertheless, I learnt a surprisingly large number of mechanical signal boxes were still operational in London, and since labour market forces in that part of the country would ensure vacancies would be harder to fill, an application to be a signalman would be more likely to be favourably received in the capital than anywhere else.

I had always dreamt of becoming a signalman when I was a boy; now at last there was chance to realize that dream. But matters are never as straightforward as one would hope; becoming a British Railways' signalman would prove to be no exception. An initial approach by letter in May 1980 elicited a response that merely stated I should re-apply once I moved to London. A very frustrating couple of weeks then followed as I attempted to get the point over by telephone that I could not move to London till I had a job to go to. Eventually an interview was arranged at British Railways' Area Manager's Office, Willesden Junction, London NW10, for Tuesday 17th June.

On that date I put on my best suit and went to Lime Street station at about 09:00 hours to catch a train for which I had been given a free pass. As I stood around the station concourse waiting to board, my managing director walked by on his way to work. Impeccably dressed as I was, it was impossible to hide the fact that an event of some significance was under way. With a foolish grin wretchedly hanging from a reddened face, I lied to the managing director that I was visiting someone. Since I had officially booked the day off, my superior had no alternative but to listen impassively to the fabrication presented to him.

Upon arrival at London Euston station, I could find no trains on the indicator board to Willesden Junction, so resorted to a roundabout route via Broad Street station and the North London Line. I did not know that times of local trains to Watford via Willesden Junction were tucked away in a corner, not immediately visible from the centre of the concourse. After a not uneventful journey from Liverpool, I eventually arrived on time for interview at 14:30 hours. The interviewer took great pains to point out disadvantages of being a signalman. I would have to work seven-day weeks, all bank holidays and one week in three would be night shift. When mates went to a football game, I would have to be on duty on Saturday afternoon. This barrage of bad news certainly unsettled me, but did not change my mind. I think the senior manager conducting the interview wanted to be sure I understood how much of a commitment I would have to make. He said, frankly, "You're over-qualified for the job." He could have added I was over-dressed, too.

Despite doing his best to discourage me, the senior manager must have concluded I was fit material for the position of signalman, for a letter soon followed calling me to attend a medical examination at Euston station on 26th June. I had always enjoyed good health, but was naturally nervous. A crucial part of the examination was an eyesight test that included colour recognition, a vital faculty for all railway workers. Happily, a telephone call to Willesden Area Manager's office the following day revealed I had passed the medical examination. But another week or two of agonizing uncertainty followed as I awaited further communication. Finally, a letter from the Willesden Area Manager dated 8th July formally offered a position of temporary Trainee Signalman at a commencing wage of sixty-seven pounds fifty-five pence per week. Starting date would be Monday 11th August 1980, coincidentally exactly twelve years after the fifteen guinea last steam train. At last, a signalman I would be.

So it was that the planet of Liverpool's night life initially drew me towards it, then by not providing a partner, allowed me to pass by, the city finally launching me in a new direction through its railway connections. I spent thirteen years in Liverpool, a large slice of anyone's life. Spare time was not entirely wasted, as I obtained a Higher National Certificate in Business Studies at Liverpool Polytechnic. The city continued the process begun by a Birmingham waitress of transforming a country boy into someone who could move around with ease in the intricate theatre, in the unfathomable maze of urban life - of transforming a country boy into metropolitan man. Thanks to the generous and effervescent character of the people of Liverpool, to their friendliness, to their wit, I left that city a less stuffy, more erudite, more balanced, a more human person than when I first arrived.

The most insignificant event can have a most profound effect. At work one day I walked into an office to find the woman in charge obviously struggling to cope with the day's workload, her usually bright face lined with concern.

"What's the matter?" I asked her.

"Oh, I dunno, Mitch. I suppose I'm just having a bad day," the woman replied.

"Bad day?"

"Yeh. Don't you ever have bad days, Mitch?" she asked.

"No, never," I said confidently.

I left the office manageress to sort out her problems. Some time later it occurred to me that the claim never to have had a bad day – otherwise known as just one of those days – was dishonest. As a junior manager, I felt a need to assert everything was one hundred per cent under control all the time, hence the lie. Days on which more things seemed to go wrong than on others were put down to my own failings, a fact I kept to myself of course, but one which had privately troubled me. The office manageress's approach of blaming woes on the day rather than on herself was far preferable. Even a whole string of days when nothing seemed to go right - when one might grumble of a Hate Deaver Week - might now be brushed aside. Labelling an unpleasant experience as simply a bad day would prove invaluable for evening out work's up and downs, and was an important item of self-preservation armour acquired during Liverpool years.

PART TWO

SIGNALS

CHAPTER ONE

"The first thing I would like to do Mitchell is to welcome you to British Rail," said Ron Dillington with alacrity.

The date was Monday 11th August 1980. I sat nervously in a small room, one of many such rooms forming the Willesden Area Manager's Office, which was no shiny glass and concrete edifice but a collection of old buildings wedged amongst a tangle of railway tracks collectively known as Willesden Junction. Ron Dillington was a supervisor of signalmen. The position once bore the title District Inspector, which title in recent times had been changed to the less elegant but equally meaningless Movements Inspector. My new employer was the British Railways Board, but the marketing name of British Rail had displaced use of the full title in all but legal documents.

A lean man with pronounced facial features, Ron Dillington continued in a spirited manner. "There's a few things I have to go over with you on your first day. First, we've got to get you a high visibility vest." He scrabbled in a drawer, eventually to drag out a crumpled piece of bright orange material which he straightened into a waistcoat-sized garment. "Bit mildewy, but it'll do. You must wear this whenever you're on or about the tracks. You'll be working at Kensal Green Junction signal box which means you've got to walk alongside main tracks to get to it, but I'll show you that later," said Ron Dillington continuing the induction programme. "Normally, Mitchell, what we do with new signalmen is we put them through signalling school, but we're not going to do that in your case; we're going to teach you on the job, in the box. You understand?"

I nodded. Ron Dillington spoke forcibly, thrusting his head in my direction whenever he wanted to place emphasis. "I'll be checking your progress. It'll be my job to make sure you're properly trained. You're going to be with Fred Abbott at Kensal Green. He's a good man, one of the old school, if you like," said Ron Dillington smiling broadly as he sensed a preference in me for working alongside an experienced signalman. "Now, I'll have to get you a set of rule books. They tell me you're a bit of a signalling enthusiast." His wide eyes twinkled and widened even further upon broaching the topic. "Have you seen the *Regulations for Train Signalling and Signalmen's General Instructions*, you know, the green-covered book?"

"No, I havn't. They're confidential aren't they?" I said, hoping my respect for proprietorship would impress the supervisor.

"I know they are, but somehow they find their way out there." His voice lowered and his countenance became serious; he looked away attempting to hide regret that I was a less knowledgeable new recruit than he had hoped for. "Well, if you're not familiar with signalling regulations, that means we've got to start from scratch."

His disappointment disappointed the person who caused the original disappointment. As an eight-year old boy in Bickle signal box I had taken great pride in knowing, for example, seven beats on the bell meant Stop and Examine Train - a bell signal to the next signalman down the line telling him to stop a train because there was something wrong with it. I was still pleased with myself some twenty-five years later in retaining that information. Ron Dillington's pessimism was nevertheless well founded since such Spartan knowledge was simply not good enough for a professional signalman. In detail, regulations lay down that if a signalman has to send the Stop and Examine Train bell signal, he must consider consequences of the defective train for other trains under his control. For example, if a passenger train passed with a door open, in addition to sending seven beats on the bell, the signalman has to stop any other trains coming towards or going away from him in case a passenger had fallen out and lay injured on the tracks. It was ignorance of how to respond quickly and properly to emergency circumstances that Ron Dillington realized had to be remedied in the new man sitting opposite, which prospect sullied an otherwise pleasing occasion of an enthusiastic addition to the ranks of local signalmen.

Despite the set back, Ron Dillington quickly returned to his normal cheerful self. "Now we need to tell you about timesheets, how you get paid, and so-on." He described the procedure for filling out timesheets, which necessitated explaining shift arrangements. Kensal Green Junction signal box was typical of many in having to be open twenty-four hours a day, seven days a week, 364 days a year, closing only on Christmas Day. It had to be manned continuously. If there were no one in the box, signals would be held at stop, trains could not move, and nothing could be done about it till a signalman were found.

Three permanent signalmen were allocated to such boxes, but since their working week comprised only forty hours, they had to put in extra time to ensure the installation stayed open. Sunday was officially outside the normal working week but, by agreement, was generally covered by the regular men. Of the remaining six days, one was considered to be a rest day, but again usually worked by the man who covered the other five. A night shift rest day would be of little use since nothing could usefully be done at night, so it was transferred to one of the daytime shifts. Consequently, men would work, say, one rest day on the morning shift and two rest days on the afternoon shift, there being no rostered rest day on a week of nights. (In 1950s Bickle, men never worked rest days, their absence being covered by a rest-day relief man.) It would appear, then, that men never had a day off, but that was not quite true, as will be explained later. A decades-old union agreement endorsed these complicated schedules.

After completion of the induction programme and after I had been measured for signalman's uniform, Ron Dillington had more information. "You'll be starting in a week's time at 22:00 hours, 10 p.m. What I want to do now is take you along to meet Fred Abbott so you both know who you'll be working with on Monday night."

The Movements Inspector led the way through a labyrinth of passages in Willesden Junction Station, along a platform for local trains to Euston terminus and up a staircase to platforms of the North London Line which were at a higher level: the North London Line passed over main line tracks into Euston. Whilst walking along the high level platforms Ron Dillington suddenly stopped beneath a suspended circular contraption displaying a horizontal black bar. "I'll show you something while we're here," he said. "You see that banner repeater."

I looked up at the round sign.

"That's a banner repeater for your Up home," said Ron Dillington. "Sometimes it sticks in the 'off' position, and then you can't give a Line Clear to High Level box. All it needs is a clout with a broom handle or something. That'll fix it."

A point being made here was that signalmen were expected to do what they could to repair faulty equipment before calling in technicians, and wielding a broom handle was certainly not beyond capabilities of signalmen. If a paraffin signal lamp went out, signalmen were expected to relight it; if accumulation of snow hindered operation of a signal wire, signalmen should endeavour to clear it away. With Lesson Number One in elementary signal repairs out of the way, we continued our journey. We walked to the eastern end of Willesden Junction high level platforms, down the platform ramp, and along a ballast-strewn wide way between Up and Down Platform Lines towards Kensal Green Junction signal box. After crossing a pair of lines we climbed the signal box steps to arrive on a small landing outside the signal box door. Ron Dillington politely tapped on the door and entered.

"Hello Fred. How's things?" asked the Movements Inspector.

"All right, yer know," said a smiling Fred Abbott.

"Good, good," said Ron Dillington. "Now I want you to meet Mitchell Deaver. He'll be starting with you next Monday night then."

The tall, well-built signalman beamed a welcoming smile and outstretched his hand for me to shake. I grinned and met his hand with mine. His firm grip crushed my fingers whilst we exchanged pleasantries.

"I suppose your relief'll be here soon," said Ron Dillington looking at his watch.

"About ten minutes," replied Fred Abbott.

"I just wanted you two to say hello, so you know where you are on Monday. C'mon Mitchell, we'll get out of the way and let these men change shifts in peace," said the Movements Inspector, whereupon he whisked me straight back to the Area Manager's Office. Ron Dillington was coming to the end of his shift too, which meant my day was also nearly over. He concluded a first day on British Railways with typical broad smile and by wishing me good luck in a forthcoming career, a warm handshake saying he was almost as pleased to have me working for him as I was in fulfilling a twenty-five year-old ambition to be a signalman.

CHAPTER TWO

One week later, with orange reflective vest wrapped round a chest exploding with pride, I marched off the platform ramp at Willesden Junction, along the wide way towards Kensal Green Junction where, for the first time in my life, I was actually going to work in a signal box rather than visit it. Not since boyhood days in Bickle would a signal box give up entirely secrets of its lever numbers and idiosyncrasies. Exercising due care, I crossed the pair of lines to reach the signal box steps. With loud confident footsteps I climbed the wooden staircase towards faded paintwork of the signal box door. I looked through the panes, grinned, turned the handle and walked in. Fred Abbott returned my grin, directed me to a corner where I could place a bundle of belongings, and invited me to share a pot of tea with him.

"D'yer take milk, Mitchell?" asked Fred Abbott.
"Yes please," I replied.
"Sugar?"
"No thanks."
Sound of block bells interrupted tea-making. The signalman acknowledged bell code 3-1-2 from Gospel Oak signal box signifying an electric multiple unit passenger train had just left there. As Track Circuit Block Regulations were in force between Kensal Green and Gospel Oak, all Fred Abbott had to do at this stage was write the time of the bell signal in the train register book.

Track Circuit Block Regulations were and are the modern way of signalling trains, Absolute Block Regulations the old way. To explain the difference, a very basic signalling concept needs to be stated: a railway is divided into clearly defined (but varying) lengths, or blocks, and a signal at the entrance to each block tells the train driver whether he may enter that block, and if so, under what conditions. In Track Circuit Block, track circuits (wiring through rails that detect whether a train is on them) are installed the entire length of a block, typically a thousand yards long. Through this technology presence of a train in a block automatically holds the entrance signal at red. When the train moves into the next block, that colour light signal will change to yellow and eventually to green once the train has travelled far enough down the line. In this way signals at the beginning of each block automatically grant or refuse entrance into it. Some Track Circuit Block signals may be held at red by the signalman. Because track circuits actually do the signalling, all a signalman has to do is let his colleague in the next signal box know what kind of train is on its way; he simply describes the train, as the procedure is referred to. At Kensal Green this was done by sending codes on a telegraphic single-beat bell. Clearly, Track Circuit Block Regulations require that the entire length of railway between two signal boxes be equipped with track circuits (or with some other means of detecting trains).

In Absolute Block Regulations, railway between two signal boxes need not be track circuited. Only one train at a time is permitted between boxes. Telegraphic block indicators, such as those I knew at Bickle, are used to indicate whether or not there is a train between signal boxes. These are used in conjunction with single-beat bells.

Absolute Block signalling involves three stages, the first being a need for the signalman to ask by bell code permission to send a train, which his colleague down the line grants by repeating the bell code and by giving a Line Clear indication on a block indicator. Next, when the train passes the first man, the Train entering Section bell signal, two beats, must be sent, at which point the second man must turn the block indicator to Train on Line. Finally, when the train has passed the second signal box, the Train out of Section bell signal, 2-1, must be sent and the block indicator needle returned to the Normal (or Line Blocked) position. Another train may then be offered. Absolute Block is far more laborious, yet has proved reliable for a century or so and, even into the 2010s, is still in use on many segments of the British railway network.

Block indicators I remembered from Bickle signal box were like large mantelpiece clocks, one for sending trains and one for receiving trains in each direction, a total of four. Along with single stroke bell units, they were attractively encased in polished hardwood. British Railways produced the equivalent in a six-inch plastic cube, with all three block instruments stacked on top of one another, the sending indicator on top, receiving indicator in the middle and block bell at the base. The result was a cheap-looking affair that men referred to as Woolworth's blocks. The term Line Blocked used in older instruments for the vertical needle position was replaced by the word Normal.

Kensal Green signalled to four different signal boxes. Track Circuit Block Regulations applied to Gospel Oak and to Willesden power box,

Absolute Block Regulations applied to Willesden High Level Junction and Willesden New Station. Apposition of Track Circuit Block and Absolute Block Regulations was just one example of a mix of old and new found in many 1980s signal boxes.

CHAPTER THREE

The first few minutes of the first day in Kensal Green continued at a relaxed pace. "You'll be able to use the spare locker 'cause there's a vacancy here," said Fred Abbott. "Maybe when you get trained you'll be able to take the vacancy, I don't know."

"You mean I won't get it automatically?" said I.

"No," said Fred Abbot in his soft London accent. "Somebody with more seniority could apply for it. We'll see."

Though from opposite ends of the country and a generation apart, conversation flowed freely between trainer and trainee and centred on antecedents and my lifelong interest in railways, particularly signalling. An exchange of bell codes on the high-pitched bell from Willesden High Level Junction halted colloquy. Absolute Block Regulations being in force, Frank Abbot attended to the eighteen inches-high plastic block instrument. After working the Morse code key, or bell tapper, he turned a white wedge-shaped knob, the commutator handle, from the six o'clock position to the four o'clock position, which moved it from the word Normal on a white background to the words Line Clear on a green background. The dial needle above it responded in exactly the same way. He then thrust his grey duster in my hands and said, "Number 56."

"What?" I said, flabbergasted at being entrusted with the lever frame after being in the box only ten minutes.

"C'mon, you've gotta learn," urged the senior signalman.

I got up, walked over to short-handled red lever number 56 labelled Up Platform Line Home 1, and attempted to pull it, but it would not move. The levers I remembered from boyhood had a trigger handle behind the main stem; these levers had none.

"Use the stirrup," said Fred Abbott.

I attempted to pull up a hoop of metal fixed to the front of the lever, but it would not move.

"Nah, push down," said the signalman. "Don't worry, I had trouble myself when I first worked these frames. I was used to Great Western frames with the handle behind."

After I had struggled to get number 56 out of the frame, Fred Abbott told me to pull number 53 Up Platform Line Home 2 and number 43 Up Main Starting, which were also short-handled and coloured red. What ought to have been a simple and smooth operation of pulling "off" three colour lights degenerated into a clumsy battle between man and metal as this apprentice struggled to execute the most basic of signalman's skills. The pathetic effort had cleared signals for a passenger train on the Up Main. The Up direction was eastwards, or from right to left when viewed from the box, Down opposite. All three signals were colour lights and therefore required little effort to move levers - or should have required little effort but for a tiro's inept operation of the stirrup handle. To pull "off" a signal, or to clear a signal means, put simply, to change the signal from stop to go.

Once all three stop signals had been cleared, one would have expected the Up Main distant, number 58, to be pulled to tell the train driver all following signals were "off" and that he may proceed with all speed. This was not possible as the distant had been disconnected a year or two earlier. Number 58 was a traditional semaphore distant signal with yellow fish-tailed arm and matching black chevron that was mounted beneath Willesden High Level Junction's home signal. It had at one time been mechanically worked by steel wire until a new bridge constructed over the West Coast Main Line left no room for a wire run. So the signal was disconnected to remain fixed at caution, the long-handled yellow-painted lever frustratingly secured back in the frame.

To have an old-style semaphore signal as distant for modern colour light stop signals was the opposite way round to the expected. Conventional thinking has it that if there must be a mixture of semaphores and colour lights, it is preferable to have a colour light distant as its electric light gives a clearer indication of the road ahead than the semaphore's paraffin lamp, and mechanical distant signals sometimes need considerable effort to operate them, a condition which does not improve over time. On the Midland Region of British Railways there appeared, on the face of it, to be a partiality for semaphore distants governing colour light stop signals, but this was merely because stop signals had come up for renewal first.

Whilst on the subject of number 58 lever, its neighbour in the frame, number 59, was an oddity in being painted green, a rare colour in mechanical lever frames. At one time it had worked a lineside gong for communicating with traincrews when the entrance to a siding was obscured by thick fog. In those days there was also a lever next to points letting into the siding for traincrews to ring a gong in the box, a gong which was still in place behind the lever frame, redundant. Number 59 green lever now worked nothing, free to be pulled and pushed around as much as one wished if the urge were there, otherwise remaining in desuetude.

(On page 219 of *A Pictorial Record of L.N.W.R. Signalling* by Richard Foster is a photograph of the gong inside Kensal Green box. The book includes two other interior shots, one being of detonator placers on page 225. On page 266 can be found an illustration of the cast iron name plates behind levers 23 to 26 which date from a time when the Platform Lines were referred to as lines for Kensington. This suggests that tracks to Kensington were once the main lines rather than tracks towards Richmond; the two diverged at Willesden High Level Junction.)

To return now to the first few minutes of the day, out of breath from struggling with stirrup handles, I sat down on a battered, pale blue wooden chair at a kitchen table. The table's plastic surface was blue gingham check. This table and deep kitchen sink in a corner gave the signal box a domestic feel. Fred Abbot eased his muscular frame back into a worn but comfortable brown leather easy chair. He did not sit long. Two beats on the bell told of the passenger train's passing Willesden High Level Junction. Fred Abbot sprang up, acknowledged the message by replying two beats on the tapper and by turning the commutator handle on the block indicator from the four o'clock position to the eight o'clock position, which the needle above copied by swinging over from green-coloured Line Clear to red-coloured Train on Line. The signalman wrote in the train register book. After its stop at High Level station, the three-car passenger train soon passed by, its silent electric motor drawing current via pick-up shoes rubbing along a 600 volt direct current third rail adjacent to the running rail. The only sound heard was that of wheels rattling over pointwork. The train was described to Gospel Oak on the bell, and after I had been ordered to put levers back in the frame, Fred Abbott was able to give High Level Junction the Train out of Section bell signal, 2-1. Via the commutator handle, he returned the block indicator needle to its white-coloured vertical position labelled Normal.

This procedure is followed for every train when Absolute Block Regulations are in force.

CHAPTER FOUR

One could not have wished for a better tutor than Fred Abbott. When Inspector Ron Dillington had referred to Fred Abbott's being of the old school, he meant the man matched exactly the popular image of a signalman - insofar as there is a popular image of this small craft of workers - in being an older person, of stable disposition and exuding an air of dignity. His very name, its ordinariness, was typical of signalmen. From the handful of signalmen I had known in Yorkshire and from the many I would come to know on the North London Line, it seemed as if all had been named by taking everyday Christian names and common surnames, by tossing those names in the air and by allowing them to be paired wherever they fell. Doubtless a Julian Witherspoon or a Marmaduke Farquahrson could be found in a signal box somewhere in Britain, but I never heard of them.

Fred Abbott had once retired from service, but had been asked to return owing to shortage of signalmen. Despite his age, he kept a straight back and square shoulders; he had been athletic in youth. Flashes of dry humour offset a sometimes stern demeanour. On the illuminated signalling diagram that sat on the block shelf, the signal box itself was represented by a small red rectangle containing a line and a dot showing relative positions of the frame and the man who worked it. Fred Abbott would refer to this symbol as the envelope. Presence of trains was indicated on the diagram by pairs of red lights that illuminated in sequence as trains moved from one end of the area of control to the other – left to right or right to left. The senior signalman would occasionally walk up to the diagram and, with perfect timing, blow on the last pair of lights just as the train moved off giving the illusion he had extinguished the lights with his breath.

Notwithstanding his own innate sense of humour, Fred Abbott had to contend with a new brand his pupil brought to the signal box. Tracks on the illuminated diagram were broken into individual track circuits, each with a pair of red lights. The track circuits were shown in different colours (the actual palette having little significance) purely to identify where one ended and another began. Noting the colouration, I pointed outside and said to

Fred Abbott, "Why aren't the tracks out there coloured in the same way as they are on the diagram?"

"Rain washed the paint off." He looked me hard in the eye to underline the fact his reply, no less rapid than it was droll, was funnier than the question.

We were walking round the box one day to check I knew the purpose of each piece of equipment and on arrival at a window, I pointed to the casement and asked "Window?"

Fred Abbott chuckled and nodded that I was quite correct in identifying the pane of glass as a window.

"Ah!" I cogently added, "but what's on the other side?"

The signalman's chuckle broke into resounding laughter.

Despite occasional light-hearted banter, I set about the serious task of learning the lever frame and identifying the trains that passed Kensal Green Junction. Concurrent with learning how to work the box, I had to study rules and regulations to qualify as a signalman generally, and accordingly spent part of the day dealing with trains under the watchful eye of Fred Abbott, part of the day burying the nose in rule books. Parallel courses of tuition lasted several weeks.

CHAPTER FIVE

In *Regulations for Train Signalling and Signalmen's General Instructions* I had to be conversant with both Absolute Block Regulations and Track Circuit Block Regulations, for both were in effect at Kensal Green. A signalman also had to know those parts of the Rule Book that referred to him.

Three signalling regulations dealt with unsettling eventualities: Regulation 20 with a train that had broken in two, Regulation 23 with a runaway train and Regulation 22 with a runaway train running away backwards. The chances of any of these alarming circumstances arising are greatly reduced in present times thanks to the continuous air brake being connected throughout trains. The air brake is so set up that if couplings – heavy chains fastening rolling stock together - break under load, air pipes between vehicles rip apart exhausting compressed air to the atmosphere, which action automatically applies brakes to both halves of the train stopping them. Even with the air brake, in rare circumstances runaways can still occur, and that is why these regulations are retained. Some years ago a parked locomotive was not properly held by a handbrake and began to move out of a siding on its own. The driverless locomotive eventually found its way onto the main line, which was downhill, and careered out of control for many miles. The runaway engine was dealt with in accordance with Regulations 22 or 23 until it was successfully diverted into a siding.

Up till the 1950s most freight trains were not fitted with the continuous brake, the brake on a heavy steam locomotive plus the guard's van's hand brake being sufficient to control a train. Where heavy loads and steep gradients greatly increased risk of couplings breaking under strain and portions of trains running away, spring-loaded catch points were installed on hills in such a manner that trains passing over them in the right direction were unimpeded but anything moving in the wrong direction would be thrown off to the side. I wondered how often the emergency of a runaway train occurred in days of predominately unfitted freights. At some point I asked around. Despite an abundance of anecdotal evidence, no one contacted could come up with reliable first-hand experience of such a nightmarish happening.

Absolute Block Regulations 20, 22 and 23 essentially said that a signalman must do whatever he can to mitigate consequences of a train running out of control. He must consider diverting errant vehicles towards a line where there is a rising gradient to slow them down or he must consider diverting them into a siding. The prescribed bell signals were 5-5 for a divided train that was still moving forwards but in two separate parts, 4-5-5 for a runaway train, and 2-5-5 for a train running away in the wrong direction. Since the last two bell codes were very similar, a mnemonic would be to consider that the number four was for a train going forward. Mercifully, I would never have to deal with an out-of-control train.

Despite studying assiduously all rules and regulations, both the apocalyptic and the mundane, the recurring problem of being a slow learner resulted in tuition taking longer than both Ron Dillington and I had hoped. In particular, I had the utmost difficulty in remembering two conditions which must be met before a train could examine the line between two signal boxes owing to something untoward, as laid down in Absolute Block Regulation 15.

"Now Mitchell," Ron Dillington would ask in one of his periodic visits, "what do we need to examine the line?"

"Er, Train out of Section and...er..." I faltered because I could not remember the second of two requirements.

"You need Train out of Section for the previous train and telephone communication between the two boxes concerned. You've gotta remember this Mitchell if you want to pass your signalman's test," the Movements Inspector would say testily.

Rules and regulations were not the only books a signalman needed to master. He had to know of course which trains went in which direction and the order in which they ran. To that end, signal boxes were issued working timetables (as opposed to the simplified versions available to the public) which, one would have thought, would remove any doubt as to the sequence of trains. But it was not quite that simple. Three completely separate working timetables existed in 1980, one for passenger trains, one for mandatory freight trains and one for conditional freight trains, though the latter two were combined at a later date. Even three timetables did not give all information about train running because special notices were delivered to signal boxes daily telling of additional trains and cancellations; they had to be thumbed through for anything relevant. In the event the special notices seemed to be primarily about trains not running to and from Corkickle, Whitehaven, which was about two hundred and fifty miles away. WILL NOT RUN the notices would shout from their stencilled sheets, as if security of the nation would be threatened if trains did run to Corkickle.

The number of documents from which signalmen gleaned information about trains was still not complete as a weekly publication called the W1 listed excursion trains such as football specials, mystery tours, and so on. The pamphlet was normally delivered on a Friday afternoon, so the man coming on duty on Saturday morning had to remember to read it immediately in case a special train was due just after he had signed on. Finally, separate papers were issued for ballast trains, trains used by civil engineers for track maintenance. Thus it was by no means a simple matter determining what train should be running where at a particular time of day. Having said all that, establishing in which direction trains should go at Kensal Green Junction was not too onerous because most went straight up and down the main lines. Even so, Fred Abbott had written a list of timetabled trains that diverted and pinned it above the train register book, such enumerations being termed a simplifier. They were found in most signal boxes.

Other booklets delivered regularly to boxes were the weekly operating notice (the WE-1) which demanded continuous scrutiny as it listed permanent and temporary changes to operating practices. The periodic operating notice (the WED-1) was a mind-numbing catalogue of changes to rules and infrastructure that mostly had gone before, but occasionally contained completely new instructions, so had to be gone through with equal diligence.

In many signal boxes the frequency of service left a moment or two between trains, but a signalman need not fear running out of reading material to fill the void, for two further tomes were placed in each box, the General Appendix to the Working Timetable and the Sectional Appendix to the Working Timetable. The soporific blue-backed General Appendix supplemented the Rule Book by listing sundry other requirements in operating the railway. More interestingly, the green-backed Sectional Appendix set out for the benefit of both signalmen and traincrews which signalling regulations applied to which running lines, where signal boxes were located, and, especially fascinating, listed any special instructions that applied. Though I had to be aware of their contents, I would not be grilled on either of these publications. Nevertheless, in quieter times I would flick through pages of the Sectional Appendix to read of other signal boxes on the railway network.

CHAPTER SIX

The lever frame at Kensal Green, technically a London and North Western Railway tumbler frame with levers spaced every five-and-a-half inches, proved relatively easy to learn. I soon mastered which points had to be thrown for which routes, and in any case the illuminated diagram showed which levers worked which pieces of signalling equipment should there be doubt. I gradually learnt which trains went where, and time eventually arrived when all agreed I was both fit to work the box and was capable of passing a rules test. The two had to be considered separately, but were disposed of over a three-day period.

On the day I had to pass out in the box, Fred Abbott left me on my own with Ron Dillington's colleague, Inspector Henry Knowles, who watched me do everything correctly to keep trains moving. Accordingly, I was passed out as competent.

A final handshake with Fred Abbot was amongst many shared in three days. Even though the senior signalman and I got on well together, in one area I had not been the best of pupils. I had ignored a plea to be in no rush to report for duty so that he had time to settle in at the beginning of the shift. Despite the request, ever conscientious, I would turn up just a few minutes after the signalman himself had arrived. In due course I would learn it is very disconcerting for a signalman to be interrupted in the first moments of taking up duty as he needs time to put away his belongings and read all necessary paperwork before receiving guests. As much as Fred Abbott appreciated an eager learner, because the tuition period had lasted longer than expected and because I had consistently invaded his incipient private time, he was glad to see me go. A year or two would pass before remorse descended on me over letting the man down in these respects, by which time he had retired for a second and last time, presenting no opportunity for atonement.

To pass the rules test, I had to report to Euston House at the station of that name on Wednesday 1st October 1980 at 09:30 hours. On arrival, my normal state of nervousness was heightened to such a pitch I could hardly give my name to the clerk whose task it was to show me to a document-cluttered examination room. My watch showed 09.45; "He must be running late," I thought. Ten o'clock passed, then 10:30. It was now 11:00 hours. By the time the examiner walked into the library-like room at 11:10 hours, I was so fed up with waiting all nervousness had drained away and I just wanted to get the ordeal over with. The delay may well have been planned to achieve exactly that result.

The senior inspector took his seat and, with little formality, painstakingly and patiently plodded through just about every regulation and special instruction that applied to Kensal Green. He wore the dark blue three-piece uniform of signalling personnel, but of better quality material reserved for higher grades. With perfectly laundered shirt, smart tie and meticulous grooming, the senior inspector transformed railway uniform into a Savile Row suit. A quiet spoken Scot, his gentle brogue and uncommon courtesy eased away any last vestiges of nervousness. All British Railways' supervisory staff were straightforward people of easy-going nature who exercised authority only when needed, but this genteel dapper senior inspector, impervious to the madding crowd, an island of decorum in a sea of brashness that was London in the 1980s, retained a civility that was exceptional.

The verbal examination seemed to go on for ever, but probably took about ninety minutes. Thanks to Ron Dillington's sedulity and to hours of punching rivets of signalling rules into a steel sheet brain, I passed the examination. The urbane senior inspector turned to me and said I had done very well. He added in his soft tongue, "It seems to me you had a railway background before you joined us?"

His comment momentarily startled me, but was probably invited by use of railway slang in some answers. "I've been interested in signalling all my life," I said.

"Well you know, being a signalman is quite different from just having an interest in the subject," said the senior inspector sagely. "But you should do all right. The best of luck Mr. Deaver."

We exchanged smiles and shook hands. After a brief call on the roster clerk, the man whose job it was to ensure all signal boxes were manned when they should be, I left Euston House a signalman at last. I had vowed not to wear uniform picked up a week or two earlier till I had earned my wings, now I would wear it with pride. The illustration on the front of this book shows me in the three-piece signalman's uniform, plus a signalman's cap. I did not wear the cap very often, partly because it was ill-fitting, which in turn was owing to a full range of sizes not being available as demand for headgear was low.

In due course comforting news came through I had been awarded the vacancy at Kensal Green Junction.

CHAPTER SEVEN

North London Line electric passenger trains that ran from Broad Street in the City to Richmond, Surrey, cheerfully sped through a rainbow of suburbs in the northern half of the metropolis conveying commuters to work, children to school, sightseers to Hampstead Heath, Kew Gardens and Richmond, shoppers to Camden, suitors to Islington, girlfriends to Gunnersbury, aunties to Acton and railway workers to Willesden. In so doing the service provided an invaluable corridor to those wishing to travel in a direction perpendicular to the capital's prevailing flow of traffic.

Passengers paid little attention to and were mostly unaware of a succession of traditional signal boxes that controlled the North London Line, beginning with Broad Street box where Up and Down main lines fanned out into four terminal platforms. Signalling there followed a pattern often seen in terminus stations in that only distant and home were provided for incoming trains. It always struck me as odd that in such cases the distant signal could actually show "off" when the line was coming to a dead end. I suppose the rule that a distant can only display "off" when all home and starting signals that follow are "off" was being observed, and that drivers' route knowledge which of course included an awareness of buffer stops ahead ensured trains did not career into the station concourse.

At Dalston Western Junction, the next box along the line, lines from Broad Street joined two others. They continued as four-track railway as far as Camden Road Junction signal box where the main North London Line turned northwards and a branch continued westwards to join the Euston main line at Primrose Hill. Gospel Oak signal box returned the North London Line to a westerly direction and brought in a branch from the Tottenham direction to continue through Hampstead Heath tunnel and on to Kensal Green Junction. The three mile stretch from Gospel Oak to Kensal Green was a railway bottle-neck in that numerous freight trains crossing London had to squeeze between North London Line passenger trains in order to reach points east and west of the capital.

Kensal Green Junction was situated in north-west London at a mid-point amongst suburbs of Kensal Green, Kensal Rise, Willesden and Harlesden. The suburbs were largely unknown outside London, for none enjoyed the literary fame of Hampstead Heath nor the cinematographic connotations of Ealing nor the governmental connections of Westminster nor the mixed reputation of Soho nor the cultural opulence of Covent Garden. Yet anonymous Kensal Green and neighbours structurally and economically were a sizable portion of the capital, with railways playing an important role in their financial well-being.

The mass of pointwork that formed Kensal Green Junction sat in a shallow but wide grassy cutting dotted with trees and shrubs, the whole being boxed in by residential properties to the north, the Harrow Road overbridge to the west, the Wrottesley Road overbridge to the east, and an empty office block on a continuation of Harrow Road to the south. Kensal Green signal box stood on a low wide bank on the northern edge. This graminaceous relief from the endless march of London's suburbia, in its bosky wilderness, shamed the plainer but better known nearby Wormwood Scrubs. The handsome signal box nestled in greenery like a diamond set in gold, not that signalmen recognized the gem in which they worked, as the complete view was enjoyable only from Wrottesley Road bridge. Glazed on three sides and with a narrow exterior walkway for window cleaning, the signal box featured decorative bargeboards, finials set against boarded gable ends, cream woodwork and a brick base.

From construction of the first signal boxes until the 1980s, signal box architecture had never been thoroughly analyzed, so several knowledgeable enthusiasts, wearied through having no nomenclature to describe a multitude of styles, set about classifying the buildings. Their work, published in the 1986 book *The Signal Box*, subsumed Kensal Green and all others like it in a classification known as London & North Western Railway Type 4.

At Kensal Green twin tracks of the North London Line split three ways which, together with a siding off the Down Platform Line, gave an impressive view from the signal box of no less than seven tracks. One branch, the City Lines, led to a modern electrical signal box known as Willesden power box. Another branch hooked up a short distance away with the Euston to Watford suburban line at a box called Willesden New Station. The North London Line itself continued westwards to meet the next box a third of a mile away, Willesden High Level Junction. At that time the bracket structure of High Level's Down home semaphore signals mounted on a bridge over the Euston main line was a familiar sight to passengers from north-west Britain nearing journey's end.

Kensal Green Junction marked one corner of a vast complex of railway lines centred on Willesden power box. The power box was alongside the former main line of the London and North Western Railway, now Network Rail's West Coast Main Line, that gouged a wide multi-track channel through the area. The Willesden Junction complex contained acres upon acres of sidings and, depending how far the net is cast, about a dozen manual signal boxes, plus a couple of shunting frames. A shunting frame is a facility operating points and signals but not signalling trains. A dense cluster of mechanical signal boxes defying progress - even with Willesden power box in their midst - was a delightful surprise to this signalling enthusiast. In the 1980s, juxtaposition of modernized and unmodernized signalling equipment was widespread throughout the London Midland Region of British Railways. High cost of renewals was the explanation. I had heard the cost of replacing a simple one-arm semaphore signal with a colour light was in the region of ten thousand pounds. The large sum is explained not only by the exchange of old for new, but also by the installation of track circuits, wiring to connect track circuits to the new signal, alterations to the signal box lever, wiring and diagram and by amendments to a multitude of records scattered about the network. The cost of completely abolishing a manual signal box was huge. For that reason many lever frame boxes continued to work colour light signals on the West Coast Main Line.

A microcosm of London Midland Region's technological blend of electronics and brute force, the sixty-lever frame at Kensal Green worked nine points, two locks for points, three semaphore signals, four mechanical disc ground signals and nine colour light signals. Days when signal boxes contained uniform rows of levers identical in every respect except colour were gone. Levers merely making electrical contact for colour lights and power-operated points were sawed down a few inches. Through rationalization of layouts some levers became spare and were painted white. Some white levers were cannibalized to repair others, some removed altogether. Thus the lever frame in Kensal Green, like many others, looked bitty. Yet it retained the comforting propriety of all levers being in perfect alignment when sitting back in the frame.

As for the signals themselves, one semaphore, the Up New Lines home 2, was a simple straight post signal having the familiar red arm with vertical white band; it was sited on the wrong side of the tracks owing to space restrictions. A second semaphore was the Down Platform Line starting, with High Level Junction's distants fixed at caution on brackets beneath. The Down home 2 bracket junction signal, just east of Wrottesley Road bridge, comprised a main post on top of which was fixed a horizontal platform with railings. On this platform were fixed three dolls (or posts), each doll carrying two semaphore arms, one above the other, the whole arrangement resembling a tree with branches at right angles. All arms were red except one yellow distant arm. The left doll read towards Willesden New Station signal box and bore that box's fixed distant beneath. Both the centre doll and right doll carried beneath the main arms subsidiary arms – smaller semaphore arms with red and white markings running horizontally rather than vertically - the purpose of which will be explained later. The centre doll, the tallest, read towards Willesden High Level Junction, the right-hand doll towards Willesden power box. A fourth doll was redundant and bore no arms. This magnificent array, this local landmark must have been one of London's most elaborate mechanical signal structures to remain in use during the 1980s, if not *the* most. I will henceforward refer to it as the junction signal.

A railway is a beautiful thing. On the subject of beauty James Joyce has this to say:

> ... beauty is beheld by the imagination which is appeased by the most satisfying relations of the sensible.

The beauty of a railway lies in its innocent utility. Over-bridges leave just enough space for trains to pass through: too little space would have rolling stock scraping abutments, too much space would squander masonry. Station platforms seem to nip the railway as it passes between them, yet do no more than escort it briefly through a confined space, then release it to charge onwards. Points deflect trains from one track to another at just the right curvature for the governing speed: not too sharp to throw vehicles off, not too elongated to waste resources and space. Mile after mile of irrefutably parallel steel ribbons at precisely four feet eight-and-a-half inches apart fixed to evenly spaced sleepers provide an indisputably permanent way. Trains of uniform dimensions glide along those rails on flanged wheels honed to ride with perfection.

It was, then, amidst this uncorrupted symmetry, this celebration of imperial orderliness and predictability known as the railway, that I began a new career.

CHAPTER EIGHT

A glow radiating from the round face of Jim Waters approved of my being on time to begin night shift; it was 21:22 hours. Shifts changed officially at 06:00, 14:00 and 22:00 hours, but management had no objections to men's mutually acceptable private arrangements; at Kensal Green Junction unofficial changeover times were 06:45, 13:30 and 21.30 hours. Jim Waters was one of three responsible for continuously manning the box. Fred Abbott was of course another, and I was now the third man. We three were regular mates, as was signalman's jargon.

"The kettle's boiling for yer, Mitch," said Jim Waters nodding in the direction of a large aluminium kettle gently simmering on the oven located against the back wall. "Everything's okay, no problems. See yer later."

The large young man grabbed his duffle bag from the kitchen table, hurried his bulk across the brown linoleum floor, left the signal box and sped off into a mild October night to catch the next Broad Street train home. Jim Waters, a lively character whose eyes flashed like Belisha beacons as he spoke, imported an undeniable sparkle of youth to the signalling grades, yet he would prove capable of astounding devotion when marriage eventually came his way. Unlike the extended time spent with Fred Abbott, little opportunity arose to get to know Jim Waters well because he always rushed to leave the box once I arrived - which is how relief should take place anyway. Nevertheless, he found time to confide on one occasion that he, too, had always wanted to be a signalman as a boy.

I signed on duty in the train register book, began reading the clutch of special notices hanging on a bulldog clip above the register, and dealt with 3-1-2 passenger train bell codes. Code 3-2-5 on Willesden High Level Junction's high-pitched bell signified approach of a freightliner train, a train of specially designed flat wagons carrying containers. Containers had not only revolutionized handling of merchandise in ports, but had introduced an entirely new kind of train to the rails. The signalman at Acton Wells Junction (about two miles away) telephoned with identity of the train just belled.

"Ah, good evening. That's the ol' Southampton, Mitch," said my regular mate, his salutation consequent upon the first telephone exchange of the night.

Men who worked the same shifts as oneself but in a different box were also referred to as regular mates. Over time friendly working relationships grew. My regular mate in an adjacent box, Willesden New Station, would telephone about 22:30 to gossip. He was a member of the Local Departmental Committee, another wonderfully evasive title. Local Departmental Committees were informal gatherings of management and workers to discuss working arrangements. My regular mate was thus privy to many issues to which the rest of us were not.

The "Southampton" freightliner was the Southampton to Ripple Lane, Ripple Lane being on the Thames estuary. The prefix "ol'" was a matey addition to all regular freight trains. This train was sometimes referred to as the Southampton 'liner, which begot a second nickname, the QE2. A train from Millbrook, near Southampton, to Stratford in East London was another freightliner that also ran in late evening, and as both were hauled by Class 47 locomotives, the two were almost indistinguishable. Shipping line names on container sides probably would have reliably indicated which train was which, but it was the colour of containers that I noticed: the Southampton to Ripple Lane had more red containers, the Millbrook to Stratford more yellow and orange containers. We never knew of course what was inside all those huge secretive boxes, but a similar mix of colours each evening suggested similar merchandise being conveyed on a daily basis.

It seemed odd that freightliners and other trains had the same mix of traffic each day, but the pattern might be explained by needs of industry. Suppose, for example, a factory needed one tank wagon of raw materials each day and dispatched one box van of finished product each day. It was more economical to have one tank wagon and one box van delivered every twenty-four hours than to have ten delivered at once, which would involve extra shunting, require extra siding space and incur demurrage.

Of all changes that had taken place since I knew railways as an eight-year old in Bickle, probably the biggest change, certainly the one I had most difficulty getting used to, was virtual abolition of the guard's van. Most freight trains were fitted throughout with either the air brake, or, in older stock, the vacuum brake, and since risk of a train uncontrollably splitting in two was deemed low, did not convey a guard's van at the rear, the guard now generally riding in the rear cab of a locomotive. Several months would elapse before I stopped staring at the end of a train looking for a guard's van with its smoking chimney. A red paraffin lamp called a tail lamp hanging from the rear vehicle now confirmed the train was complete.

Another major change was to classification of trains, in that they were no longer Classes A to K but Classes 1 to 9 plus 0. Classes A and B, express and stopping passenger trains respectively, became Classes 1 and 2 with the same bell codes. Classes C, D and E freight and parcels trains had been spread amongst new Classes 3, 4, 5, 6, 7 and 8. Classes F, H and J freight trains without continuous brakes had become Class 9. Class G light engines, that is, engines without trains, had become Class 0. Freightliners were a Class 4 train, but with a unique and extravagant bell code of 3-2-5. The bell code may have been more a musical celebration of their success than a necessary identification, for in time the bell code would be abandoned, to be replaced by the standard Class 4 code of 3-1-1.

Bell codes, whilst adequate for block signalling, did not tell a signalman at a junction which way to send a train. Train whistles and special bell codes were possible means of giving directional information, but on the North London Line freight train destinations were passed on by telephone.

Broad Street to Richmond passenger trains ran every twenty minutes in both directions. Two or three freight trains an hour had to be slotted between the passenger service. This North London Line cocktail of passenger and freight prevailed till about midnight when the passenger service ceased. The last two electric multiple units in the Up direction terminated in Willesden Junction high level platforms to become empty coaching stock, one going to Watford, the other to a bay platform in the station's lower level. Once passengers had detrained, both units travelled from the station to Kensal Green Junction stopping east of the Wrottesley Road over-bridge, at which point they changed direction and were signalled through a crossover towards Willesden New Station signal box.

After the two empty stock trains were disposed of, the night belonged to freight trains.

CHAPTER NINE

A quiet spell after midnight allowed signalmen to catch up with paperwork, to make a pot of tea, and to watch London's suburbs slowly wind down from the helter-skelter of daily life. One by one tiny bright specks of bathroom and bedroom lights extinguished, like a nightly version of the solemn *tenebrae* church service, leaving only a necklace of street lamps to keep vigil. The last red double-decked bus ran westwards along Harrow Road. As Cimmerian darkness flooded the metropolis, vehicular traffic steadily dwindled till about 02:00 hours when only night revellers and those who had catered for them spottily passed along the main road opposite the signal box. One of London's ubiquitous black hackney cabs may well have been the very last vehicle. The city slept.

Whilst the population slumbered, freight trains thundered across a line that not only linked east and west London but four corners of the country: the line was a pulmonary artery at the heart of Britain. Signalmen watched every train go by for anything amiss. In carrying out that duty, I could not help but admire the urgency, the determination, the constancy, the evenness with which trains of vital commodities passed in front of the signal box all night long.

The Cliffe to King's Cross ferried its load of building materials from Kent across South London, over the River Thames, along the North London Line to a yard close to that well-known terminus station. The outline of its bogie hopper wagons looked like the arched back of some prehistoric animal about to pounce on prey. (Bogies are two pairs of wheels close together on one assembly; normally two bogies are fitted to one vehicle.) The train, hauled by Class 33 diesel locomotives, later retraced steps back to the southern bank of the Thames estuary, much of the well-planned operation being executed under cover of darkness.

The Westbury, Wiltshire, to Chadwell Heath in East London hauled metal-sided open wagons, code-named MSVs, filled with stone for highway construction. The train was nicknamed in rhyming slang the Ted Heath, a reference to a former Prime Minister rather than to the bandleader. Several of the train's wagons were loaded not with gravel nor crushed rock, not even with portions of strata such as that found at the foot of cliffs, but with boulders in some cases so large only two fit in a vehicle. I wondered how such colossal lumps of stone were loaded without demolishing the wagons, obviously not by dropping them from great height. I was spellbound by the train's sisyphean cargo and would chatter excitedly to colleagues about the mountain lumps that rolled by. Mates were not moved by the spectacle.

The procession of freight trains at the rate of about four an hour continued through the night without abatement: trains of tank wagons filled with oil, trains of specially designed double-decked automobile-carrying vehicles called cartics (derived from articulated car carriers) van trains filled with motor car parts feeding hungry factories with just-in-time deliveries, trains of yet more wagons filled with stone, each train to a different destination, each requiring a telephone call to identify it. A Class 3 parcels train to Basingstoke was the only train running under bell code 1-3-1; it alone required no identification. For the locomotive enthusiast, diesel engines hauling these trains were mainly Classes 31, 33, 37 and 47. All were painted in British Rail's shade of marine blue. A time before all traction was equipped with a bright headlight, the period is now identified by enthusiasts as the blue era.

First hours of night shift up till about 04:00 were perhaps the most varied, the most interesting, even the most exhilarating of the entire twenty-four hours at Kensal Green. After that, as darkness dampened the spirit, as darkness dripped from every object outside painting them in ever more obscuring shades of dark grey, romance of the night freights (a phrase originally used to describe black and white photographs of American steam engines by O. Winston Link) began to lose its appeal. The body's natural inclination to lay down and sleep fought with a need to remain not only conscious but vigilant of all that took place. Answering bells, pulling levers, observing tail lamps - all undemanding in daylight – required all the physical and mental strength a man could muster as a mantle of weariness cloaked the soul, as feet, hands, jaw and eyelids began to feel like lead. At about 05:00 hours, as the first vehicle of the morning ran along Harrow Road (perhaps a bread roundsman) as birds began their matins, as dawn approached to displace night's heaviness, breakfast of boiled egg and toast brightened an otherwise bleak time. Brushing teeth after signal box breakfast raised a problem. I had always routinely brushed teeth after breakfast and before bedtime, and a month or two elapsed before I realized the two now coincided on night shift. I had to remember to brush again after getting up in the afternoon!

For someone who had been awake all night, six o'clock in the morning was the nadir of human alertness, but about this time Kensal Green signalmen had to execute shunting moves involving much pulling and pushing of levers to change direction of three trains. We were not alone, for early morning was an exceedingly busy time in signal boxes across the country as empty coaching stock trains were signalled into position for the rush hour. Two movements at Kensal Green were the reverse of the previous night's exercise. Empty electric multiple units signalled from Willesden New Station box changed direction at Kensal Green to begin the Richmond passenger service from Willesden Junction high level platforms.

The third change of direction shunt involved the empty Scotland to London mail train that had to be turned round each morning so that equipment for picking up and dropping off mail bags on the move would be on the outside (cess side) for the return journey. Known officially as the Travelling Post Office but colloquially as the postals, the train would leave Euston with diesel locomotives at each end, reverse a short distance down the West London Line (which linked Willesden Junction to Clapham Junction) as far as Mitre Bridge Junction where it would change direction and travel to Willesden High Level Junction, thence to Kensal Green where it would change direction again via the crossover to traverse the Down City Line towards Willesden power box. A simple triangle would have accomplished the move far more efficiently, but no such formation existed locally. A freight or two on the City Lines often ran amongst this frenzy of shunts between 05:50 and 06:30 so signalmen at Kensal Green worked hard when almost spent.

Mercifully, a brief lull descended on the signal box a few minutes before relief arrived allowing time to tidy up, put the kettle on, and gather one's senses for the journey home. As regular as the North London Line passenger timetable, as reliable as the block bells, the always neatly-attired and clean-shaven Fred Abbott climbed the box steps and entered at 06:40 hours. I was fortunate to have such excellent relief. With eyes moist and red at the edges, I left for the journey home.

A brisk walk along the ballast in invigorating fresh air woke me up. Then the electric multiple unit's sough and soporific sway on the journey home made eyelids once again heavy. Yet, another bracing march from Hampstead Heath station to a bed-sitting room in Belsize Park pumped new life into a night-weary body. Once home I was sometimes too shaken by being alternately revived and soothed to easily fall asleep. Occasionally I resorted to strong beer to induce sleepiness, but never finished the bottle. Nevertheless, as inevitable as the rising sun that refereed the whole process, sleep came. In those delicious moments of teetering on the cusp between being awake and being asleep, in an ephemerality that defies measurement when fragments of dreams flitted in and out of a brain that was both conscious viewing the unconscious and unconscious enjoying the fleeting images before it, the delirium, the bliss, the ecstasy of being free to fall asleep was over all too soon. The night shift worker finally tumbled into the arms of Morpheus.

After the very first Monday night shift, I slept till 17:00 hours. Thereafter I usually awoke no later than 13:30. Colleagues told me extended slumber on the first occasion followed by only about six hour's sleep on all other occasions was the usual pattern. Perhaps a depressed level of energy on night shift drew less on corporeal systems so that we needed less sleep, or the sleep we did enjoy during the day was so deep we needed less of it, or mid-afternoon warmth and brightness simply made lengthy slumber impossible. One advantage of night work is free time during the day to run errands. Another is that it forbids alcohol consumption, a not completely unwelcome discipline for someone who would imbibe three or four times a week if he were free to do so.

CHAPTER TEN

By Thursday the unstoppable cavalcade of night freights had begun to take its toll. Exchanges on the telephone with mates during small hours grew increasingly curt as the week progressed, though men always stopped short of losing temper at once again being hauled out of a comfortable upholstered chair to answer the block bell. Friday night brought some relief in that a couple of trains that had run near dawn did not run at all on Saturday.

Almost without exception I wore uniform for night shift, including in winter months a long-sleeved waistcoat long the mark of a signalman (but without gold pocket watch carried by signalmen of my youth). Each evening during the week I strode proudly bag in hand to Hampstead Heath station sneering at the *canaille* denied the privilege of wearing signalman's uniform, looking down on those deprived of the honour to guide night freights through the metropolis. Nothing got in the way of a signalman's resolute journey to work. Not even a damsel in distress. I remember hearing a young woman's call from an upstairs window to the effect she needed a hand with something, an entreaty this bachelor had to ignore afraid a possible dalliance might make him late for work.

On Saturday, the previous five evening's conceit crumbled as, in sombre midnight blue uniform and with head hung low, I envied the young and not so young dressed brightly and casually for the evening's celebration as they happily threaded their way through northern suburbs to public houses, night clubs and parties on their weekly night out. (Only in London did the distinction between generations become unclear, blurred or otherwise confused so that one could not easily guess age.) Temptation to turn about and go home reached the greatest when passing a public house where loud dance music blared out, where a hoppy aroma and warm light oozing from an open door invited all to enter and enjoy. Only a teetotaller, a prosaist, a man of the cloth and a signalman on his way to night shift could resist. I would glance in, but with heroic stoicism would walk straight by, and with unfaltering metronome-like steps, safely complete the journey to Hampstead Heath station. Arrival at the signal box put all worldly distractions behind as the night's business demanded attention.

When time came on Saturday night to put two empty passenger trains to bed, one went in the direction of Willesden New Station box as usual but the other was stabled in the siding between Up and Down Platform Lines at Kensal Green, the only occasion in the week the siding was used. The movement involved crossing the empty stock from Up Main through the crossover to Down Platform Line and sending bell signal 3-3-2 Shunting into Forward Section to Willesden High Level. This permitted the train to pass starting signal number 9 in order to reverse into the siding through points that were ahead of signal 9. Once the train was inside the siding, eight beats on the bell withdrew the shunt.

The timetable had no trains running on Saturday night, but men at Kensal Green, like many others, invariably had to deal with what were termed Engineer's Possessions. This procedure involved handing over control of part of the railway to the Civil Engineer's Department for repair and maintenance, in accordance with Section TIII of the Rule Book. Several steps had to be taken to protect the work area including placing metal collars over signal levers leading into the possession, turning the block indicator to Train on Line if Absolute Block Regulations were in force, and an appropriate entry in the train register book signed or dictated over the telephone by the man in charge of the possession.

An Engineer's Possession taken one Saturday night would remove from service till Sunday evening the Down Main between Kensal Green Junction and Gospel Oak. In order to maintain a passenger service, at 06:00 hours on Sunday a procedure called Single Line Working would be instituted allowing trains in both directions to use a track normally used in one direction, in this case the Up Main. Since no public transport existed to get people to work at 06:00 hours, personnel had to report for duty the previous evening. They began to arrive in the signal box as last passenger trains ran.

First was a member of the permanent way staff who, when I was a child was called a platelayer, but who was now called a trackman. His task as Blocked Road Man was to place a red lamp and detonators at the entrance to the possession. After we had exchanged pleasantries, he made himself comfortable in a corner of the box. A permanent way inspector in charge of the possession arrived next, and immediately began making telephone calls to ensure all was laid on for the night's work. The door then opened to a member of the supervisory staff who donned the title Responsible Officer to oversee Single Line Working. Finally, a relief signalman, who burst through the signal box door mouthing profuse apologies for being late, would act as Pilotman. The Pilotman had to be on each train during Single Line Working to ensure two trains could not enter the single line from opposite directions simultaneously, a gloriously simple device and one hundred per cent foolproof.

Roomy Kensal Green box now became scene of an elaborate farce the likes of which the Marx Brothers would have been proud. As I struggled to throw levers, work bells and make train register book entries, the Responsible Officer and permanent way inspector fought over the desk carrying both the telephone and train register book as they endeavoured to make their own arrangements. The Pilotman, still flustered through tardy arrival, nervously danced about the signal box floor as he tried to find a few square feet of sanctuary, but was constantly chased by two officials and me as we wove about one another trying to finish our work. Only the Blocked Road Man escaped the *melee*. From his refuge in the corner of the box, he watched with silent amusement as four agitated men trying to complete their duties swirled around like undisciplined dervishes.

Such riotous behaviour was not typical of Saturday night Engineer's Possessions. On the night in question, pandemonium eventually abated and, with everything in place, peace at last befell the signal box allowing each man to find a place to sit down, though I gave up the easy chair to no one. Little more would happen on this night till the small hours when Single Line Working began.

CHAPTER ELEVEN

Saturday night shift officially ran from 22:00 to 08:00, the extended hours being part of a weekend schedule that gave one of the three regular men, in this case Fred Abbott, the whole of Sunday off. The man who had worked late turn on Saturday, Jim Waters, came back at 08:00 hours to work an eleven-hour shift till I returned at 19:00 hours. No matter who worked the day shift on Sunday, they always succeeded in arriving promptly at 8 o'clock. Jim Waters would bustle in bright and fresh as if returning from a week's holiday, would throw his bag on the kitchen table, and would sit on the table beside his bag as a clear signal for me to go and for him to take over.

Signalmen on Sunday night shift enjoyed only four hours of 3-1-2 bell signals with very little freight activity. Moreover, it marked the end of a week of nights, of being shackled to a temperate life in darkness, of fighting the temptation to fall asleep in favour of running the irrepressible night freights with their multi-coloured containers, their slick oil, their lumpy stone, their gleaming motor cars, and all.

Highlight of Sunday night shift, for me, was the last Down passenger train because it was the only train in the entire timetable to run straight from Down Main to the Down New Lines. It was the only occasion in twenty-one days when signalmen operated number 2 arm on the junction signal. When time came I would grab dusty number 2 red lever and heave the little-used semaphore signal to the "off" position, using more effort than was needed to make most of the occasion.

Oblivious of the joy his train brought to at least one signalman, the driver had to contend with a series of poor signals. He met a yellow aspect in automatic signal KG63, a yellow aspect in Down Main home 1 (worked by short-handled number 7 lever), Willesden New Station's distant fixed at caution beneath number 2 arm on the junction signal, a yellow in R3 which automatically repeated signal 3 and red in number 3 starting signal itself, which eventually would change to green. Signal R3 was opposite the signal box, yet signalmen had no direct control over it because it functioned automatically as part of the Camden Junction to Watford unique system of signalling; Kensal Green Junction was one boundary of the system.

Absolute Block working between Kensal Green and Willesden New Station had complications too involved to mention here. Indeed, excessively complex signalling on such a short stretch of double track was tolerated because only six trains a day used it. It was referred to as the New Lines at Kensal Green, as Branch at Willesden New (differing nomenclature often being found in adjacent boxes) as the City Loop by the Electrical Control Officer (in charge of electric supply for motive power) and as the Number 1 Curve by the Civil Engineer's Department! All in all, the connection was a fussy little piece of railway.

A delight of working Absolute Block to Willesden New Station was the block instrument, not a standard British Railways plastic item but an elegant, antique, polished wood-encased instrument to the design of G.E. Fletcher of the London and North Western Railway. It, too, stacked all three functions on top of one another but did so much more stylishly. A height of twenty-one inches earned the design a nickname of tombstone block. The example in Kensal Green had a beautifully mellow ring.

After the last passenger train movements on Sunday evening, very little happened till about 05:00 when the Severn Beach to Bow tank train heralded in a new week of freight trains on the North London Line. One more 6 o'clock scramble rounded off the week of night shift. At 06:45 Jim Waters, bleary-eyed and splenetic, would slump into the signal box with hardly a word to say, sharp contrast to the previous morning's sunniness. The double-back from Sunday day shift to Monday early turn always taxed signalmen. I would hurry home from night shift, sleep for about four hours, return to relieve Jim Waters, and by beginning a week of late turn, that is to say, afternoons, would round off the weekend's leap-frog of shifts.

CHAPTER TWELVE

On Monday afternoon after a week of nights, walking along the wide way from Willesden Junction to the signal box felt like rising from the dead, felt like being injected with some miraculous elixir taking ten years off one's life! Properties behind the signal box that had been lifeless inky black forms were once again homes with people in them. Rails were no longer silver arrows floating on unseen ether but solid shiny metal secured to timber sleepers of varying hues. Even on a rainy day, elation at seeing the sky could not be contained. Light-footed, I would climb the signal box steps to greet Jim Waters who had recovered from lassitude of a few hours previous.

The shift allowed some time to read a newspaper between trains. Strictly speaking, reading material other than rules and regulations was not allowed, but I never heard of men being disciplined for having a newspaper in the box. On the way to work I usually picked up *The Daily Telegraph* whose rich coverage of news and whose regular lighter features provided more than enough reading, though its position was a little too far right for someone politically colourless. *The Times* I found too imperial, *The Guardian* too difficult. To be able to set aside a minute or two here and there to read a newspaper and to enjoy a cup of tea whilst doing so struck me as an entirely civilized way of conducting business.

The late turn shift saw ever-reliable electric multiple units, officially known as Class 501, tearing up and down every twenty minutes. Men sometimes referred to passenger trains as simply the passenger, or in reference to the electric current that powered them, the DC or the juice. Most commonly they were called the motor, which was probably an abbreviation of electric motor train once used in regulations to distinguish them from a steam engine. As a boy I remember being baffled by the term motor train, twenty-five years later I discovered what it meant.

Freight traffic ran patchily during the first half of late turn. A lull in stilly hours of early evening was followed by a steady increase in freight train numbers, so that by the time one's relief arrived at about 21:20 a busy spell was under way. Several freight trains returned eastwards after delivering cargo in the morning.

In the westbound direction two freights were noteworthy in that drivers had to reduce speed to a crawl when passing Kensal Green because High Level Junction's distants fixed at caution gave no clue whether that signal box's home signals were "off" or "on": drivers had to be sure they could stop their trains should signals be "on". One train was the Mark's Tey, Essex, to Acton comprising MSV metal-sided open wagons loaded with sand. The train was fitted throughout with the vacuum brake, but the heavy, densely-packed wagons wanted to keep rolling even with brakes applied.

The other train difficult to stop was the Temple Mills (east London) to Acton mixed freight. It had a continuous brake through only the front part of the train, and was therefore one of few to convey a guard's van at the rear. At the time I did not give the matter much thought, but it seems likely the train was partially fitted because half of it was fitted with the air brake, the other half fitted with incompatible vacuum brake. The train was nicknamed the Dan and Doris because its bell code of 1-2-2 for a Class 7 train had the same beats as signature tune for BBC radio's perennial "The Archers".

Trains in the Down direction that enjoyed an unimpeded run were those heading straight along the main line and where a Line Clear had been obtained from Willesden High Level Junction signal box. With a Line Clear, number 7 colour light could be cleared straight away, followed by number 9 semaphore starting signal and number 8, the semaphore home on the junction signal. The last two had to be pulled in that order because the signals were close together. This meant signalmen on every occasion had to turn sideways to reach lever 8 between levers 7 and 9 already pulled over, a task not as easy as it might seem because levers in Kensal Green were chest high, taller than most.

Without going into detail, mechanical and electrical systems reduced trains' speeds in the Down direction for any movement other than proceeding straight along to High Level. An example has already been seen in Sunday night's last passenger train making a left turn for Willesden New Station.

If a light engine headed in the High Level direction arrived at the junction signal and a Line Clear was not forthcoming, number 11 arm, beneath number 8, could be cleared to move the engine as far as number 9 starting signal. Number 11 was a small semaphore arm coloured with red and white horizontal rather than vertical bands. Raising this arm revealed a letter W behind the arm (illuminated at night by a mirror from the signal's paraffin lamp) meaning "Warning, the line is clear to the next stop signal only".

Number 11 signal was not much use because a train of normal length standing at number 9 would block the junction. I recall using number 11 for a light engine on only one occasion. From time to time we had route learning trains where a locomotive pushed around an observation coach for drivers to learn the railway. Sometimes I would deliberately slow the train down so that number 11 lever could be used, an action much appreciated by the instructor on board. Number 11 arm was eventually taken away.

For trains making a right turn at the junction signal for the Down City Line, number 10 arm was cleared. Between Kensal Green and Willesden power box the Down City Line was permissive, meaning that freight trains were allowed to queue behind one another, rather than one having exclusive occupancy as is the case on most stretches of railway. When the line was already occupied, number 12 small arm, beneath number 10, was cleared which revealed a letter C (illuminated at night) for Calling-on, which train drivers understood to mean there was already a train ahead.

Theoretically signalmen at Kensal Green could send freight trains along the Down City line continuously as there was no numerical restriction on how many trains could occupy the track, but since it was only a mile long there was a practical limit. The timetable listed only a handful of trains using the Down City Line each shift, and as they were an hour or two apart, chances several would fill up the Down City Line were slender. Until one day, that is.

I think a freightliner was first, for which I cleared full-size semaphore arm number 10 giving the right away for the Down City line. The train rumbled happily by. Shortly after, Gospel Oak described another Class 4 train for the City line, this time a cartics train. After being checked at number 7 signal, the cartics train crept down to the junction signal. I hovered over lever 12 waiting for the train to get close, occasionally depressing the stirrup handle to see if the electric lock released. View of the approaching train was obscured by Wrottesley Road bridge, so pulling lever 12 was guess-work, but once the nose of the engine appeared in the bridge archway, one knew for sure the lever would release. After being given number 12 signal, the cartics train trundled by the signal box to stop behind the freightliner train whose tail lamp was about half a mile away. I do not know to what extent drivers close in on a train ahead in these circumstances; they probably reduce the gap to the minimum required to make a safely controlled stop. A few tense moments elapsed till the end of the cartics train complete with tail lamp cleared the junction points. Had it come to a stop straddling the junction, the passenger service would have been brought to a stand. In the event, there was a little spare room.

Meanwhile, Gospel Oak had belled on a light engine for Willesden. I initially dithered over running it onto the Down City Line, but on its arrival bravely pulled lever 12. The locomotive took the signal, and gently rocked its way over the mesh of metal forming the junction, grumbled beneath the signal box windows, and came to rest just behind the cartics train and just outside the box. All junction track circuits had extinguished, but, displaying no confidence in the illuminated diagram, I went out onto the track to ensure no train passing in the Up direction would graze the light engine. It would not and I rejoiced in seeing the Down City Line filled to its limits. The locomotive was described to Willesden power box with the Class 0 bell signal of 2-3. A telephone call told the power box it was for Willesden.

A minute of sheer delight was abruptly terminated by a ring on the telephone I had just used. It was the power box supervisor. "'Ere..." he began.

"'Ere" was a term commonly used in London to hail a person, a verbal equivalent of the railway's one-beat Call Attention bell signal. The term usually preceded a rebuke, as it did in this case.

"That light engine you just sent us," continued the power box supervisor.

"Yes," I answered nervously.

"Well, you should've told us it was coming, and we would've got rid of this stuff," said the supervisor. "Now it's blocked in, and we need that engine."

"Oh," I said, crestfallen.

The supervisor's expostulation did not end there. "Or, if you'd told us about it, we could've sent it down to Acton Wells and he could've put it through South West Sidings. As it is we've got a train held up now with no engine."

I gulped, then apologized: "Sorry about that."

"All right," said the supervisor.

Stung with a humiliating reminder that prime aim of a railway is efficient handling of traffic and not entertainment of staff, I slumped despondently into the easy chair. All would end well though. The freightliner and cartics trains on the Down City line soon began to move. Before long the illuminated diagram showed the track to be empty, meaning the light engine had been freed for service.

CHAPTER THIRTEEN

For those who are not early risers, and for those with a proclivity to drink, two not incompatible traits, a late turn shift suited admirably. I usually went to work in mufti allowing freedom to do whatever pleased once the shift was over. On the Monday evening, what seemed like an unquenchable thirst drove me to the first public house I could reach after work which, whilst living in Belsize Park, was a hostelry close to Hampstead Heath station. I would dive into the bar, dance from foot to foot waiting impatiently to be served, quickly order a drink and down the first pint in very little time. After Monday, any licensed premises in north-west London was fair game provided it could be reached from Kensal Green before last orders at 23:00. More often than not, though, taverns would be within walking distance from home. Apart from Saturday evenings when I tended not to drink at all, only the greatest fortitude prevented drinking every single night of late turn.

After an undemanding Saturday late turn came a double-back to the long Sunday shift commencing at 08:00. Initially I used the Underground to get to work, but after a few months decided it was easier to walk. Bag in hand I would leave Belsize Park at 07:00 hours to strike out through suburbs of Swiss Cottage, Kilburn, Queen's Park and Kensal Green to arrive at 08:00 hours. Oddly, bad weather never intervened, so the walk was always pleasant; perhaps Saturday's reduced commercial activity cleansed the air for Sunday.

Normally by 08:00 all Saturday night Engineer's Possessions had been given up, so Sunday started quietly. The timetable dictated a first duty of signalling the electric unit from Kensal Green siding to Willesden high level platforms for the Richmond passenger service. It was essential that not only regular signalmen at Kensal Green but every relief man who ever worked the box knew that the unit was stabled in the siding on Saturday night and that it began service from there on Sunday morning. To give another example of a simple yet vital railway duty, traffic managers based at Willesden Junction drew up rosters for passenger guards based there.

If this were not done, guards would not know when to go to work and the whole local passenger service would collapse.

Having the right personnel in the right place at the right time with the right knowledge was crucial to every single railway operation. It mattered not whether the task was easy or difficult. To their credit British Railways always had staff to meet every need. A counter argument to set ways of doing things is that people might be inflexible. I found this to be true when extra trains were diverted via Kensal Green (which happened from time to time) as I struggled to work at a faster pace.

To return to the long Sunday at Kensal Green, for ten hours the signalman dealt with hardly anything else but bell code 3-1-2 motors every twenty minutes each way. To relieve the monotony, on the way to work I bought a *Sunday Times* from the mountain of newspapers stacked like crates of cabbages at the north end of Belsize Park. The first few hours went quickly as one enjoyed a leisurely breakfast, and happily ploughed through the multipartite newspaper. By early afternoon, however, the brain could absorb no more political, social or scientific revelations nor ponder any more erudite opinion nor admire any more skillfully written investigative journalism. *The Sunday Times* was set aside. Around this time some strange force known only to signalmen working the long Sunday appeared to slow passage of time so that each hour seemed like two. With nothing useful to do between trains, I would squirm in the armchair in abject boredom wondering if the shift would ever end. By late afternoon, however, the same unidentified force now exerted power in the opposite direction so that 16:00 hours came round as a shock. I had to rush tea, hurry to polish the floor, and scramble to tidy up for Fred Abbott's arrival a little before 19:00 hours. It was now my turn to double-back to early turn Monday.

CHAPTER FOURTEEN

A signalman's three-week cycle of shifts meant he never had to face Monday morning malaise suffered by the rest of the working population because on early turn he had already been at work the previous day, likewise for Monday's late turn. On night shift he had all day Monday to prepare himself.

With trains passing in rapid succession like machine-gun fire and levers slicing back and forth like books pulled off shelves for a quick read and put back again, early turn was signalling at its best. Mind you, there was still time to enjoy a first cup of coffee and eat breakfast of boiled egg and toast at about 07:00 hours. The shift went quickly, in part because we actually worked only seven hours owing to the privately agreed changeover times.

Because both office workers and schoolchildren needed to reach their destinations by 09:00 hours, to relieve overcrowding on the North London Line the Richmond to Broad Street passenger service was augmented each morning by two trains from Watford branching off at Willesden low level station, climbing the short gradient to Kensal Green, and continuing to Broad Street. The supplemental service brought welcome use of the majestic Fletcher block instrument to New Station box. As school finished an hour before offices closed, no two matching trains ran in the evening.

Passenger seating was not the only case of rush hour overcrowding on the line. The timetable around the time of the second augmentative Watford to Broad Street train stretched the line's capacity to its limits. A new freightliner service that started from Garston, a suburb of Liverpool, used the West Coast Main Line to reach Willesden Junction where it gained the North London Line via the Up City Line to reach its final destination of Tilbury. Its reporting (identity) number was 4E91. The long heavy train was christened Big Bertha, an admittedly over-worked nickname dating from the second World War when it referred to a monstrous German long-range gun. The train was normally hauled by two Class 37 diesel engines in multiple, that is to say, the locomotives were coupled in such a way both could be operated from the leading engine. (In steam engine days, no such economy was possible; double-heading required crews on both units of power: the locomotives operated in tandem.)

Some days when 4E91 was exceptionally heavy the driver asked signalmen at Willesden power box if they could arrange a good run to avoid stalling on the gradient between the power box and Kensal Green. This required signalmen at both Willesden and Kensal Green to clear their signals together. In such circumstances I let the power box know when I had been able to pull "off" all signals, which were numbers 47 Up City Line home 1, 46 Up City Line home 2, 43 Up Main starting and 48 Up City Line distant, all short-handled levers working colour lights. Number 48 was slotted with the power box's last controlled signal, a term which meant in this case that signalmen in both boxes had to pull "off" for the signal to show green. (More will be said on slotting later.) On hearing from me, the power box cleared their controlled signal to give the driver four green signals in a row. In due course train 4E91 roared by. The driver would wave his thanks, which I would acknowledge by holding up a hand and grinning at a successfully coordinated effort.

This impressive show was all very well, but care had to be taken not to delay the passenger service. The timetable listed (from memory) an Up passenger from Richmond passing at 08:18, 4E91 at 08:29½, the Up passenger from Watford at 08:31, and another Up Richmond at 08:38. I ran 4E91 in its timetabled path one morning, but it confirmed my worst fears by badly delaying following passenger trains - knocking them, was the slang term. I never did it again. Why was the timetable drawn up this way? The answer may lie in the method of preparing timetables whereby straight line graphs of train speeds are used to ensure adequate margins. One can only assume that the timetable as written would have worked for a freight train the usual length of a quarter-mile, but did not work for one approaching twice that length.

Once the rush hour was over at 09:00 hours, levers crashed about with all the finesse of a blacksmith's forge as depots in east London opened flood-gates to release a procession of freights onto the North London Line destined for points west and south. Ripple Lane facility dispatched a daily service of uniform hundred-ton tank wagons carrying aviation fuel to be unloaded at Langley for Heathrow Airport. Also from the same stable was an occasional oil train to Staines, which, inspired by a television advertisement for detergent that began with a view of soiled linen and an announcer uttering disgustedly the word "stains", we nicknamed the Dirty Washing. Other westbound tank trains from Ripple Lane went to Thame, Newbury and Thatcham. The Ripple Lane to Salfords tanks turned left at Willesden High Level Junction to travel the West London Line.

Taking the same route as the Salfords was the Temple Mills to

Sheerness, a train of scrap metal carried in MSVs for the steelworks there. The vehicles' sides were punched outwards by tortured chunks of metal rammed into them. Open wagons were the most interesting type to watch go by because one could see what was in them. As the MSVs passed clangorously by, tops of their loads offered tantalizing glimpses of motor car engine blocks, steel girders, pipes, steel sheeting and such things that once led a useful life but that were now destined for melting down and reviviscence as something new.

CHAPTER FIFTEEN

Absolute Block signalling was at its most rewarding when handling a procession of trains in the same direction. As soon as the signalman ahead gave Train out of Section he was offered another, sometimes immediately followed by the Train entering Section signal of two beats – in and on at the same time, as this was known. Progress of trains being checked by too many following closely together was called working block to block. When three freight trains, the maximum possible, ran between passenger trains on the North London Line, the signalman at Kensal Green was kept on the hop, not because he had an excessive number of levers to pull, but because equipment was scattered the considerable length of the sixty-lever box. Most signal boxes had levers for principal running signals located at the extremities of the frame, partly through a desire to match arrangement of levers with geography of the layout controlled (to avoid point rodding and signal wires having to criss-cross) and partly through convention. So Kensal Green's most-worked levers were numbered 7, 8, 9, 43, 53 and 56. In some newer installations main running signal levers were placed in the centre of the frame for the benefit of signalmen.

In the past when traffic was even heavier than it was in the 1980s, Kensal Green's position was elevated to controlling all trains entering the North London Line in the Up direction. Signalmen at Bollo Lane (beyond Acton Wells), Acton Wells and High Level had to ask Kensal Green's permission before releasing a train. As the number of trains declined, the routine was abandoned and signalmen simply let trains onto the North London Line at their discretion, and told Kensal Green after the event.

One day, I ran a freight that had been waiting on the Up City Line immediately behind a passenger. Acton Wells told me of a freight he was also releasing and then told me of another that Bollo Lane had let out, so we now had the maximum permitted number of freights between passenger trains. In response to a bell signal from High Level, I gave a Line Clear for what I assumed to be one of the freights Acton Wells had told me about, but much to my dismay, the signalman at High Level telephoned to say it was a freight he had just unloaded onto the North London Line at *his* junction. There were now four freights running between passenger trains, which inevitably delayed the service, and which I could do nothing about. Control Office in Euston telephoned imputing blame to me for letting out the City Line freight when three others were on their way. Arguments that no mechanism existed to prevent four freights being let out simultaneously by four different signal boxes failed to impress Control Office, and I was held responsible for the late-running passenger train.

From time to time managerial and technical personnel toured lines in a train comprising an observation coach and engine, the train being referred to as an Officers' Special, an evocation of the military atmosphere that once prevailed on railways. Paperwork stated that the Officers' Special would be inspecting the North London Line one morning, and that it would briefly recess in Kensal Green siding – at about 10:15 from memory. Of opinion that sparse use of the siding was waste of a good amenity, I looked forward to the event with excitement far greater than the unspectacular movement warranted.

As the appointed hour approached, I swept the floor, tidied the box and straightened the tie in readiness for guests. Gospel Oak had not described the train by 10:15, so I telephoned the man there, but he had no news. Now, I seldom ate lunch in the box on early turn, but on this day for some reason I had chosen to do so, and as mid-day approached with disappointingly still no sign of the Officers' Special, I placed a prepared meal in the small oven to heat. About twenty minutes later Gospel Oak belled on the Officers' Special. The train arrived whilst I was in the middle of eating the meal, so I had to break off and, amid a flurry of other traffic, had to shunt into forward section to put the Officers' Special in the siding. Soon a host of officials, young, old, in casual corduroy, in business suits, detrained and clambered up the box steps, entered, and darted about the box looking at different pieces of equipment. I reddened with embarrassment at the half-eaten meal laying on the table; I cannot remember what it was, but it was by no means *cordon bleu*. The party soon left to re-join their train, leaving me to choke down the remainder of the meal, and to scramble to put the box back in order for Fred Abbott.

Acton Wells Junction periodically ran into problems with signalling equipment which would invariably bring the line to a standstill. On one such occasion, Inspector Ron Dillington raced to Kensal Green to see what could be done to minimize delays to passenger trains. The next train in the Down direction was a tamping machine, a piece of equipment normally employed for maintaining track but which (in a re-location movement) was travelling under its own power to Acton. Ron Dillington, with a twinkle in his eye, turned to me and said, "Put that tamper in the siding then, Mitch." My elation at using the rusting piece of track was matched only by the supervisor's amusement at a signalman enraptured by the simple act of backing a train into a siding. Tamping machines and similar devices were strange looking pieces of equipment, not the boxy outline of a conventional train, but with hydraulic arms and other working parts exposed to the elements. I often wondered what passengers waiting for a normal train made of the bright yellow contraptions as they trundled by. This unlucky tamper was bundled into the siding and released when the service was back to normal.

In another instance where Acton Wells had signalling equipment problems, a train of mixed traffic arrived at the junction signal. It may have been the Dan and Doris. Since no supervisor was present in the box and Euston Control was so busy dealing directly with the problem they could not be reached, I took the initiative. When the train driver telephoned from the junction signal I told him of the circumstances.

"How many wagons do you have?" I asked.

"About twelve," came the reply.

"You should fit in the siding, then," I said.

"Should do, bobby," said the driver, the term bobby dating back to earliest days of signalling when policemen were hired to control trains.

We agreed to put the train in the siding. Shunting proceeded with the train first drawing forward then reversing, the guard at the rear ensuring the train did not hit buffer stops. Alas, the train did not fit; the engine came to a stand on number 37 points, points in the siding that must be thrown back to allow normal running on the main line. A grim-faced driver dismounted, strode to the box, climbed the box steps, entered and without emotion gave his report: "The train is in the siding but the engine won't fit. The rear wheels of the engine are in but the front wheels are still sitting on the points."

I threw up my arms, spun on the ball of one foot and stomped to the far end of the box in despair. The train was about twenty feet too long.

"Don't worry, matey," said the driver consolingly. "I've got an idea. If you can get me the road up to High Level and then down to Mitre Bridge, I can take the engine to Acton through South West Sidings and we can leave the train here."

Relief replaced despondency. "Right. Good. We'll do that then," I said ecstatically.

The driver's route knowledge, wisdom and good nature saved what could have been a very unpleasant hour or two in, first, having to explain the predicament to Euston Control, and, second, having to sort out the mess. Henceforward I was much more studious before pressing the siding into service. The day after the incident, when problems at Acton Wells were cleared up, buried amongst entries in special notices about trains not running to and from Corcickle were details of an exceptional train that would depart from Kensal Green siding and run to Acton.

CHAPTER SIXTEEN

Saturday morning, at a somewhat easier pace than weekday mornings, concluded both the week of early turn and the three-week cycle of signalmen's shifts. It was time for the weekend off we told ourselves, though of course it was only one day off, Sunday. After rising at 05:40 for six days I was so exhausted that sometimes on Saturday night I would just find the nearest public house, drink myself silly, slump into bed, and pass out for twelve hours.

On Sunday during the weekend off I would escape the cramped, one-roomed accommodation that London's property market imposed, and make for the incomparable open spaces of Hampstead Heath to trace its well-worn footpaths, to wander its grassy meadows, to admire its lines of stately trees, to observe genteel Monet-like groups of strollers who likewise chose to spend the afternoon in the most refreshing of public open spaces. Only once was the park's tranquility shattered. It happened when laughter filled the air as a pair of mallard ducks hopped a ride on a radio-controlled model boat to go round and round a pond entertaining all who watched.

By Monday I had had sufficient time to relax and to prepare mentally for the next week of darkness. I never objected to working nights, rarely taking time off from the shift, regarding it as a kind of sacrifice, a masochistic necessity. (Night shift's self-denial even extended to the breakfast table where it forbad marmalade on toast.) There had to be some price to pay for arriving at the perfect vocation in life, for that was how I saw being a signalman, and that price was a week of nights.

When first employed by British Railways I had not been entirely happy about the prospect of virtually continuous working, of working twenty days out of twenty-one. Indeed, looking back from a distance, such a work pattern still seems formidable. But the routine proved to be not quite so demanding, as reduced activity at weekends gave the signalman a break. Had the job continued at its weekday pace throughout all twenty days I for one could not have done it. Another factor was bank holidays. In the first case they extended the easier weekend period by one day and in the second case men were granted a day off in compensation for working a bank holiday, a day which could be taken at any time. Annual leave entitlement of course allowed further time off. Thus there were not too many instances of working a complete cycle without some form of relief. Changing shifts every week might have been thought difficult, but I experienced no problems. On night shift a man could look forward to late turn, on late turn to early turn, and on early turn to the weekend off.

    I saw the three-week cycle of shifts as one week of asceticism, one week of indulgence to make up for the week of asceticism and one week of signalling in its most perfect form. Doubtless colleagues did not view the trimerous work schedule quite so dramatically.

CHAPTER SEVENTEEN

No matter which shift, the signal box becomes home the entire eight hours a signalman is on duty. Through the way he adjusts lighting, the manner in which he scatters belongings about the box, even the way he signals, he puts his stamp on the place. Signals obey levers, bells ring at the touch of a key, and with autonomy the envy of many, a signalman is king of the castle for duration of his shift.

Personally, I acquired an affinity for not just the signal box but the entire stretch of railway overseen by Kensal Green, which included three colour light signals on the Down Main that functioned automatically through track circuits. Numbered KG61, KG62 and KG63 in continuance of the sixty-lever frame, the signals were not easily reached from the public highway. I visited them at least once just to see what they looked like - and found they looked just like any other colour light. I came to know KG63 a little better than the other two when one winter's day, after finishing early turn, I volunteered to stand at KG63 on overtime to verify each passing train was complete with tail lamp. This was done because we had an electrical failure that disabled the signalling system. Confirmation of a train passing with tail lamp allowed Gospel Oak to release the next train.

Railway between Kensal Green Junction and Gospel Oak consisted of plain double track without a single siding (though there had been many in the past). As if to compensate, no less than six small stations existed in three miles between Kensal Green and Hampstead Heath tunnel: Kensal Rise, Brondesbury Park, Brondesbury, West Hampstead and Finchley Road and Frognal. Initially I gave them little thought, but in time embraced them as part of the infrastructure towards which I felt a responsibility, even a paternal responsibility.

As much as everyone would like trains to run perfectly on time all the time, I am afraid instances arose where either signalling equipment failure or train failure held up the Broad Street to Richmond passenger service. It fell to Euston Control office to deal with problems, to get the service back to normal as soon as possible. Often matters were so complicated

Control did not have time to constantly relay progress by way of the circuit telephone to stations and signal boxes along the line. No informational devices other than blackboards were installed at smaller stations, and I imagined passengers pacing up and down the urban platforms wondering what on earth had happened to their train. I imagined the ticket clerk besieged by irate travellers declaring they could not understand why she did not know when the next train would arrive. Whenever possible, I would telephone the little stations if I had news.

"Train for Broad Street in about five minutes," I would hurriedly say to each station.

"Thank you, dear," a female voice would say, warmth in the words expressing gratitude for the supererogation.

Though telegraph instruments of one design or another took care of signalling trains, telephones were a vital supplement; Kensal Green had no less than eight. Direct lines, hot lines if you will, were installed to Gospel Oak, Willesden power box and Willesden New Station. Circuit telephones linked the box directly to Euston Control and to the Electrical Control Officer, the latter telephone emitting a disgusting buzzing noise on the few occasions it ever rang. A concentrator provided telephone connections to Willesden High Level and Acton Wells, and to many more in the past. A box sitting on the block shelf displayed eyeball-like orbs for incoming calls from trains standing at signals, which were answered using an old-fashioned telephone operator's peg. Finally, the instrument seeing most use was a conventional rotary-dial telephone sitting on the train register book desk.

Most telephone calls were the simple act of telling the next signal box destination of a freight train. Some calls were unexpected. I was surprised to receive four beats on the bell from Willesden power box, because the code signified a Class 1 train and I knew for sure no excursions were running that day. The power box signalman spoke on the hot line: "That's a light engine for Dalston, going to assist a breakdown."

My initial reaction was to say the bell code should have been 2-3 for a Class 0 light engine, but fortunately stopped myself in time. I had known as a youngster in Bickle that four beats on the bell stood not only for an express passenger train but for a snow plough or breakdown train going to clear the line and for a *light engine going to assist a breakdown*. On the only occasion it ever cropped up I momentarily forgot. (I cannot remember where the engine was going, I have used Dalston for convenience.)

Signalmen's slang bespattering conversation tended to enervate significance of operations. The act of describing a series of trains in Track Circuit Block Regulations was sometimes referred to as poking them along, an allusion to trains being reduced to no more than moving coloured lights on a diagram, like billiard balls on a billiard table. Signals were often called pegs or sticks. On a less derisive level, a home signal might be referred to by drivers and signalmen alike as the home board, a description from long ago when signals were rotating boards. The term distant board could also be heard occasionally. But it seemed to me that the words home board more than any other slang instantly evoked the long history of railways. Railway workers found very satisfying the practice of sharing terms and expressions that were dated and that were peculiar to their employment, as if indulging in some private language.

Small diesel shunting engines known as the Class 08 were nicknamed Jockos. They had a cab at one end only, unlike most modern motive power with controls at both ends. When an 08 engine's duties changed it was sometimes convenient to have it facing the other way. To turn one round involved its taking the same roundabout route as the postals train, or sometimes the reverse route. This complicated procedure for small gain included the usual change of direction at Kensal Green. So the engine would be belled by Willesden High Level Junction as a Class 0 light engine followed by a three-word telephone message succinctly laying out the plan: "Jocko for turning." I had heard of new men at Kensal Green attempting to send the engine on to Gospel Oak thinking Turning was a suburb in east London.

Light engines, sometimes contemptibly referred to as rail polishers, from Willesden power box were typically headed for Stratford or Ripple Lane, but time came when their destinations proved a source of mirth. One day my regular mate in the power box - whose imperturbability, incidentally, made him one of the best men to work with - told me an engine was for Thames Haven. This was unusual, so when I repeated the name back to him I did so with raised voice of surprise and disbelief. This reaction evidently amused the power box sufficiently for them to embark on a series of little jokes by dispatching engines for other exotic locations such as Barking and Dagenham Dock. At some point I realized the jest, but played along by ensuring responses were no less theatrical than response to the Thames Haven engine had been. All along I gave no hint of deliberately over-acting, though power box staff may have ultimately concluded that was exactly what I was doing. In each case the engine probably was for Ripple Lane, but since Ripple Lane, Thames Haven, Barking and Dagenham Dock were all in the same general vicinity, there was no risk of motive power being misrouted.

CHAPTER EIGHTEEN

Light-hearted telephone exchanges were not uncommon. For example, a Ripple Lane to Earley (near Reading) tank train invited quips about its running early or late. Some signalmen were more amenable than others to chatting on the telephone, one being Dave Smith. We had much in common in being the same age and same height, in having recently joined the railway after a career in commerce, in not objecting to an odd pint of beer now and then and in borrowing freely from the creativity of much loved comedians Tommy Cooper, Frankie Howerd, Benny Hill and Peter Sellers. I wonder if this leaning towards jocosity was generational, a light-heartedness found in people born just after the Second World War. Our history teacher in secondary school, referring to boys in the class, once remarked, "Each class has its idiot. Form 2B you're all idiots!"

Dave Smith would sometimes give details of a freight train in the form of a crossword puzzle clue: "What we've got next then is 'Richards is on his way to the angry monarch', 'Richards is on his way to the angry monarch'." Dave Smith would repeat the clue in deep bass voice redolent of the hidden announcer once heard on radio's "Twenty Questions".

"Ah, the Cliffe to King's Cross," I would say.

Dave Smith's clue of "Nellie Dean is going to see Shakespeare" referred to the Millbrook to Stratford freightliner.

Another humorous telephone conversationalist was Bob Williams, a family man whose equanimity earned him friends the length of the line. He telephoned shortly after I had been passed out to work Kensal Green. The message was unsettling: "You only just passed, you know."

"What!" I exclaimed.

"They said you only just passed out. You only just to say made it," repeated Bob Williams.

"I thought I did a pretty good job," said I, wounded.

"Nah, I'm only kidding. You did fine," said Bob Williams with a chuckle. Apparently it was a popular ruse to tell a newly-qualified signalman he had only just scraped by.

On a later occasion when I called Bob Williams he said he was busy talking to a signalman Jack Thompson on another telephone, and asked me to hold on. "I don't think I know Jack Thompson," I said, just for something to say.

I could then hear Bob Williams say to Jack Thompson, "Mitch Deaver says he doesn't think he knows you," to which Jack Thompson appeared to respond by saying something equally insignificant. Bob Williams returned to speak to me. "Jack Thompson says you'd just better watch what you say about him."

"He didn't say that at all," said I laughing.

Bob Williams could then be heard saying to the other signalman, "Mitch Deaver says don't be a smarty-pants, or he's gonna come over there and sort you out."

"Hey Bob, you pillock," I yelled down the telephone, "I didn't say that at all."

I could hear Jack Thompson laughing on the other telephone. Bob Williams then returned to me to say, "Jack Thompson says less of your lip, or he's gonna come to Kensal Green and re-arrange your face for you."

"He said nothing of the sort!" I said with a laugh.

"Mitch Deaver says you'd better watch it, or he's gonna come over there and knock you into the middle of next week," said Bob Williams to Jack Thompson.

"You rat-bag, Bob," I shouted down the telephone.

Bob Williams could no longer disguise merriment in his voice as he relayed false threats back and forth. However I had had enough of tongue-in-cheek taunts, and told him I would call another time.

Signalman John Edmondson, in being a compact man who kept his hair short, and in being given to occasional bouts of silliness, was not unlike the author. Whilst talking on the telephone and dealing with trains at the same time, I said to him, "Well, I'll say ding-ding, then." By that I meant I would say Train entering Section rather than ring two beats on the block bell. Soon afterwards John Edmondson gave Train out of Section on the bell, at which point I said to him, "Why don't we say the bell signals instead of ringing them? I'll say ding, you can say dong." John Edmondson agreed with a chuckle, and we continued our conversation until the next train.

"Ding," I said, one beat being the Call Attention bell signal.

"Dong," came the reply.

"Ding-ding-ding-ding-ding," I said asking a Line Clear for a Class 6 freight train, five consecutive beats on the bell.

"Dong-dong-dong-dong-dong," said John Edmondson granting the Line Clear.

For Train entering Section I said ding-ding, John Edmondson said dong-dong.

When time came for John Edmondson to Call Attention for Train out of Section, he said, "Ding."

"No, you're dinging when you should be donging," I said.

"Er...sorry. Dong," said John Edmondson.

"Ding," I replied.

"Dong-dong dong," he said, giving the 2-1 bell signal.

"Dong-dong dong," I replied.

"You're donging when you should be dinging," he said.

"Er...sorry. Ding-ding ding. Oh, that's enough of that," I said irritably.

"Yeh, I've had enough as well," said John Edmondson with a testiness matching mine.

The tomfoolery came to a sudden end because the game was easy as long as one signalman was sending bell signals and the other receiving; reversal of roles by the second man having to send Train out of Section muddled both of us.

John Edmondson was once victim of a prank, one that did not involve telephones, but one that bordered on the inappropriate for a signal box. He was training at Kensal Green when his trainer (not me) feigned nodding off. The man training him then pretended to wake up suddenly. He leapt to his feet, and shouted at John Edmondson, "LOOK WHAT YOU'VE DONE!"

A frightened John Edmondson looked at the illuminated diagram, looked up and down the lever frame, looked outside on the track, looked back at the illuminated diagram. "Wha...what?" he said trembling.

"Ah...nothing. I was just pulling your leg," said the trainer.

John Edmondson buckled at the knees, staggered to the nearest chair, sat down and put his hand on a heart that was racing. "You rotten..." he said.

Perpetrator of the mean trick was supposed to cultivate sound railwaymanship in a pupil, not scar John Edmondson's nerves so badly he would take weeks to recover. The cruel hoax breached professional standards and was a disgrace to the signalling grade. It was also very funny.

CHAPTER NINETEEN

To return to social telephone calls, not all were light-hearted. Some were serious, many humdrum, a few fell into no easy category. I used to get occasional calls from mates on rules and regulations, not because I knew them all, for poor memory forbad extensive knowledge, but because I knew in which book to find them. Many conversations had no connection with the railway.

The topic of natural history popped up now and again. On one occasion Dave Smith and I discussed newspaper articles telling of vast herds of cattle reared to meet global demand for hamburgers. Reports voiced concern that methane in the animals' natural gaseous discharges would cause too many of the sun's rays to be trapped in the atmosphere thus overheating the planet to the detriment of all. (This was prior to the term greenhouse effect entering widespread use.) I said to Dave Smith that large numbers of big animals and their associated bowel movements was nothing new. Consider the dinosaurs, I said. Consider the monstrously nauseating spectacle of a Brontosaurus breaking wind, of a Lambeosaurus letting off, of a Fabrosaurus feeling a need to release gas. I then suggested the popular theory of dinosaurs being wiped out by an asteroid was unadulterated tosh, and that the real reason for their extinction was that their accumulative flatulence brought about their own demise. I may have expressed it more pithily.

We humans are members of the animal kingdom too, and our mating rituals became subject of conversation one night when the eyebrow-raising phenomenon of mixed couples arose. That darker-skinned men might possibly have the edge over paler counterparts when it came to romance, that growing up in multiracial districts might affect choice and that some individuals were simply non-conformists were all discussed – with no judgement passed on anyone I hasten to add.

The topic occupied thoughts for some time, but I gradually came round to thinking that mixed couples were no more than one manifestation of a broader and not uncommon circumstance, that of a man and woman who were generally and perhaps erroneously perceived to be mismatched. This idea formed premise for further reflection that there might be a common thread running through all lop-sided liaisons, especially in particulars of their first meeting. In search of that thread I drew on memories how different people reacted to one another in Liverpool's discotheques, recollections which in due course revealed a converse situation, that of two people who might be expected to form a pair but who did not.

Kensal Green phrontistery then threw up another question: were there demographic reasons for odd couples? Large numbers of men, went one line of thinking, took themselves out of the marriage market, which forced women to look further afield and to pair off with someone unexpected. For example, some men enjoyed healthy relations with the opposite sex but dodged permanent relationships. Others lacked self-confidence, had no money, or were socially inadequate. A small percentage of men simply had no sex drive; they had no interest in women, nor in men, were otherwise quite normal but would never marry.

All these lucubrations eventually coalesced into something I thought colleagues might be interested to hear, but first a note of caution about rushing into judgements. More than once I have been startled and dismayed to see a relatively young woman socializing with an older man. It seems likely, however, that the disquiet was unjustified because in each case the meeting was probably no more than father and daughter meeting for a chat.

CHAPTER TWENTY

Bob Williams would be the first lucky signalman to hear of an intellectual breakthrough. Choosing a period on night shift interrupted by few trains, I said over the rotary-dial telephone that I had been thinking about couples one sees around who do not appear to be a very good match. "Now, suppose you saw a smartly dressed man with a tattily dressed woman," I said.

"What are you on about, Mitch?" said Bob Williams.

"I mean, wouldn't you wonder how they met in the first place?" I asked. "You see, I've been thinking about that, how people who seem very different end up being together."

"So, what are you saying?" said Bob Williams impatiently.

"I've got this theory, it's called the…" I hesitated. "It's called the Pyramidal Theory, you know, like pyramids." A chuckle came from the telephone, and after it had subsided I continued, "It's like this. Suppose two people are in the same room together, and they're the kind of couple who wouldn't normally meet, maybe different races, or they just don't look as if they'd go together. Then, they just happen to be standing next to one another and one of them, knowing that the other is someone they would not normally associate with, out of politeness makes a special effort to be nice and asks the time, or something like that. Pleasantly surprised, the other responds by being extra nice as well. This returned pleasantness prompts the first person to warm even more to the other, which invites a similar warming. They sort of reach out to one another and eventually end up forming a friendship. It's as if they were stepping down from a distant position and at the same time moving towards each other, you know what I mean."

All Bob Williams could utter was a muted "Hmm."

"So it's like…it's as if…" – the deliberate tautology built up to the main point I was about to make - "they both had been on the steps of two pyramids opposite one another, and with each kind gesture they stepped down a step, and in so doing moved closer, eventually to come together at the foot of the pyramids. I call this the Descending Pyramidal Theory."

I paused to allow a response, but since none was forthcoming, continued. "Then there's the opposite of what I just said. Suppose there are two people who ought to be a good match, and they know it; they're both on the same level, kind of thing. One of them, usually the girl, doesn't want to let the other know that she really likes him, so she acts cool, distances herself from him a bit, and tries to elevate herself – playing hard to get, you know. It's as if she steps back and upwards. The bloke, on seeing this, thinks to himself that she must be classier than he thought. So he puts it on a bit, and maybe tries to pretend he's better than he is. The girl sees this as being stand-offish, so just in case he's not as keen as she thought he was, she cools, taking another step back and away, figuratively speaking. This stepping back and elevating, it's all mental, you know what I mean, they're still talking face to face.

"So this is the reverse of what I was talking about before," I continued. "It's as if the two people were together at the foot of two pyramids to start with, but their changing attitudes of backing off and becoming aloof were like stepping back up the pyramids. By elevating themselves they ended up further apart than when they first met. So I call this the Ascending Pyramidal Theory. So there you are, that's the Pyramidal Theory."

Bob Williams chuckled nervously. "All righty, Mitch," he said. "Anyway, I've got a couple of things I want to do here. Catch yer later."

The conversation with Bob Williams ended abruptly. I was surprised and disappointed he did not want to talk further. Whether he simply had no time for such excogitations, or he felt embarrassed on my behalf, I do not know. Whatever the case, he obviously wanted no more of the Pyramidal Theory. Undeterred, a week later I spoke to Dave Smith on the telephone.

"Hey Dave, are you busy?" I began in a cheerful voice hoping to encourage a lively discussion.

"No mate," replied Dave Smith.

"I was talking to Bob Williams the other day," I said, roping in the name of another signalman in a shameful attempt to spread blame for what I was about to say. "We were talking about how you see couples together who you wouldn't expect to see together, sort of mismatched, you know, and I was thinking about this and had an idea..."

I told Dave Smith of the Pyramidal Theory both in its Descending and Ascending forms, though more concisely than the rambling monologue delivered to Bob Williams. I paused here and there for the listener to interject, but interject he did not. At conclusion of the conspectus I said, "So, whaddya think?"

Dave Smith thought for a second, then said in his deep bass voice, "Amazing." Silence then told he had nothing further to say.

"I just thought you might be interested," I said, now struggling for some way to close a conversation that had disappointingly failed to expand. The railway came to the rescue. "Anyway, next train on the Down will be the ol' Southampton."

Dave Smith's one word response was not praise but a statement of utter disbelief that, first, a person could have dreamt up such a zany idea, and, second, that that person could have been bothered to explain the lengthy but insubstantial reasoning to someone else. Nevertheless, he could not have been entirely dismissive, because I would soon discover that the theory had somehow reached the ears of John Edmondson, and I think it was Dave Smith who told him rather than Bob Williams.

The following week John Edmondson bounced into the box to relieve me at Kensal Green when I was on early turn. He had a gift for mimicry. As I gathered belongings together and prepared to leave, he squared himself opposite me, looked me straight in the eye, smiled, then said in a voice remarkably like mine, "My friends, the Pyramidal Theory."

Taken aback by a revelation that the theory had travelled further than two men originally forced to listen to it, I coloured, grinned foolishly and said, "That's right, that's the theory." I then made straight for the door leaving John Edmondson standing with arms outstretched waiting for a response that never came.

Introducing the idea to Bob Williams and Dave Smith had disappointingly failed to engage interest, yet in reverse circumstances of having the proposition sprung on me, ironically I too was dumbfounded. Had I known beforehand, I would have been mentally prepared and would have stayed in the box to talk. Therein may have lain the problem. Conversations on signal box telephones were normally on day-to-day matters. When I unloaded the Pyramidal Theory on two signalmen, they were ill-prepared for an avalanche of spurious arguments on an issue some would say hardly deserved to be called an issue. It is unsurprising they had little to say. And when caught off guard, architect of the theory himself could not put together an intelligent response.

Signalmen forgot the *recherché* theory with a celerity matched only by the suddenness of its introduction amongst them. A weakness in the theory was that actual distances between real Egyptian pyramids at Cheops were far too great for the argument to be convincing about people standing at the foot of them. No more than a signalman's frivolous diversion, the Pyramidal Theory lacked the science normally accompanying such surveys. That is not to say the subject is completely without merit for serious analysis. A student of behaviour however would be hampered, firstly, by having to identify a couple he thought to be poorly paired, secondly, by the treacherous ordeal of having to tell those two people exactly what he thought, and thirdly by then having to persuade them to talk about what he considered to be their misalliance.

To return to the topic itself, one could compare the mating process with what economists call a perfect market. A perfect market requires large numbers of buyers and sellers, and requires good communication amongst parties. The stock exchange and racehorse betting are examples of perfect markets. Typical arenas for boy to meet girl such as night clubs and public houses usually contain large numbers of both sexes, but such places fail the perfect market test through lack of good communication. All males are unable to talk to all females and *vice versa*. Worse, a person might converse with no more than a handful of strangers the whole night. I make no apologies for labelling the dating process a market place; after all, both men and women do their utmost to sell themselves. Speed dating, whereby unattached people are organized to spend just five minutes in conversation with a succession of prospective partners, is an improvement on the randomness of night clubs. The internet may bring couples closer to the economists' model. A flaw with all dating processes, it has to be said, is denial of the fact some people are emotionally unsuited to remain with one person for any great length of time, and a lack of honesty by the people concerned and by the people pursuing them in not facing up to that reality does nothing but perpetuate strife.

Another slant on the unpredictability of matchmaking is that men might perceive asymmetry in a couple owing to belief that they themselves would better suit the woman concerned. Some men have only themselves to blame for finding themselves in that position. Coxcombs, poltroons, misogamists, those of parsimonious bent, those for whom consuming the maximum amount of beer in the minimum amount of time is of greater importance, notoriously stand around bathing in their own misplaced contentment whilst others win over the woman. If they fail to act when opportunity presents itself, they leave the gate open for the opportunist, the confident, the charismatic to charge in and claim a prize. Let those lethargic men now wallow in purse-lipped, teeth-grinding envy at an ill-match precipitated by their own failure to approach the woman just stolen.

No amount of rationalization can make sense of the aleatory nature of mating. The Ascending Pyramidal Theory may explain failure to cement a friendship in a few cases. If it were ever possible to establish the facts, we would probably find the main reason why more relationships are not formed is apprehension on both sides about meeting someone new, which in turn is explained by fear of rejection. Given enough time though, most do eventually settle down with someone, and it is inevitable in a sea of apparently well-matched partners, the lone rock of two that are not will occasionally jut out. In times of high divorce rates, who knows whether a weld of sameness is more likely to last than an attraction of opposites.

Whenever men and women are thrown together in a broth of mingling humanity of such richness it is impossible for at least two of their number not to become acquainted, it is the initial conscious and subconscious exchange of signals that determines which man and which woman will pair off. How and why this signalling should on occasion give rise to couples whom the general throng by some unwritten but universally agreed code deems ought not to be together we shall never fully comprehend. As Thomas Hardy lamented in *Tess of the D'urbervilles*:

> ...why so often the coarse appropriates the finer thus, the wrong man the woman, the wrong woman the man, many thousand years of analytical philosophy have failed to explain to our sense of order.

To a bachelor, thoughts of where and how to meet members of the opposite sex were never far away, and that preoccupation played no small part in formulation of the Pyramidal Theory. More will be said of personal romance later.

CHAPTER TWENTY-ONE

It is with great pride I say I never lost a day's work through ill-health during time as a British Railways signalman. But I came very close.

Part of a signalman's duties was to keep the box clean and tidy. I extended that duty to taking care of the box exterior by nailing back on a finial that had fallen off the west end, above the staircase. Addressing years of accumulated grime on the outside of box windows was not so easy. At weekends I set about cleaning one pane at a time with abrasive pad and scouring powder. After six months of labour windows were sparkling clean, if somewhat scratched. Bright new light now pouring into the box picked out dust and debris between the lever frame and front windows, an area in which we seldom trod. Tired of looking at the filth, one mid-morning I enthusiastically grabbed a broom, and, head down, began sweeping at the left-hand (east) end of the box. Such was spring-cleaning fervour, I did not see the corner of the block shelf jutting out at head height and marched straight into it cracking the top of my skull on the hard wood projection. I recoiled at a sharp jab of pain, cursed, rubbed my head with the palm of the hand, and continued brushing, though less industriously than before.

Moments later I felt warmth on the top of the head. Exploration with the finger found a pool of blood. I dropped the broom, hurried to the sink, and irrigated the ruptured area with cold water. Colliding with the block shelf had burst open the skin, my head was bleeding profusely. In order to deal with trains at the same time as administering crude first aid, I had to dash round from sink to lever, to sink, to block bell, to train register book and back to the sink to once again mop up the haemorrhage. I thought of telephoning for help, even for relief, but fortunately the flow of blood steadily decreased till it stopped altogether. By the time my mate arrived, I had cleaned all traces of blood from sink, floor, messing table and train register book desk. On my way home to Belsize Park I called at the Royal Free Hospital where the Casualty Department put several stitches in the wound. I can still feel the scar on top of my head to this day, at least one way in which Kensal Green Junction left its mark.

To reach another case of nearly losing time through sickness it is necessary to take a circuitous route via occasions when signalmen met outside work for a social drink.

A measure of *camaraderie* ran through the North London Line work force, but was strongest in linking together a group of signalmen in their twenties and thirties, including me, who joined the ranks in the late 1970s and early 1980s. Friendships over telephone lines seemed unnatural without face-to-face contact, so I would endeavour to meet fellow signalmen outside work, usually in hospitable confines of a public house. Arrangements were not easy since our homes were scattered across London, and not all worked the same hours, some men working twelve-hour shifts. Various combinations of various signalmen met from time to time, a few outings deserve special mention.

Affable Bob Williams was a family man, for him to spend an evening drinking was tantamount to shirking responsibilities towards his wife and children. Nevertheless, because we had spent so much time chatting on the telephone, I insisted we met person to person, but was able to persuade him to go out for a drink on just one occasion. Conversation not unsurprisingly centred on work, and after several pints I felt an uncontrollable need to talk about the junction signal at Kensal Green.

"You know, Bob," I began, "that signal's got four dolls on it. One of 'em's empty now, it used to read to the Down Goods when it was there. So now there's one for the Down New Lines, one for the Down Platform Line – to High Level you know – and one for the Down City Line. But even with three dolls it's still a really big signal!" With those last few words I stretched arms out sideways to their limit firstly in a gesture to emphasize words just spoken, and secondly, with straightened spine intended to represent the main post, in a hopelessly inadequate and idiotic imitation of the twenty-five feet wide signal itself. Bob Williams laughed uncontrollably at the spectacle of a signalman trying to impersonate a signal. He would remind me now and again how ludicrous the act was.

It was Dave Smith with whom I met most frequently, if irregularly, for a drink. We were sometimes joined by signalman Eddie Jones, a thin man with long hair who, though economical with words, was good company. Visiting any public house in Greater London brought great pleasure, but those in the East End of London, central London and Richmond were especially enjoyable. The East End, home of the Cockneys, struck me as apart from the rest of London as much as Liverpool was apart from the remainder of Lancashire. Inhabitants of the East End shared with inhabitants of Liverpool a sharp edge to their dialect, a sharp edge to their humour, unspoken tribal loyalty, and an irrepressible zest for life. Taverns in the East End radiated warmth and friendliness, but additionally swarmed with young women of captivating prettiness and sapling-like outline, a look made famous by a certain East End model a few decades ago. I would discover East End girls were largely spoken for.

Dave Smith and I signalled passenger trains to Richmond all shift long on early turn. The temptation to hop on the first train there after work more than once proved too great to resist. The town's unique combination of endless park, graceful Thames and inviting riverside amenities rewarded all visitors. Dave Smith fondly remembers two incidents. The first involved an attack of Monty Python humour when, as passers-by looked agog, I walked on my hands along the pavement in The Quadrant. Since I am no acrobat the inverted walk lasted but a couple of seconds. I cannot now remember the joke, but it seemed funny enough at the time to justify upside-down behaviour. The second vignette took place whilst discussing over beer something of a sexual nature that must have dated from adolescence, when I said in jest, "How was I to know, I was only twenty-eight at the time." My coeval companion told me a middle-aged woman sitting at the next table had been listening to all carnal disclosures, and that her eyes nearly popped out of her head when she heard this final utterance.

CHAPTER TWENTY-TWO

As enjoyable as occasional outings were, I felt need for celebration, for something on a grander scale. Friendships were valued (such as they were, for we each lead separate lives) but I thought we should commemorate the joy of being signalmen, even applaud the signals and signal boxes of our livelihood. Could this mean hiring the Albert Hall for a campanological concert of tuned block bells, or throwing a banquet of boiled eggs, toast, coffee and whatever else signalmen ate on duty? No, nothing so dull. The gala day, in its imaginativeness and enterprise, would surpass anything Willesden Junction had ever seen before. A gang of us would go out and get drunk. Dave Smith, after thoughtful consideration, agreed to this suggestion (the other suggestions I wisely did not put forward) and would contact other men.

A Friday evening on a week of early turn was the only date to suit all parties. I met with Dave Smith, Eddie Jones and three others hitherto unknown to me at Willesden Junction to begin the night's festivities. After cleansing the palate at the local railway club, we caught the North London Line to Hampstead Heath station, immediately tumbling into the establishment there to quench a formidable thirst acquired on the long, hot, dry ten-minute train journey from Willesden. After each throwing down a pint, we hauled ourselves up the steep slope of Pond Street, past the antique dealer whose window display never seemed to change, to turn right onto Rosslyn Hill. We stopped in a hostelry that specialized in draught Guinness, which I ordered. Staff took care to pour the Guinness slowly, periodically turning off the spigot to allow stout to settle before adding more. So diligent was the bartender in ensuring a perfect pint of Guinness, my compeers, who had ordered other brews, had just about finished theirs before I started mine. They stood around glaring as I gulped down the rich creamy dark ferric liquid as quickly as I could, a haste insulting the bartender who had meticulously prepared it.

At last I finished the drink and wobbled out of the premises to rejoin friends impatiently waiting in the street. We continued uphill towards

Hampstead. I was bloated like an overfilled hot water bottle, and suffered a sensation of one's body being fuzzy round the edges making it unclear where feet ended and pavement began. With an urgency fuelled by thirst, the quick-marching coterie stormed up Hampstead High Street noisily taking up more than their fair share of the wide pavement, other pedestrians having to give way. Lagging behind was a balloon-like person uncertain whether his feet were meeting the ground. Once in the centre of Hampstead, we piled into a public house and decided to stay there for the evening. Since the time was only about 20:00 hours, early by standards of the drinking population, we were able to claim a table.

I have little recollection of the ninety minutes or so that followed. Without the interruption of promenades between hostelries, the pace of drinking increased, with pints of beer poured down throats like swilling a yard, a pace I could hardly keep up with. We continued to buy rounds, but with a full stomach and a degree of inebriation not experienced for a very long time, I declined a pint here and there, eventually switching to gin and tonics.

In the company of alcohol, boorish exchanges amongst men are inevitable. At one stage I annoyed Eddie Jones, causing him to rise to his feet. To counter his action, I rose to my feet too, which annoyed him even further. Fortunately, we quickly saw conflict was out of place on such an occasion, so we sat down and resumed conversation with the others. As evening progressed, ribald conversation grew louder. Hearty guffaws filled the room, the din intensifying to a level approaching the intolerable in Hampstead.

Amid obstreperous raillery, Dave Smith's experienced eyes darted about noting turned heads and icy glares from bar staff. "Hey, let's quieten it down a bit fellahs," he said, "or we're gonna get thrown out." We heeded his advice, slumped back in our chairs, changed subjects, and reverted to speaking in more conversational tones.

Some time later, I ran out of words and ran out of ability to listen. As I looked at an almost empty goblet wondering how many more gin and tonics to have, a novel idea crossed my mind: maybe I should have no more at all. I stared at infinity through a circular polished wood table covered in pint glasses with varying levels of ale in them. Two alternative plans strove for supremacy. The first plan was to leave immediately because I had work in the morning. The second plan was to remain with the four men (one had left) who were now in excellent humour enjoying life to the full. Free-flowing conversation blended pleasingly into the good-natured civilized hubbub that prevails where intelligentsia are said to live. Signalmen were enjoying the peak of their night out, an evening for which I had long campaigned; for me to leave would spoil the moment and defeat the whole object of the evening. (A third choice would have been a compromise of staying for just one more drink, but an advanced state of drunkenness eliminated the brain's capacity to deal with options numbering more than two.)

Still gazing through the cluttered table, I wrestled with the dichotomy. Then, as if a brick had been tossed on them, the scales of decision swung violently towards the side of leaving immediately. I congratulated myself, firstly, on still being capable of making a decision, secondly, on the fine decision itself that two pints of Bass, one pint of Guinness, four pints of Young's and three gin and tonics were adequate refreshment for one night, and that it was time to go.

Abruptly, I stood up and announced, "I'm gonna go."

"You're not leaving *now* are you Mitch!" said Dave Smith.

"Wassa matter, can't keep up with us?" said Eddie Jones.

"You're right," I slurred. "I'm not used to drinking so much. Gotta be up in the morning."

"So have I!" said Dave Smith.

"So have I!" said Eddie Jones.

"I know, I know," I bleated, "but I've gotta go."

I walked away from the table. Drinking companions briefly watched the ungraceful exit with mouths agape, then sharply returned to revelry as if I had never been there. I politely but unsteadily eased my way through the crowd that now filled the establishment this Friday evening, and left for the long, mercifully downhill tramp to a bed-sitting room in Belsize Park.

CHAPTER TWENTY-THREE

A faint whistle came from some place, I knew not where. It slowly grew in volume to a shrill piercing screech that penetrated the skull as disagreeably as a dentist's drill. After a short period of bewilderment, I concluded I was fast asleep, and that the intracranial sound was that of the alarm clock trying to wake me up. The only way to stop the beastly noise was to do what the device was trying to get me to do, that is, to climb out of a precipitously deep alcohol-induced slumber, gain consciousness albeit a sickly headache-laden consciousness, and switch off the electronic alarm clock. The clock had been a farewell gift from co-workers in Liverpool who knew I would be needing it, but who I am sure would have preferred it not be used in the distressing circumstances in which the author found himself this Saturday morning. After a moment or two of staring at uninteresting cream paintwork on a bed-sitting room ceiling, I dragged myself out of bed, washed, dressed, grabbed my bag and left for work looking forward immensely to the first cup of coffee in the signal box. The train journey to work allowed a little more time to wake up.

I bid my mate a grumpy good morning as he left. I settled in. Block bells seemed far too loud this morning. When throwing levers, I had to bring them gently to rest in the reverse or normal position to reduce noise, rather than crash them about as I usually did. Though a little nauseous, I felt surprisingly well, especially after breakfast. The Saturday morning should not be too troublesome. At about 06:50 the telephone rang.

"Kensal Green," was my standard response.

"Oh… you're there," said a voice.

"Yeh, I'm here. Whaddya mean?" I responded.

"That's okay, if you're there it doesn't matter," said the voice I now recognized as belonging to a relief signalman who worked the North London Line. He hung up the telephone abruptly to cut short further discussion. This relief man had not been with the party last night, so what was the purpose of his checking I was there? Had word travelled fast fostering a general concern about my welfare? The call was inexplicable, and moved the story of the Signalmen's Night Out into a phase of mystery.

I set about dealing with the next train. Though nausea gripped the stomach, a headache pounded between the temples and weakness visited the limbs, none of these impeded operation of the box; I looked forward to going home at 01:30 hours for a few more hours' sleep. Shortly after the first call, the telephone rang again, it was Euston Control.

"Mitch," said the controller.

"Yes," I replied.

"We're a bit puzzled that you're there. We had you down as being sick today," said the man in Control. I had never met the controller, yet he was a man with whom I had always enjoyed the friendliest of working relations.

"I'm not sick," I said indignantly. "Feel a bit rough, but I'm not sick. I'm here, aren't I?" I added ungrammatically.

"Yeh, I know Mitch, but we've got you down in the book that you called in sick," the man insisted.

"I never called in sick," I said, my stance changing from argumentativeness to belligerence. "If I'd called in sick, I wouldn't be here!"

"Okay, Mitch," said a perplexed controller. "We'll let it go at that."

Puzzle of the relief man's telephone call was now compounded by someone calling me in sick without my permission. My initial feelings were that if anyone had to call me in sick, I was the person to do it, not somebody else. But I then wondered whether there might be no conspiracy at all, just a case of someone doing me a favour. That person thought I was in such a wretched state last night I would not make it to work – that I would go AWOL, absent without leave. Well, I proved that person wrong by turning up for work promptly and by executing duties in a proper manner. Indignation swelled to annoyance as I struggled to think who had called. The most likely person was Dave Smith, he was a good enough friend to act on my behalf in such a manner. Still, I was annoyed he did so, and snatched up the telephone to ring him. After he answered I asked crossly, "Hey Dave, did you call me in sick?"

"Not *me* mate," said Dave Smith, his words fading as he backed away from an obviously hostile telephone call, his normally jovial disposition running for cover in the face of unpleasantness.

"Well somebody did. All right, then," I said mollifying a confrontational tone, and put the telephone down.

I thought again. The way Dave Smith said "Not *me* mate" suggested he knew of someone who had made the call. It must have been Jonesey. Eddie Jones and I had never met enough times to become close friends, not close enough for him to do this kind of favour anyway. Tensions had risen the previous evening when we reared up against one another. Had he sought revenge for a confrontation in which he perceived I had gained the upper hand? Was it he who tried to spoil my faultless attendance record by calling me in sick? He was the only other person in the crowd who knew my full name to call me in sick. Anger grew as a net of suspicion closed in. There was only one way to find out, so with hands trembling with rage, I grabbed the telephone to spin numbers of the signal box in which he worked.

Eddie Jones answered drowsily.

"Why did you call me in sick?" I snarled down the telephone.

"What?" came the response.

"Why did you call me in sick?" I repeated with increased menace.

"I don't know what you're talking about," said Eddie Jones.

His voice sounded as if he were trying to apply a polished edge in order to render words more convincing. He was obviously lying. "Sod off Jonesey!" I said bitterly.

"Sod off Deaver!" said Eddie Jones returning the vituperation like exchange of pistol fire.

I slammed the handset back on the telephone, missed, fumbled with it, drew a breath, then more carefully placed it where it belonged. Still smarting from the cruel trick, still shaking with rage, I collapsed in a heap in the armchair. There I sat brooding over events of the first half hour on duty. To begin, I had received a nonsensical telephone call from a relief man, then had learnt a person unknown had told my employer I would not be reporting for duty owing to ill-health.

As the morning progressed, an explanation of the relief man's call slowly emerged. Acting on information I would not be at work on Saturday morning, Euston Control had arranged a substitute. I could only assume the relief man had been running late, had intended to speak to the night man to let him know he was on his way, but finding I was on duty, told Control he was evidently not required. This prompted Control to call me. Had the relief man been on time, two signalmen would have reported for duty at Kensal Green that morning, which would have been even more perplexing.

Someone calling me in sick was not easy to explain. Dave Smith's prevarication suggested he knew who had perpetrated the crime. Eddie Jones' response was laden with guilt, though it was not at all clear what Eddie Jones hoped to achieve since I was going to report for duty regardless of any telephone call. I comforted myself that more information might come to light in due course, and was therefore content to consider all mysteries solved and returned to concentrate on work.

Traffic on Saturday mornings was kind to a signalman with a hangover. Passenger trains obliged with twenty-minute regularity, freight trains ran sporadically. Still, a headache stubbornly drummed out its punishment and the digestive tract continued to complain of abuse inflicted on it twelve hours earlier. A burst of activity about 10:00 hours brought frequent use of the telephone, numerous entries in the train register, many visits to the block shelf and much swinging of the lever frame. Until now I had felt remarkably well. Until now I had been unaware how much a signalman had to rotate around the box from one piece of equipment to another in the course of duties. The continual spinning had a predictable effect on an over-taxed stomach whose contents now churned, rumbled, heaved, expanded and generally caused acute distress to the owner of the stomach. The said stomach contents welled up like hot magma bursting through a dormant volcano plug. But a bell had to be answered, an entry made in the train register book, so I clenched the back of the throat to stem the flow temporarily, then dived over to the sink, opened the mouth, and spewed the Technicolor slurry over the sink's entire enamelled surface. After, I washed myself and the sink, and felt a little better, that is, till the next busy spell when exactly the same thing happened.

I allowed my mouth to hang open so that the lower jaw pressed against the gullet to discourage further eruptions, an action that unavoidably slurred speech. The Southampton to Ripple Lane freightliner passed, I belled 3-2-5 to Gospel Oak, but did not lift the telephone to speak as was customary, hoping the signalman would be able to guess the train. He did not guess, and immediately rang for clarification. I tried to say Southampton, but unable to close the mouth to form consonants, it came out as Wer-WER-wer. I dashed once more to decorate the sink, then returned to tell Gospel Oak more successfully the train's destination. Mental capabilities were unaffected, but as continual visits to the sink and consequent cleaning up were interfering with operating the box, I telephoned for help.

Thirty minutes later a Traffic Manager arrived; he would operate the box whilst I recovered. By midday the stomach had ceased to eject its contents, but nausea persisted; if I resumed working the box consequences would be predictable.

"Do you mind if I go home?" I asked the Traffic Manager.

"Well, the idea is that I would work the box and you'd just keep an eye on things," he said.

"I feel pretty lousy," I said. "I think I'd like to go home, if you don't mind."

The inspector shrugged his shoulders.

"It won't affect my record though. I mean, it won't be put down as being off sick?" I asked.

The Traffic Manager shook his head in the negative. He took a dim view of my leaving. He concentrated on working the frame, and chose not to watch as I sheepishly crept down the signal box steps. As fresh air purged the sickly feeling, shame overcame me for deserting the post. Nevertheless, a decision had been made. When home, I flopped onto the the bed and fell sound asleep. I did not go out for a drink that Saturday night.

CHAPTER TWENTY-FOUR

A feature of the signalman's job in those days was free time between tasks during which there was nothing to do but keep watch. During the day at Kensal Green, seldom more than a minute or two passed between throwing levers, working the block shelf, using telephones, and writing in the train register book. Even those spare moments were meant to be used to keep up-to-date with publications and to look out over tracks to ensure all was well. At night, however, with much reduced frequency of trains, even the most industrious amongst us would occasionally run out of things to do. In such moments I would just sit with one leg cocked over the battered old easy chair arm allowing thoughts to float like dandelion heads in a breeze, to alight on whatever took their fancy.

I sometimes thought about women. I sometimes thought about how much money I did not have in the bank and wished I had. I sometimes thought about where I would like to spend a holiday. In the dying art of daydreaming, all manner of things could be touched upon. Sometimes I just looked at the signal box and trackwork outside, marvelling how Kensal Green Junction was just one vast machine that began at signal levers, extended through the bewildering but ingenious grid of ironwork on the ground floor that mechanically interlocked the frame, through steel wires that left the foot of the box to cross under tracks, to pass over detector beds, to run to the foot of signals, and finally to travel up the signal post to work a semaphore arm. Rigid rodding, whose profile was an inverted U, similarly connected levers to points and facing point locks utilizing bell cranks to turn rodding through ninety degrees where required.

Detector beds were laid out alongside and connected to pointwork in such a manner they allowed operating wires to pass through to pull signals "off" only when point blades were hard against the rail and set for the route governed by the signal. Detector beds prevented signalling trains over points that were gapped, therefore avoiding a possible derailment. Both mechanical interlocking and detector beds – the latter becoming increasingly rare - were fascinating pieces of equipment whose ingenuity could only be appreciated when parts were moving. Whilst on duty I was never able to watch them of course. Occasionally I went downstairs to gaze at the interlocking which was like a finely-meshed portcullis. Pull of a lever caused a component to move vertically which, by bearing against other components, caused them to move horizontally locking other levers in place, or freeing them. I could make little of the mechanism. Nevertheless, ignorance did not prevent me from appreciating the sprawling ingenuity of a mechanical signal box.

Now and again I would ponder the train driver's task but would always conclude a signalman's job suited far better. A train driver had to think continuously about the train's speed, taking into account the prevailing gradient, the authorized maximum speed, any temporary speed limitations, the weight of his train, its braking capacity and, not least of all, the signals he is governed by. This linear kind of thinking, this extruded method of organizing one's thoughts probably would not have suited me as well as the signalman's job where a great number of separate tasks are executed rapidly, sometimes simultaneously, throughout the day.

Thus in quiet times nothing restrained the mind as it pondered the next place to visit in search of the fair sex, as it dwelt on the expansive mechanical machine in front of me, as it planned domestic chores such as shopping and going to the launderette. During such carefree moments, the brain was always receptive to anything that came its way, but one image that briefly popped up then evanesced was puzzling. It was the picture of a telephone kiosk, of a red telephone kiosk found everywhere in Britain. The first time the kiosk flashed before the mind's eye I thought nothing of it; on the second and third occasions I wondered why this should be, but could supply no answer.

Some time passed before another perplexing image began to materialize, that of the open pages of a pocket diary I always carried. The two icons would periodically and mysteriously appear and disappear, like headlamps of two cyclists lost in fog. After a time, the two separate visions came into sharper focus, the telephone kiosk now stood on a hill, the diary now opened to a page of telephone numbers. Then, during a quiet moment on night shift whilst sitting in the easy chair, the two objects converged and crystallized into one clear memory. The memory now suddenly recalled was of my standing in a telephone kiosk on the hill between Hampstead and Belsize Park, of reading the telephone number of Euston Control from the diary, of dialling that number and of telling the controller I would not be coming into work the following day because I was sick. I could even now remember being pleased with myself at making the telephone call, as pleased as I had been at the decision to leave the public house earlier, that latter memory not having been lost. Months had passed since I had got pitifully drunk in Hampstead. It was not until now that I realized with devastating opprobrium that no one had called me in sick, I had done it myself.

At the moment of truth, the signal box and everything around transiently melted like a Salvador Dali painting, then reformed solidly as history re-arranged itself. A sorry state of intoxication had wiped out memory of making the telephone call; indeed, I had no recollection whatsoever of walking home. Memory of telephoning in sick evidently did not even last till reaching home, for I stupidly failed to switch off the alarm clock. Then, completely oblivious of saying I would be absent, reported for work in the normal way. (One wonders if I had switched off the alarm clock and slept till, say, 10:00 hours, whether I would have awoken, panicked, and made another telephone call to Control apologizing profusely for not turning up for work.) Memory is odd. It appears to be the case that a trauma such as concussion or, in my case, far too much beer, does not necessarily destroy memory but merely locks it away for a time.

As story of the Signalmen's Night Out moved into its third and final phase of denouement, the horror of what had taken place overcame me like a virulent fever. Suffering under a heavy carapace of ignominy, my face became hot. I pushed back into the armchair as if to escape my own iniquity. I broke into a sweat over the ineluctable truth of getting drunk, calling in sick, forgetting I had called in sick, going to work, and accusing someone else of calling me in sick.

I had been rude to the man in Control, a man who did not deserve such treatment.

When I had challenged Dave Smith about the matter, I had read his emphasis on the word *me* in "Not *me* mate," as a pointer to his knowing who the real culprit was, whereas the emphasis had no such significance. By suspecting culpability I had endangered a valued friendship, by misinterpreting intonation had set a wrong course.

Eddie Jones had said the words "I don't know what you're talking about," airily, a response to wrongful vilification. His London accent, amplified through innocent emotion, had reached my northern ears as affected and therefore disingenuous. Rocked by a sequence of unexpected events that Saturday morning and with a brain not as sharp as usual, judgement had been impaired. I had been unable to see the obvious implausibility of Eddie Jones' spitefully calling me in sick when he could have inflicted far greater damage to my reputation by doing nothing and allowing me to go AWOL. Eddie Jones, a likeable and uncomplicated person, a fellow signalman, a sound companion, deserved better.

Being an incurably straightforward person, my immediate reaction once the truth became apparent was to call Dave Smith and apologize for casting aspersions and to call Eddie Jones to apologize for the calumny, but could not find words. I did not know whether to blurt out the whole story straight away, or whether to lead up to it by first chatting about that fateful night, then gently easing out the truth. At great length I mulled over how to phrase an apology, but at the same time felt both men by now would probably have forgotten the acrimonious telephone calls. To now remind them and then to reveal truth of a mental black-out would inflict multiple blows to friendships instead of a single blow of the original telephone call.

Much time was spent rehearsing lines of atonement. So protracted were deliberations about what to say, I am no longer absolutely sure whether apologies were actually offered or not. I rather think they were not and that I chose to burke the whole business, in which case the truth has remained hidden for thirty years, only finally revealed on publication of this book. Upon publication it is my intention to convey sincere apologies to Dave Smith. I have long lost contact with Eddie Jones and therefore cannot do the same for him. My wish is that some day he will read these words: the humblest of apologies, old fellow, I hope you will forgive my wronging you.

CHAPTER TWENTY-FIVE

Apart from occasional beery get-togethers, signalmen normally did not come into contact with one another except when relieving and being relieved. I do not know the extent to which signalmen across the entire network met outside work, but I did hear one story from Liverpool that two men who worked in adjacent boxes for eighteen years till one retired never met in all that time, and even failed to meet after retirement. One would have thought the two men would have made an effort to meet at least once, even if only through curiosity.

At one time signal boxes with lengthy frames were so busy they needed more than one person per shift, but most of these splendid boxes were swept away with the advent of electrically-powered operation. So a signalman's lot was generally a lonely one. Picture the monasticism of working a box in the northern fells with only howling wind for company, with only a sparse train service to keep the mind occupied. Needless to say signal boxes around Willesden Junction were far removed from such bleak romantic solitude, London's screaming economy never being far from earshot.

Colleagues in nearby signal boxes offered telephone companionship, as has been seen. Working relationships could be so close a signalman could recognize a regular mate's ringing on the block bell; he might even discern what kind of mood his mate was in by the way the bell rang. (Certain relief men were easily identified too, one rang slowly and deliberately, another used to hit the key so hard the bell at the other end almost jumped off the block shelf.)

Still, it troubled me that if a man never met those with whom he worked, those colleagues were in danger of being reduced in status from human to just a block bell that interrupts at awkward times. Sour humour and strained friendships would follow. It is for these reasons, and also through inquisitiveness, that I made special effort to meet face-to-face at least once all men with whom I regularly worked.

One man was difficult to work with. He seemed to send only two kinds of bell signals, one was one-and-a-half beats (a beat on the bell plus a click) which stood for Call Attention and Train entering Section, the other was a slur of beats and clicks which stood for all other bell codes. His telephone manner was gruff. Possibly this man had no friend on the North London Line. Out of concern I telephoned him one day to let him know I would be calling by to say hello. On arrival at the signal box door, I politely knocked and waited. He beckoned me in. For a while small talk passed back and forth between two people with little in common. Then the man's eyes softened as tension drained from his face; he sank back in the armchair and in softer voice said in reference to my visit, "You're the only one who's done this."

On seeing the man had been moved by a small gesture of kindness, my eyes moistened, I became more relaxed and allowed an almost imperceptible smile to creep across my face. But when he saw my empathy, he decided for reasons known only to himself to discourage any more friendliness, and with features hardening and eyes turning cold, immediately reverted to his usual crusty self. This rapid switching of moods threw me off balance, so I backed off and said to the man, "Anyway, gotta couple of errands I have to run. Talk to you tomorrow. 'Bye now." I left the anchorite to enjoy his loneliness and hastily left the box.

Notwithstanding this failed attempt at friendship, just how important it was to meet everyone was brought home when, for one reason or another, some time had elapsed before face-to-face contact was made with a certain new recruit. We had spent much time on the telephone in which he had asked questions about signalling to a depth that would confound many. His way of speaking, in addition to revealing he was an Irishman, somehow painted a picture of a squab, elderly, round-shouldered and bald man, an image which became as clear in the mind as a portrait in oils.

He would be finishing work early one Saturday morning and said he would walk along the track to see me. Imagine my shock when a tall man of slim build (as many Irishmen are) with an astonishing head of hair (as many Irishmen have) sauntered along the permanent way impeccably dressed in a two-piece suit and tie. Till he stopped on the far side of the tracks opposite the box and called out in his rich Irish brogue, I could not believe it was the man I had come to know so well over the telephone and whose appearance I had imagined to be the opposite of the actuality now presenting itself. We exchanged a couple of pleasantries. He surprisingly declined an invitation to come up into the box, and instead chose to continue strolling along the track, eventually to disappear in the distance.

I was disappointed, and a little hurt, that he rejected the overture. Could it be that my appearance to him was as great a shock as his to me? Could it be that he had exactly the same mental image of me as I him? (I did not have his height nor luxuriant head of hair, but I was not stout, elderly nor round-shouldered.) The oddest aspect of this story is that when we resumed our usual telephonic exchanges the following week, the image I had had of the man would not go away; the picture of an older person persisted even though meeting him in the flesh had proved how egregiously wrong that was.

Meeting colleagues from neighbouring boxes required extraordinary effort, but a signalman could expect through the working week a trickle of visits from other railway employees. A weekly visitor to the location if not to the box itself was the lampman whose job it was to renew all paraffin lamps in mechanical signals. Only once did he come up to the box, when he told me of all the manual boxes that used to control the main line in Willesden before modernization. He used to keep a note of every lamp he had to service, in other words, of every full size signal and every ground signal around. He regretted not keeping the record.

Technicians from the Signalling and Telecommunications Department were frequent visitors, either to carry out planned maintenance or to effect repairs. The most common problem was failure of track circuits in showing occupation by a train when there was no train there. (Such a false indication held a signal at stop resulting in train drivers having to be instructed by the signalman to pass the signal at danger and to proceed with caution.) I recall a comment by one technician that colour light signals were immensely easier to repair, but he conceded a semaphore "was a better signal". By that he meant a semaphore arm was a stronger signal, at least by daylight. (It is noteworthy in the 2000s some semaphore signals were being retained but with paraffin lamps replaced by electric lights.) Men from the Signalling and Telecommunications Department, usually referred to as the S and T, were not without humour. Every time one technician entered the box he asked if he could wash his feet in the sink, his sportive request being matched with one from me to tighten the electric wire that ran to automatic signal KG63 because the signal was only showing a pale green!

During weeks of early and late turn signalmen were usually visited by either a Movements Inspector or a Traffic Manager, sometimes both, because it was part of managerial duties to do so. One week Movements Inspector Henry Knowles brought with him a visitor from Japan to look at the box. The visit was going well until the oriental guest intimated to the Inspector he needed to use the toilet. Now, the toilet at Kensal Green was of the chemical variety that required a nest of toilet tissue placed in the bowl before solids could be deposited therein. Henry Knowles, who did not smile a great deal, felt even less inclined to do so at this juncture as he had hoped to impress the Japanese visitor with British Railways' high degree of organization. Instead he was now faced with not only having to tell the guest about the box's primitive facilities but also having to demonstrate how the latrine should be prepared for use. As the Movements Inspector's duties now came perilously close to that which his title might suggest, Henry Knowles' fine porcelain skin turned cadaverous and his eyes enlarged with horror. Seeing the frightful predicament, I dashed forward, tugged on the visitor's jacket sleeve (for he spoke little English) and led him to the toilet on the landing by the entrance door. In the small room, I laid toilet tissue in the bowl, and with the kind of obsequiousness revered in the visitor's home country, gestured towards the privy, bowed, and backed out. A short while later the guest re-appeared a little flushed. He grinned at Henry Knowles and me, thanked us in broken English, but explained he only wanted to wee.

CHAPTER TWENTY-SIX

Visits from management higher than Movements Inspector or Traffic Manager were rare, but a sequence of events would precipitate such a call from high office.

Improvements to rolling stock and track had resulted in maximum speed on parts of the West Coast Main Line being raised to 125 miles per hour, which in turn prompted a notice to that effect on the back of official publications such as the W1. Printed in large type were the words HIGH SPEED RUNNING ON THE WEST COAST MAIN LINE followed by a message that all staff must now be prepared for same.

Use of such a large typeface was not common in railway printed material, employees being more accustomed to scrutinizing small print for instructions. The message HIGH SPEED RUNNING ON THE WEST COAST MAIN LINE jumped off the page to cudgel the brain as if words had been stamped on it with a branding iron. The exhortation kept repeating itself over and over in the mind like a gramophone record played loudly by an annoying neighbour. It cried out for response, and respond I would. I sent a letter to the Regional Operations Manager in Crewe (whose title appeared on official documents) that went something along the following lines:

> Dear Sir,
> New ideas and new thinking in management are always appearing, and it is vital that every industry should be aware of such changes so that they remain at the forefront in their field. Sometimes this involves discarding old, worn-out routines, and embracing something revolutionary. In current times Japan is one of the most successful industrialized nations in the world, many would argue we have a lot to learn from them.
> One notion common to all Japanese companies is that a healthy workforce is a productive workforce. It seems alien to Europeans, but

Japanese companies insist that their workers incorporate a keep-fit regime into their day, so part of the working day is given over to exercise.

I was delighted to see that British Rail is now following the Japanese example. I am writing about notices on the back of the W1 imploring staff to join in in high speed running alongside the main line. I think this is an excellent idea that will result in much fitter and healthier employees which in turn will benefit everyone. Presumably they will participate before their normal shift starts, and that they will wear high visibility vests. Doubtless all this will be undertaken under the protection of Section T II of the Rule Book, with handsignalmen keeping a look out.

I was really excited about joining in, but, unfortunately, the other day I twisted my ankle whilst out walking, so I am excusing myself from the exercise.

Yours faithfully,
a signalman in the Willesden area

P.S. the notice says 125 m.p.h running, this must of course be a misprint and should read 12.5 m.p.h.

(Reference to Japan both here and in the previous chapter is coincidence. The two incidents occurred at different times, and may even have happened in reverse order.)

The letter was duly posted without the sender's address; I hoped the recipients would find it amusing. I gave the matter little further thought until, a week or two later, the Area Manager himself called at Kensal Green box. He hesitated at the door and looked me straight in the eye as if to gauge my disposition. I welcomed him in, then we briefly talked about the job.

Conversation halted as the Area Manager pulled a crumpled piece of paper from his pocket, a letter I instantly recognized, one that had obviously passed through many hands. "Did you write this?" asked the Area Manager thrusting the document at me.

The last thing I expected was the letter about high speed running to find its way back to me. I coloured, but uncertain of the consequences of admission, offered no reply. Trying to regain composure, I took the letter and read it. It seemed funnier now than when I originally wrote it, and as I handed it back I could not suppress a broad grin. At that, the Area Manager broke into a short laugh. "We read it, and we roared with laughter," he said. It was a relief to know the missive had been received with the same humour with which it had been dispatched.

"I said to the people in Crewe that it could have been written by one of two signalmen I knew to be wags," said the Area Manager.

The plenipotentiary then looked at me for response, but for the second time received none. At the outset I had not owned up to being the author, and felt the best course now would be to maintain an ambiguous position.

A foolish grin hung on the face as I fidgeted and exchanged uncomfortable glances with the senior manager. He seemed disappointed I did not confess. "Ah well, I'll see the other signalman with it," said the Area Manager. He left shortly afterwards.

The Area Manager, a quietly spoken and much respected man who kept in reserve the far-reaching authority bestowed on him, deserved greater honesty from his servant. I should have been grateful for his conciliatoriness. A more imperious official could have taken a very different view of an absurd letter sent by one of the most junior members of staff to one of the most senior members, and could have asked if I had nothing better to do. The Area Manager really wanted me to admit to the jest so that we could share the ludicrousness of confusing 125 miles per hour trains with twelve miles per hour jogging railway workers. A cautious stance disallowed what could have been a natural and entirely amicable conclusion to a mischievous escapade.

CHAPTER TWENTY-SEVEN

Whether or not we had visitors, the rigid three-men three-week cycle of shifts remained unbroken with signalmen working all their rest days. When I was a child in Yorkshire signalmen were compelled to take off rest days, their absence being covered by a rest-day relief man. Annual holiday entitlement and any sickness were covered by a general purpose relief man. The position of rest-day relief man still existed on the North London Line in the 1980s, but he was found work filling signal box vacancies; it was for this reason that not all signal box positions were filled. General purpose relief men were also extant.

Approximately twenty relief men were qualified to work Kensal Green, and whenever Fred Abbott or Jim Waters took annual or compensation leave, I never knew who would replace them till I saw them in the box. Some relief men appeared oftener than others, but from time to time a man would appear at the signal box door I had not seen for, say, a year. It was always a delight to see them, I am not sure why. It may have been a simple joy of renewing an old acquaintance or there may have been hint of a returning prodigal son. The best explanation for a sudden onrush of joy is that whereas only droplets of goodwill are measured out to a friend one sees daily, towards a colleague long absent the equivalent amount of amity gushes forth in one unstoppable deluge. A similar uplifting of spirits occurred whenever a permanent way inspector I had not seen for a while appeared on Saturday night to take a possession.

Over the years train drivers based in Broad Street and signalmen on the North London Line came to know one another even if only to the extent of recognition and exchanging waves as trains passed the box. From the large number of signalmen I knew well, and from what I knew of North London Line drivers, both groups of men had one thing in common: about one third of their numbers were railway enthusiasts. This shared propensity to view the railway as not only a place of work but as inspiration - even if leisure pursuits such as steam engines or railway modelling had little connection with the North London Line - formed a loose bond between drivers and signalmen.

Although one third of signalmen may have been railway enthusiasts, another third looked upon the career as just a job: they had no love for the railway at all. I do not say that disparagingly, because a strong case could be made that such men made the best signalmen, the most convincing evidence being errors of judgment this signalman made through over-enthusiasm. Those men who were not railway enthusiasts were just as reliable as men who were, and often seemed more willing to work extra hours additional to those already worked. The remaining third of signalmen, those who were neither railway enthusiasts nor who looked upon the railway as just a source of income, struck me as people who had no interest before they joined the grade but who acquired a fondness for railways as time went by, even if they would never admit the fact.

To turn now to meeting people who were not railway employees, passengers of course came very close to signal boxes as their trains swept by. They would not normally come into contact with signalmen except in a few instances where boxes were built on station platforms and where passengers would sometimes enquire of the man on duty how trains were running, such interruptions not usually being welcomed. Part of our duties as signalmen was to watch every train go by in case a defect required seven beats on the bell (Stop and Examine Train) to be sent to the box in advance. As we peered down from our glassy towers at electric passenger trains silently speeding by, we checked that no axles were over-heating, that every door was securely closed, and that all was in order. A pretty face would not escape notice either.

The closest I came to meeting passengers whilst on duty – and it was not very close at all - was an occasion when something was amiss on the Up Main towards Gospel Oak. Train drivers had to be cautioned, but since Up Platform Line homes 1 and 2 colour light signals did not carry telephones, the caution had to be issued face to face. This was achieved by waiting till trains had almost come to a stand at Home 2 signal number 53 (about a hundred yards away) pulling the lever to clear the signal, then immediately displaying a red flag from an open signal box window to stop the train. A passenger train responded to this procedure and stopped opposite the box for me to shout across the message. Once the caution was delivered, I followed rules and then hung a green flag out of the window for the train to proceed. As the train pulled away, I glanced at its occupants. I made eye-contact with a woman in her early twenties in the process of slumping back in her seat obviously displeased at what in her opinion was a signalman doing nothing more than playing to the gallery. For 249 days of the working year she shot by the trackside shed without incident, on this day she would be late for work because railwaymen were playing trains.

MITCHELL DEAVER

In his sequestered existence a signalman relished his independence, valued telephone exchanges with colleagues, appreciated box visits, welcomed long-lost fellow workers and, from his royal box position, enjoyed the wispiest of contacts with the travelling public.

CHAPTER TWENTY-EIGHT

In such manner four years passed at Kensal Green Junction during which a signalman's life settled into a regimen of familiarity, of predictability, and of generally feeling at home. But such contentment could not last because time never stands still, even for a monolithic state industry such as British Railways.

Routines changed. An early casualty was use of destination to identify trains. Around 1983 we were directed to stop the colourful practice of giving place-names for trains, instead to employ lifeless four digit reporting numbers printed in working timetables. First component of that number was class of train. Second was the British Railways region to which the train was destined: E for Eastern, M for London Midland, S for Scottish, V for Western and O for Southern. Various letters were used for trains that did not leave the region of origin. Z was used for special trains, X for out-of-gauge trains. Last two digits of the code were a serial number. Thus the four Southampton freightliner trains seen each day were no longer - as comfortable as an old pair of jeans - the "Ol' Southampton" but severe 4E66, 4E78, 4O79 and 4O60.

Describing trains from Kensal Green to Willesden power box had always been by a block bell of London and North Western Railway design comprising an oblong black box on short metal legs with the bell dome itself suspended underneath, an instrument I nicknamed a rat's coffin. The bell had now been replaced by a computer visual display unit comprising monitor, modem and keyboard. To describe a train to Willesden power box, its reporting number was typed in and a key pressed which placed the reporting number on the monitor's representation of the Down City Line, the description then being automatically forwarded. By a similar process reporting numbers of trains coming from Willesden power box appeared on a representation of the Up City Line, a short, shrill electronic tone announcing the fact.

The remainder of Kensal Green box continued to use hundred-year old technology, and it was unfortunately that antiquity which threatened secure positions of signalmen. Ever since signal boxes were first built in quantity, railway companies have constantly been searching for ways to economize by reducing numbers. Such schemes as replacement by West Hampstead power box of numerous manual boxes on the former Midland Railway main line out of St. Pancras forced many signalmen to seek work further afield, but isolated closures of boxes here and there still took place. Movements Inspector Ron Dillington called by to disclose one such plan.

"You see, Mitch," he began, "they're looking at doing away with either Kensal Green or High Level. One of 'em's going to go."

"Well, that's easy," I said confidently, "all they've got to do is put High Level on here. We've got plenty of spare levers. They'd just have to make High Level's points motor operated."

Ron Dillington gave a short nod, more to acknowledge a declamation than to concede merit of the argument.

"This is a nicer box, we know," said Ron Dillington in uncharacteristically low voice.

"And you could make High Level's Up home signals IBs," I said. (IBs, or Intermediate Block signals are home and distant positioned further along the line additional to the normal complement of signals.)

"Now, think about that Mitch," said Ron Dillington, his eyes flashing with zeal, his words coruscating with fervour as he saw looming a debate on signalling technicalities. "Why couldn't we have IBs at High Level?" His question remained unanswered; a blank face told him I did not know. "If the telephone has failed at an IB, what can a driver do?" asked the Movements Inspector.

"He can pass it at danger," I said limply.

"Right," said Ron Dillington. "But you couldn't have that at a junction, could you now?"

He smiled benevolently to raise spirits after I had been shot down over rules and regulations. "Anyway," Ron Dillington continued in avuncular tones, "the problem is the Warning Arrangement. The signalman at High Level has to be able to display a green flag from the box window to the driver of a train accepted by Mitre Bridge under the Warning Arrangement. So if we did away with High Level, what do we do? Do we do away with the Warning Arrangement between High Level and Mitre Bridge? I don't know. It's all being discussed by the powers that be. No decision has been made yet which box to close, if any." Ron Dillington chatted a little longer that day, then left, less than happy about the arraignment of Kensal Green Junction.

The Warning Arrangement, part of Absolute Block Regulations, was a dispensation from the requirement that a full quarter-mile be clear beyond the home signal before a Line Clear may be given. It was used at signal boxes only where expressly authorized and allowed a signalman to accept a train from the box in the rear when the line was clear to the home signal only. The accepting signalman used bell signal 3-5-5 to tell the box in the rear of that fact so the signalman there may caution a train by using a green flag, or by using a subsidiary signal marked W. The Warning Arrangement, once widespread particularly for freight trains, was in due course renamed Restricted Acceptance.

In earliest signalling, green used to mean caution and white all clear. Owing to growing numbers of white electric lights on property adjacent to railways, from the year 1893 onwards green became the "all clear" in fixed signals, but no change was made to hand signals, a green flag still meant caution. What always seemed especially inappropriate was the circumstance of a signalman being advised by bell code 5-5 that a train approaching had accidentally divided, whereupon he had to gently wave a green flag at the driver to tell him his train had split in two! The anomaly concerning hand signals remained unchanged for ninety years till the mid-1980s when the green flag for caution was changed to yellow.

Particularly at work, human nature tends to prefer routine over change; it is easier to carry out the same duties each day than to learn new ones. There is something of a Luddite in all of us as we jealously cling to familiar practices, steadfastly refusing to acknowledge that a change might be for the better, or that invariability over any length of time leads to boredom. Whether popular or not, developments in the mid-1980s materially altered appearance of the North London Line. Two changes, displacement of Class 501 three-car electric multiple units by Class 416 two-car units and closure of Broad Street station with North Woolwich becoming the eastern terminus of the line, did not affect me. A third change did.

Several months after Inspector Ron Dillington's briefing came the announcement Kensal Green box would close. A push-button panel would be installed in High Level Junction to control both layouts formerly worked by lever frames, the changeover taking place during Easter weekend of 1985. By this time Fred Abbott had retired for a second and final time and Jim Waters had become a relief man. Their replacements had fled the box because a signalman made redundant three times had no entitlement to a replacement position; this was only their first displacement but they were taking no chances on another two. I chose to remain till the end. In the final week or two, the North London Line was shut down at Kensal Green Junction as semaphore signals were felled, the junction ripped out, earth excavated, new foundations laid, a revised track layout installed and new colour lights erected. The box ceased to signal trains in a reliable efficient manner, and was instead relegated to handling only Civil Engineer's trains carrying away spoil and redundant equipment, bringing in fresh ballast and new track.

The semaphore junction signal, for decades a spectacular archway to the Willesden railway complex, remained till the very end. I did not see it come down. A British Railways employee had planned to purchase and preserve it (goodness knows where he would have erected it without breaching Town and Country Planning laws) but damage it suffered whilst being dismantled meant he had to abandon the prize; he made do with the Down starting bracket signal.

I would have liked to have been there at the very end. I presume the correct procedure would have been to send box closing bell signal 7-5-5 to adjacent Absolute Block signal boxes of High Level and Willesden New Station, then to telephone mates to inform them the box was abolished forthwith. A telephone call to Track Circuit Block Regulations neighbours of Gospel Oak and Willesden power box would have sufficed. In the event, Easter weekend of 1985 was my weekend off, so the last I saw of Kensal Green was on the Saturday morning. I understand the end was not at all clear cut, with the box merely fading out of existence during the following Sunday as connections were severed. Official abolition is recorded as 06:00 hours on Monday 8th April 1985. The structure itself was demolished a year or two later.

I had heard some men took to heart abolition of their first signal box, but I felt no great loss when the time came as emotions had been disbursed on first hearing of the box's fate. Even though Kensal Green Junction was not particularly highly thought of amongst signalman, it would always be special to me because it fulfilled a boyhood dream. As far as I was concerned its spaciousness, lengthy frame, impressive outlook and verdant setting more than compensated for lack of operational sparkle. I took care of the box and did my best to work it as it should have been worked, but when time came I was ready to move.

CHAPTER TWENTY-NINE

As a displaced man I had first pick of available jobs and chose a vacancy at Acton Wells Junction, the next box towards Richmond after Willesden High Level Junction. The vacancy corresponded to my position at Kensal Green, hence a three-week cycle of shifts remained unbroken, with the last shift at Kensal Green on Saturday morning 6th April being followed by night shift at Acton Wells on Easter Monday, 8th April 1985. A period of training lasting till the end of April inured a transferred man to demands of his new post.

Acton Wells Junction, a busy crossroads on the railway network, was located on the northern edge of the suburb of Acton. The signal box, sited on the eastern side of the North London Line that ran approximately north and south between Willesden Junction and Richmond, could not easily be seen from any highway, and was reached only by walking a few hundred yards alongside railway tracks. For the technically minded, fenestration and vertical exterior boarding classified Acton Wells architecturally as North London Type 3a. The lever frame, with levers spaced every five-and-a-half inches, was originally a North London Railway tumbler variety but was relocked with London and North Western Railway tappet interlocking secured in metal casing immediately behind the frame. Signal box interlocking was usually housed out of sight on the ground floor, but in this case was in view, though its mysteries concealed by a metal cover firmly bolted down.

Acton Wells was all that Kensal Green was…and more. Four pairs of main lines converged in a scissors formation with two sidings (Southwest Sidings) in the northern V of the scissors. The frame was more complicated and physically harder to work. Whilst most of its operation could be discerned by studying the illuminated diagram, setting up routes for Southwest Sidings had to be memorized because sequence of pulling and pushing black point levers and blue facing point lock levers could not easily be deduced.

Absolute Block Regulations, using British Railways' standard

"Woolworth's" block instruments, applied to Willesden High Level Junction to the north and Bollo Lane Junction to the south on the North London Line and to Acton Canal Wharf on a line linking the North London Line to the main line out of St. Pancras station. This line through Acton Canal Wharf was called the Midland Line. On the fourth leg of the scissors formation, Track Circuit Block Regulations were in force to Old Oak Common power box on the Western Region of British Railways, communication being by electronic train describer.

Much was new, such as bell code 1-2-1 Train Approaching. Acton Wells had to send this signal to Bollo Lane as soon as Willesden High Level Junction sent Train entering Section. This enabled Bollo Lane to lower level crossing barriers against highway traffic in Churchfield Road, Acton, and pull "off" signals in time - all exemplifying great trouble taken by the railway concerning level crossings.

A procedure at Acton Wells not met before was a run-round movement, the transfer of a locomotive from one end of its train to the other. This was undertaken between Acton Wells and Acton Canal Wharf when a train arrived from the north that had to reverse direction at Canal Wharf to take a branch into Willesden yards.

Another new form of traffic were trip workings, freight trains conveying traffic over relatively short distances, usually between yards in big cities. Because in steam engine days target-like boards were carried on the front of locomotives displaying numbers, trip workings bore such names as Target 3, Target 25, and so on. In modern reporting numbers the letter T was retained for trip, resulting in such identities as 6T03, 7T31, etcetera. A trip working from Cricklewood would arrive at Acton Wells Junction via the Midland Line, change direction and propel – push its train rather than pull it - into Southwest Sidings. It later returned to Cricklewood by reversing the movement. The train was either only partially fitted, or completely without the continuous brake, for it was one of few to retain a guard's van.

Other noteworthy trains included a rake of bogie open wagons loaded with stone hauled by a completely new class of diesel engine, the Class 59, built by General Motors in the United States. Privately owned freight wagons were not new to the railway, but use of a company's own motive power was: the Class 59s were owned by the stone quarry. Purchase of these powerful engines was accompanied by another development, the running of trains half a mile in length. Manned by British Railways' crews of course, a Class 59, emblazened with its owner's logo, would depart from the West Country with about forty bogie open wagons loaded with stone. The train would divide at Acton, one half taking the North London Line. Sound emitted by the Class 59 was like no other from a diesel engine, the locomotive hummed rather than roared.

Two very special trains put in an appearance at Acton Wells. One was world famous preserved steam locomotive, *ex*-London & North Eastern Railway Pacific Class A3 4472 *Flying Scotsman*. It went by in the Up direction under cover of darkness about 21.30 hours one night. The other was as special as any train can be, the Royal Train. Conveying Her Majesty The Queen northwards, it too passed under cover of darkness. Extra personnel were on duty in signal boxes as a precaution. Unique regulations applied, including use of the Royal Train bell code 4-4-4 and a requirement that signalmen must first obtain a Line Clear from the box in advance before they may grant a Line Clear to the box in the rear, working double block as it was known. The immaculately kept Royal Train in glistening plum-coloured livery slipped quietly by without incident.

If a signalman were to make a mistake let us hope it was never whilst the Royal Train was around. Signalmen are as human as any other worker, but the unfortunate truth is that a slip on their part could result in catastrophic loss of life, which has happened on very rare occasions in the past. Most errors are fortunately venial, the most serious I made was to send a train the wrong way. Tracks beyond Kew East Junction were not available one night owing to an Engineer's Possession; all traffic that normally took that route had to be diverted via Old Oak Common power box onto the Western Region. One train that usually went via Kew, a Class 4 automobile train using bell code 3-1-1, was offered by Willesden High Level. Without thinking, I offered it on to Bollo Lane instead of describing it towards Old Oak Common power box. The man at Bollo Lane thought I was ringing 3-1-2, the usual passenger train code, and for that reason had no hesitation in granting a Line Clear. The train had already passed me before the signalman at Kew East Junction learnt of it and telephoned to point out the blockade. The train was halted at Kew East, ran round between there and Bollo Lane, returned to Acton Wells, and ran round again in Southwest Sidings before gaining correct routing onto the Western Region. I had to apologize profusely to both the driver and to Euston Control. Arguably a signalman should have been disciplined for such an error, but I escaped punishment.

CHAPTER THIRTY

The inventory of semaphores at Acton Wells, of prime interest to a signalling enthusiast, began with the Down Main home, a short, simple one-armed signal. Only one other full-sized semaphore signal stood on the main line, a bracket signal close to the box directing traffic either straight along the North London Line towards Bollo Lane or deviating right towards the Western Region. An odd confluence of circumstances occurred one day concerning this signal.

The London Underground Central Line passed underneath the North London Line at Acton Wells Junction. Whilst riding the Central Line one day I glanced upwards as the tube train passed under Acton Wells and was shocked to see that, on the bracket signal, red arm number 28 - the Down Main starting towards Bollo Lane – had been rotated through 130 degrees so that it was pointing backwards! For a few days afterwards I could not decide whether I had been seeing things or if I had dreamt the whole episode. In time all was revealed. When telling a relief signalman the story, he confessed that he was to blame. He had pulled too sharply on lever 28 causing the arm to flip right over; he had fortunately been able to climb the signal and push the arm back in place. By an extraordinary coincidence, I had passed underneath to witness the irregular aspect during the brief period it was displayed!

The bracket signal also carried Bollo Lane's Down Main semaphore distant worked by electric motor, slotting being employed to ensure the distant could not show "off" when the starting was "on". Occasionally the electric motor malfunctioned causing the distant arm to waggle up and down when it should be showing "off". Because this behaviour resembled playing a banjo, the defect was referred to as banjoing.

All signals in the Acton Canal Wharf direction, the Midland line, were semaphores, and because that box and Acton Wells were relatively close, the two shared signals. This meant semaphore arms required levers to be pulled in both Acton Wells and Acton Canal Wharf before they would come "off": the signals were slotted.

Whilst the extent of slotting between the two boxes was too complicated to repeat here, the basic idea deserves explanation. Contrast between potency of slotting and simplicity of means to achieve it never ceased to impress the author.

The term slotting derives from original mechanisms that incorporated slots. Today's design features three horizontal bars fixed alongside one another on the signal post with operating wires running from the two outer bars to each of the signal boxes. The third bar, secured between and resting upon the other two, is connected to the signal arm. When levers in both signal boxes are pulled, the two outer bars tip downwards causing the third bar to fall by gravity which in turn pulls the signal arm "off". If only one signalman pulls his lever, only one horizontal bar drops and the middle bar, because it is still resting on the other outer bar, will not move so the semaphore arm remains "on". Weights attached to the slotting mechanism ensure it functions as intended. Electrical relays achieve slotting in colour light signals. In the most up-to-date installations, solid state electronics achieve the same end, though signalmen still use the term "giving a slot" for their moiety of clearing a signal.

Again owing to closeness of Acton Wells and Acton Canal Wharf, two distant signals had to be provided for Acton Wells in the Down direction to give train drivers adequate warning. An outer distant was installed under Canal Wharf's home, an inner distant under Canal Wharf's starting signal. Somewhat rare by the late 1980s, the inner and outer mechanical distants at Acton Wells could be cleared only for the route towards Bollo Lane Junction. Heavy coal trains took that path, and I would always attempt to pull "off" both distants in time for the train to see them. Train drivers would acknowledge the effort by a friendly wave as they passed the box. Operating the outer distant required all the strength one would expect for a mechanical signal three-quarters of a mile away round a bend. Accomplishing the feat involved depressing the stirrup handle with the left hand, pulling the lever partially over with the right, then placing both hands on the upper part of the handle to heave the lever completely over, an immensely satisfying operation.

Owing to complexity of slotting, the outer distant would normally show only a poor "off", rising about twenty-five degrees instead of forty-five degrees. Experiments conducted with co-operation of the man at Acton Canal Wharf discovered that quality of the outer distant signal depended on which signalman pulled levers first. I think we found the man at Acton Wells had to pull "off" first to produce a good signal.

Signalman's slang for pulling "off" a distant signal was "giving it the back 'un". Ever since childhood I had been fascinated by remoteness of distant signals, by the raw physical strength employed pulling a signal box lever to move a yellow fish-tailed semaphore arm that could be as far away as a mile. Some distant signals were so far away two levers were employed; through a system of pulleys one took up the slack, the other actually operated the arm. Three levers were used in extreme cases, such as the Down distant at Duston West Junction, Northampton.

To return to Acton Wells, immediately ahead of the semaphore Down home on the Midland line was a pair of throw-off trap points which would divert a train into soil if it overran the signal – put it "on the ground" as railwaymen say. Levers 20 and 22 closed and locked the trap points before the home signal could be cleared. Freight trains could be given a Line Clear when there was *not* the normal clearing distance of 440 yards beyond the home signal provided trap points were in the throw-off position. Train drivers had to be careful to stop in good time.

To give a Line Clear for the occasional excursion passenger train we saw on the Midland line, the trap points had to be closed and a full quarter-mile distance kept clear beyond the home signal, such distance stretching right through the junction. An excursion was due off the Midland line at about 09:00 hours one Sunday morning when both Acton Canal Wharf and the next box, Neasden Junction, were closed. When the next box after that, Dudding Hill Junction, asked for a Line Clear for the Class 1 train, I had no alternative but to give it, but in so doing could not accept a local Richmond train from Willesden High Level because the junction was reserved for the excursion train. The Class 1 train was a long time coming from Dudding Hill and the electric multiple unit therefore ran very late. Though maintaining I had worked entirely in accordance with rules and regulations, circumstances delaying the local passenger train were extremely difficult to explain to Euston Control.

CHAPTER THIRTY-ONE

Acton Wells was operationally more exhilarating than Kensal Green. Another way in which it excelled owes more to a signalman's filing system than to inherent qualities, it is a potential to examine in minute detail at a later date how the box was worked.

I kept a note of both signalling layouts but additionally retained copy of the regulating simplifier from Acton Wells, probably dated 1987. Extrapolated from working timetables, the simplifier listed every train, including electric multiple unit passenger trains, that passed in a twenty-four hour period. Combining that schedule with knowledge of the lever frame it is possible to reconstruct, if in a somewhat spectral manner, exactly what I was doing at any time of day in the signal box, though that reconstruction is based on trains passing Acton Wells on time. Set out below is a minute by minute account of signalling four trains about 15:30 hours, with a guess made at times of incoming bell signals. To clarify the bell signals shown in this re-enactment, the one beat of Call Attention and bell code 3-1-2 for ordinary electric passenger trains is represented by 1 & 3-1-2.

Before raising the curtain - before peeking into the past - let us limn a backdrop. The signalman's easy chair was centred along the rear wall. To the right were the messing table and chair with lockers in the far corner of the box. On the left was the train register book desk, then a small electric cooker. As I waited for the next bell signal I usually sat in the easy chair looking through signal box windows at the collection of light industries stretching from the railway boundary to Acton's Victoria Road. Sometimes on late turn I would take a whole roast chicken to work for carving into mouth-watering sandwiches. So round about 15:00 hours I could well have been sitting contentedly with a well-filled stomach:

15:25 1 & 3-1-2 received from High Level; block indicator turned to Line Clear; 1 & 3-1-2 sent to Bollo Lane; signal levers 28, 29, 30 pulled.

15:28 2 received from High Level; block indicator turned to Train on Line; 1-2-1 sent to Bollo Lane.
1 & 3-1-2 received from Bollo Lane; block indicator turned to Line Clear.

15:29 Down passenger went by; 2 sent to Bollo Lane; signal levers 30, 29, 28 put back; 1 & 2-1 sent to High Level; block indicator returned to Normal.

15:30 2 received from Bollo Lane; block indicator turned to Train on Line; 1 & 3-1-2 sent to High Level; signal levers 5 and 1 pulled.

15:31 1 & 5 received from High Level; told of train's reporting number; block indicator turned to Line Clear.

15:32 1 and 2-1 received from Bollo Lane.

15:33 Up passenger went by; 2 sent to High Level; signal levers 1 and 5 put back; 1 & 2-1 sent to Bollo Lane; block indicator returned to Normal.

15:34 2 received from High Level; block indicator turned to Train on Line; points levers 17 and 18 pulled; signal levers 27 and 29 pulled.
Old Oak Common described 6M27; 1 & 5 sent to Canal Wharf; signalman there told of train's reporting number; lever 17 already pulled; levers 23, 24 pulled, 23 put back; signal levers 11 and 16 pulled.

15:36 1 & 2-1 received from High Level.
6V52 Ripple Lane to Langley tank train went by on Down; 6V52 described to Old Oak Common; entry made in train register; signal levers 29, 27 put back; points lever 18 put back; 1 & 2-1 sent to High Level; block indicator returned to Normal.

15:37 6M27 Park Royal to Willesden van train went by on Up; 2 sent to Canal Wharf; entry made in train register; signal levers 11 and 16 put back; points lever 17 put back, points lever 23 pulled, points levers 24 and 23 put back.

15:39 1 & 2-1 received from Canal Wharf.

Of course I was not the only signalman who followed the above routine, it was enacted by regular mates. The man following me in shifts, Len Robinson, a fellow railway fan, a friendly and cheerful person, was as excellent a relief as Fred Abbott had been at Kensal Green. Len Robinson's affection for signalling extended to polishing all lever handles in Acton Wells, a chore I had attempted in Kensal Green but which I gave up as too arduous.

On the few occasions Len Robinson and I met socially we joined other signalling enthusiasts, including more signalmen, to operate a mock-up railway. Spread through several rooms in an enthusiast's house, the railway comprised small control panels with moving lights on a diagram to simulate passage of trains (as in real signal box illuminated diagrams) with second-hand block instruments used to actually signal trains, all being recorded in ersatz train register books of course. Ropes of electrical wires trailed from room to room connecting the "signal boxes". The event was of course a busman's holiday but was thoroughly enjoyable, a credit to organizers who spent countless hours building and preparing the layout for operation.

The third man at Acton Wells had few words to say, and seemed not entirely happy. He eventually handed in his resignation one day and left the railway.

Description of Acton Wells would not be complete without mention of another member of the team, Pudding the cat. It was one of a litter born in Acton Canal Wharf box where the signalman there did his best to find homes. Len Robinson agreed to take one kitten to Acton Wells which the feline friend promptly adopted as his home. Their minimum need for care and readiness to accept affection (when it suits them) make cats ideal company for the lonely job of signalman. I once saw Pudding walking on the far side of the rails opposite the box, an act which proved he was aware of danger from the live third rail because he had to have found a gap in it to cross the lines and return safely. The lengths to which we go to please cats strengthen the theory we are placed on earth purely for the benefit of *Felis catus* and not the converse. I used to entertain the cat by swinging him in a chair, until, that is, the driver of a Down passenger train spotted the behaviour.

So far in this narrative the word signalmen has meant precisely that: men who worked signal boxes. Use of the term signalman has been correct because all characters including those I knew in 1950s Yorkshire have been male. What is more, until the 1970s it was acceptable to say signalmen when referring to the entire profession even if a few were female. But in the mid-1980s two changes took place, one was a shift in the English language whereby words containing *man* or *men* came to be considered inappropriate when referring to both sexes. The other was that two women began to work signal boxes in the Willesden area. Arguably, references to colleagues hereon should properly reflect presence of both sexes in signal boxes.

I am not alone in grappling with the problem; writers of regulations had to come up with an answer too. They could have altered manuals to read "The Signalman or Signalwoman ..." but such clumsy repetition would distract from grasping the rule's essence (and would lead to a tiny increase in printing costs). Authorities in due course would do away with the term signalman replacing it by the neutral title signaller. As I desire neither to use the new coinage nor to keep repeating the phrase signalman or signalwoman, I ask women who work in signal boxes – I knew one of them very well – to please forgive continuing use of the word signalmen because I do so on the grounds that the bulk of what I have to say refers to men only, and because at this late stage in the book to begin using another expression would be both jarring and inconsistent.

CHAPTER THIRTY-TWO

The story so far might imply a person's existence did not extend beyond the railway, beyond fraternizing with people who worked on it, as if all consciousness were contained in a vast and restricting bubble surrounding the North London Line with membranous offshoots to licensed premises north and south. A suggestion of no contact whatsoever with eight million individuals who populated the capital and who did *not* work for British Railways would however be mischievous.

Whilst relishing evenings out with colleagues, I would also on occasion drift in blissful anonymity amongst multitudes who rushed about city streets on imperative missions and who paid little regard to others doing the same thing. I explored only about five per cent of London's two hundred or so square miles. Over and over I would return to favourite haunts such as Piccadilly Circus, whose brash bright lights and incessant clamour have captivated generations, as memorably described in Aldous Huxley's fictional account of a mesmerized Myra Viveash in *Antic Hay*. A change to traffic flows and extensive reconstruction in the 1980s somewhat tarnished the cartwheel of streets at the hub of the universe. Even if all roads lead to Rome, they begin at Piccadilly Circus.

As one brushed shoulders with so many, chances seemed extremely slender of bumping into an acquaintance. But a case could be advocated that since one seventh of the kingdom's population was confined within the boundary of Greater London, the chances were equally slender - given enough time - of *not* meeting a friend by chance. In fact the latter was found to be true, but only because encounters occurred in areas drawing large numbers of visitors from afar, areas I frequented oftener than others. Had I spent all spare time wandering streets of, say, Lower Sydenham, I would probably have seen no one familiar.

Colleagues from work sometimes shared threading a way through this teeming carpet of humanity. I recall two of us embarking on a leisurely evening's drinking by riding the North London Line into Broad Street station then strolling through Liverpool Street station next door. In full signalman's uniform we swaggered across the station concourse proud to be part of a sprawling railway network, yet enjoying immunity from responsibility of trains feverishly arriving and departing at the terminus. Liverpool Street station was not on our line and furthermore was on a completely different British Railways region, the Eastern Region. Only small silver jacket buttons carrying the British Rail double-arrow logo identified us as employees. I do not know if station staff recognized a signalman's uniform, but their thoughts on our lack of interest in the hectic train service as we vainly strutted through like a brace of peacocks will never be known.

If fellow railway workers took no notice, someone else did. It was the rush hour, and as groups of office workers hurried to catch trains home, I was startled by an approaching young woman's voice declaring in low but urgent voice, "It's Mitch!" Source of the exclamation hung her head low as she passed causing tumbling hair to conceal her identity. At the same moment I descried the young woman's companion who glanced at me and smiled to herself. I now recognized the pair. I had met both in a night club, but friendship with one who had just spoken my name had failed to blossom. She obviously did not want to be seen, and I had mixed feelings about her seeing me in somewhat unkempt state and in railway uniform, so the encounter passed without consummation. All this happened within a few seconds as my colleague – oblivious of the vignette – and I ambled across the station concourse.

In Brent Cross shopping centre I saw a woman from the South of England whom I had known briefly whilst still living in Yorkshire, so the association went back almost twenty years. She appeared to recognize me, but she also appeared to be with her husband. I chose to turn and walk away. I saw in the centre of London sister of a former girlfriend from Liverpool. She saw me first, but as she was with a boyfriend, she turned her head away when I looked in her direction. In Tottenham Court Road (that quintessential London street usually prefixed by the definite article along whose entire length any new arrival must walk as part of his or her introduction to the city) I almost literally bumped into an old friend from Liverpool. He also was a man without deep roots and, like me, had transplanted himself to London. We renewed our friendship and revived for old time's sake a pastime of scouring drinking establishments in search of the opposite sex.

CHAPTER THIRTY-THREE

Chances of seeing a celebrity are naturally higher in London than anywhere else in Britain, and probably equal to any city in the world. Seasoned Londoners probably attached little significance to finding themselves on the same patch as someone famous and moreover took pride in their nonchalance towards the event, but for an individual new to the capital, seeing in the flesh a person hitherto known only from films or television was dream-like.

When walking from the bed-sitting room in Belsize Park to catch a train at Hampstead Heath for Kensal Green night shift, twice I passed a tall, slim, elegantly dressed woman of great pulchritude whose bearing, taut skin and finely sculptured mouth told of position, a countess perhaps. I briefly gazed at the woman admiring her beauty. A cat may look at a queen, but a signalman may not look at a countess, so I turned my head away. The woman looked at my looking at her. When I averted my eyes, she did the same.

On first seeing this striking woman I wondered why she even bothered to acknowledge my presence, but told myself she probably thought a uniformed railway worker striding out in that part of London unusual. It was not until the second time I saw her, and only then after I had walked some distance past, that I realized who the woman was. She was none other than a famous Cockney comedienne. Smarting from self-reproach over the pretermission, I turned over in the mind how I could have addressed her by her Christian name and said hello. I feel sure she would have responded. Such are opportunities that present themselves in a city home to much of the entertainment industry. Discretion is advised before approaching anyone famous, but I think a polite exchange in this instance would not have been out of place. It was infuriating a torpid brain robbed me of an opportunity to greet someone I admired.

The explosion of British popular music in the 1960s saw countless groups shoot to fame in very short time, their ultimate fate ranging from oblivion to unprecedented global popularity lasting into the 2000s.

Some lead singers have acquired awe so great commentators run dry of superlatives to describe it, though it could be argued knighthoods have gone a long way in recognizing true worth of these gifted musicians. For lesser mortals, to find ourselves in close proximity to a member of a stellar class numbering only a handful is an occasion not to be dismissed lightly. Such an event happened twice.

An early evening stroll across Leicester Square was found obstructed by a cordoned-off area and by a large, excited crowd gathering round. Celebrities were expected at a film premiere. I joined the throng, but could not get near the ropes, so stood back in hope of a better view. After several people whom I did not recognize had walked along the reserved area towards the cinema entrance, a buzz swept over the crowd heralding arrival of someone of great fame. A spacious limousine passed containing one of the elite group of singers described above. Others had gone to great lengths to see the star: I had arrived at the right place and right time purely by chance.

The second encounter with a musician of world renown occurred in a setting more conducive to a meeting of minor and major, a night club. A by-product of continuously working twenty days out of twenty-one was a financial cushion allowing a wage-earner to buy all he needed plus a little more. No longer was there need to watch every penny, extravagances greater than a few pints of beer were permissible. A carrier of extra cash did not have to worry about his heavy burden, as many London establishments were only to happy to assist in lightening the load. One such place was a discotheque in the city centre where well-behaved, sufficiently well-heeled average Londoners could mingle with the rich and famous. I had attempted to persuade colleagues in the signalling grades to join me there. They would have nothing of it, so I went alone. Entrance was gained by a courteous mien, the necessary fee and a smart straw-coloured tweed three-piece suit bought in Liverpool where it did no more than mark a young man as respectable but where in London it paradoxically singled him out as, sartorially at least, a cut above the rest. I visited the semi-exclusive club every few weeks but took care to give no hint of wealth, an illusion the attire might create.

It was in this hybrid of night spots that I came within a few feet (though it should be said so did every other patron in the club) of another musician whom culture described as a rock mega-star. Whilst dining at a table with three women, one tall woman also being extremely well known, the musician continually looked straight ahead knowing a careless sideways glance would meet one hundred pairs of eyes eagerly looking back. Though the singer may have been less than pleased at sharing the club with London's *hoi polloi,* as far as I could see not one person in the establishment was churlish enough to invade his private night out. Whilst the night was young the celebrity and *entourage* left.

Though I concede the thrill of seeing famous people may be outdone by triteness of reporting same, the singers were nevertheless part of a series of memorable encounters that began with regular mates at work, that continued through contact with other British Railways employees, that included a meeting of eyes whilst handsignalling a train at Kensal Green and that embraced coming face to face with old acquaintances. Seeing two females whose association in both time and geography was remote and seeing the young woman of more recent history (even though no contact was made with any of them) fostered a sense that one's life was a broad brush that touched upon other people's lives, not a piece of flotsam mercilessly tossed around without purpose.

As significant as all these eventualities were, none would match the life-changing auspiciousness of a chance encounter yet to be described.

CHAPTER THIRTY-FOUR

I had read many years ago London was just a collection of villages, and whilst a collection of towns may have been nearer the mark, the intussusception of this idea greatly affected social life during early times. Despite the dubious assertion that the capital was no more than a collection of municipalities butted together, like biscuits in a tin, the notion that all one needed could be found within walking distance was interpreted by me to mean chances of meeting the right young lady were just as good in local public houses and clubs as anywhere else. Quite some time elapsed before I realized that was not the case.

After I had escaped from that foolishly self-imposed confinement, I found the expensive discotheque mentioned earlier where I would see the famed singer. It was also in that place that I met the young woman who subsequently demonstrated her indifference in Liverpool Street station. Notwithstanding the opportunity to mingle with the mighty and notwithstanding the large number of available young women in the club, it slowly dawned on me that lording around the place in a three-piece suit was nothing more than fraudulent suggestion of position, one not borne out by a mundane if respected vocation and modest remuneration that went with it. I therefore abandoned the place and hung up the expensive-looking three-piece suit. (As a footnote, it is understood the night club in question has since changed character.)

Despite a string of encounters, not one friendship struck up with the opposite sex during early London years matured. A factor may have been contrast between the more predictable nature of young women in Liverpool, to which I had become accustomed, and the multiform character of their counterparts in London. Women in capital cities behave differently to those elsewhere.

By the mid 1980s changes were overdue; many would occur in rapid succession. One was the move from Kensal Green to Acton Wells. Another change annihilated any impression of affluence, the purchase of a car no grander than a second-hand Ford Cortina, brown in colour. Before purchase

I took the precaution of taking a driving lesson as many years had passed since I had been behind the wheel. Moth-balling the tweed suit meant buying replacement apparel, this time of more casual design, which in turn prompted visiting Top Man fashion shop in Oxford Street. Completely out of touch with fashion, and feeling like a racehorse trying to take the lead from behind, I had to press a sales assistant for advice. I purchased a light grey, multi-buttoned casual jacket with green trim, a pair of grey tapered trousers with raised pattern, and pair of grey shoes to match. As I tried on the new outfit, it seemed a fitting moment to reflect how long it had been since I had confronted the devastatingly serious business of trouser bottom width or the grave topic of shirt collar style.

A further upheaval was a switch from living in the eastern half of London to the western half. I had left Belsize Park to immerse briefly in Islington's cosmopolitan conviviality only to move to more sedate Acton. Acton is probably the biggest suburb ever if the frequency of its name occurring on railway maps is anything to go by. The district's endless parade of side streets might attach a certain plainness, but I grew fond of its small crowded shopping centre whose architecture was reminiscent of market towns in native Yorkshire.

Being further removed from the city centre did not keep me away from it nor prevent a major discovery. By 1985, employing the same tactics used in Birmingham and Liverpool of observing the direction in which women were heading, I eventually found the best discotheques to be surprisingly close to Oxford Street. It took almost five years to find these night spots in back street buildings converted from storage areas or light industrial premises, matching a similar period to discover identical facts in Liverpool. Contrary to original thinking, young people in London flocked just as much to the city centre for their nights out as they did elsewhere, and I would join them. Mingling with people younger than oneself was not troubling because in London age and looks mattered less than they did in the provinces. Though now forty years old, I had retained enough hair on top of the head and took care to keep weight down. To remain trim I began exercising at a gymnasium, but had to halt because an expanding physique made clothing too tight, which threatened the horrible prospect of having to buy an entire new wardrobe of larger shirts. I need not have concerned myself unduly, women in London generally asked no more than a presentable appearance, sufficient income and avoidance of Neanderthal-like behaviour.

CHAPTER THIRTY-FIVE

As spring of 1985 wriggled free from winter's cold confinement to paint luminous green dots on gaunt trees, a change of season that traditionally turns a man's mind in a special direction found re-emergent metropolitan man breaking loose from social stagnation of the early 1980s - to paint the town, to storm through newly-found night clubs, to enjoy a second youth. A swirling mass of plangent music, dazzling lights, pervasive alcohol and nubile women called, and I answered. Smiling glowing young women with copious amounts of liquor acting as catalyst basked in the heat of advances towards them by confident well-groomed eager young men. Spurred by the tonic of new clothes, lifted by the radiance of people enjoying themselves, fired by the irrepressible beat of dance music, nights out in discotheques reached a level of heart-racing enjoyment no less than that experienced in Liverpool ten years earlier. Simple dance steps remained unaltered if tunes to which they were executed were new. The word disco was still taboo ten years and two hundred miles further on.

I am able to identify the place where a certain momentous event occurred because the establishment has since closed down: name of the night club was Bananas. I arrived at the club about 22:00 hours. During the hour from 23:00 to midnight, men's desire to make an initial approach to the opposite sex happily synchronized with a period when women were most receptive to such advances. The volume of sound system speakers reached levels that almost blew people over. Multi-coloured lights flashed rapidly to constantly change appearance of everything in sight.

Amidst this churning sea of geniality I saw a tall, slim, fair-headed young woman on the opposite side of the dance floor. She was dressed in a fawn casual jacket and brown trousers which, although both were loose fitting, could not hide a mannequin-like outline. Her height and silhouette separated her from all others in the club. I dearly wanted to stride over and talk to her, but she was amongst friends enjoying a girls' night out. To rudely barge in would likely ruin any chance of getting to know her. Then the group was lost from view as waves of revellers flowed back and forth - men pursuing women, women pursuing men, groups of females heading for the dance floor. The willowy young woman and friends were lost in endless ebb and flow of stimulated, intoxicated, sweaty, yet – thanks to generous application of perfumes – aromatic young people chasing one another. Faced with what appeared to be a lost cause, I retired to the bar.

At about 00:20 hours, after paying a visit necessitated by continuous drinking, I returned to the previously occupied position near the dance floor, there to discover a pleasant and unexpected change in the atmosphere, one not easily defined. A benign sensation, as strong as it was intangible, permeated the air seeming to say all would be well, that whatever course one took would be fortuitous. The most peculiar of events can usually be put down to some practical explanation, but at the time I had no rational answer for a dimensionless interposition into the gaudiness of a London discotheque. It has since occurred to me that the phenomenon could probably be explained by astrology: someone knowledgeable in the subject had once said to me things will change suddenly, literally overnight. Still, it is more productive not to dwell on the matter but to rejoice in events that subsequently took place.

As I stood at the edge of the dance floor, I looked to the corner where the group including the arresting young woman had been, but they were nowhere to be seen. Then, the raging froth of bodies thrown together in this dark, deafening, pulsating place seemed to open up in front of me like the Red Sea. Through the gap, diagonally across the dance floor, I saw the tall young woman standing alone: she had temporarily become separated from companions. She gazed blankly across the dance floor exuding a serenity one would have thought unattainable in the robustious imbroglio of a discotheque.

The way ahead could not have been clearer had it been directed by ten feet high flashing neon signs. I fought my way round the perimeter of the dance floor saying "Excuse me," and "Sorry," as I eased through bobbing, weaving dancers, moving as fast as I could lest the opportunity be lost. After what seemed an eternity but which in reality probably took one minute I arrived close to the young woman. At that point, I slowed down and adopted a more relaxed, nonchalant demeanour to avoid startling her. I sidled to a position alongside to say something trivial. Posterity must be robbed of actual words because I cannot remember them, but they were something in the order of, "Pretty crowded in here tonight, isn't it?"

She nodded in agreement, after which I asked if she would like to dance, an invitation she accepted. After several records had spun we sat down at a table to share a drink and to speak in sentences rather than the short, shouted phrases of the dance floor. We talked in an easy, relaxed manner rather than in emotional, postural spikes normally employed in discotheques, her conversation revealing a depth of character hitherto unmet in the opposite sex. A rich exchange of openness, honesty and joy at meeting one another sealed the friendship. I learnt my new friend was from America, in England to study, her accent having been obscured till now by the barrage of dance floor noise. I also learnt she was somewhat younger than I was, but that she, too, was just a little older than most in the club, chivalry prohibiting my revealing her exact age. When slow records began to play at about 01:00, we adjourned to the dance floor where we fell into one another's arms as if sawed off at the feet!

CHAPTER THIRTY-SIX

Did the Descending Pyramidal Theory have any part to play in this coming together of two people? On the face of it, no, because we were both fair-skinned, both slimly built, and both lacked distinctive features, so there would be no question of our being considered mismatched. But she was half-an-inch taller than I was, and though we both spoke English of course, we were of different nationalities, so there was in fact a fid of disparity. The initial approach on the edge of the dance floor was likely undertaken with a measure of politeness and respect somewhat greater than for someone not quite so tall: that complaisance may well have encouraged a warm response. Also, since I had always been intrigued by Americans, my face lighting up on learning her nationality probably was also favourably received. Thus in two small ways the Descending Pyramidal Theory could be said to have played a part.

Be that as it may, our subsequent first date took place in sober fresh air of an outdoor restaurant in Covent Garden where normal chemistry was allowed to function free from alcoholic influences and night club pother. It cemented a friendship into something destined to last. Love grew. Not the electric kind of passion fated to repulse as suddenly as it had attracted, but in togetherness found only in two people completely at ease with one another, in two people who meshed affectionately like last two pieces of a jigsaw puzzle. Twenty years of touring discotheques had at last paid off in meeting someone with whom a relationship was not a battleground but a stable foundation on which to build a life together. Here was a woman whose mastery of the English language outshone mine, who had read the inside of more books than I had seen the outside of, a woman who had a university degree, embraced philosophy, studied ballet, who had been awarded for excellence in *cordon bleu* and furthermore was graced with a poise needed to dowse the solar flares of eccentricity to which her new found friend was occasionally given. The romance with a visitor from the United States flourished, and six months after the night club meeting, we married. The whiskery old adage that life begins at forty, once thought mere solace for those entering their fifth decade, was proved true. My wife and I found a spacious, comfortable, split-level flat in a quiet Acton street to make our home.

I had never been happier. I had the job I always wanted and was married not only to someone who fulfilled all dreams but to someone whose intellect would guarantee countless hours of stimulating discourse. Her firm but placid disposition nurtured a co-existence able to smooth over small dramas that punctuate married life. Immense happiness flooded our domestic lives and accompanied us in explorations of London, in our holidays in many parts of Britain (eased along the way by British Railways' travel discounts to employees and spouses) and in a couple of trips abroad.

If combination of happy marriage and happy work sounded too good to last, it was. When we had begun to talk seriously about marriage, my wife had said to me, "You know, if we married, I can't stay here, my home is America."

"So I would have to go over there," I said flatly.

My wife-to-be could not bring forth words to affirm a gigantic commitment necessary as condition of marriage, but looked at me with pale-blue eyes awash with sympathy and apprehension. She nodded. My response was a shrug of the shoulders.

"So that would be all right, then?" she asked in a voice racked with solicitude.

"Well," I began, "I moved away from my home town in Yorkshire twenty years ago. That was probably the biggest upheaval I could ever have made in my life. I moved to Birmingham, left there, moved to Liverpool, uprooted myself from there and came to London. So I suppose it would be just another move. Just another hop, really."

I had skittered city to city and just another hop America would be, but this time a 3,000 mile hop to another country, another climate, another culture. With a wordless shrug of the shoulders I had agreed to leave Britain, to leave behind all I had grown to love – tranquility of the countryside, stimulation of city life, an evening's blissful first pint of draught bitter - all would be given up to emigrate to America. Above all, a career in British railway signalling would come to an end.

Consummate irony of the title of this book is now exposed. Through the Return to Steam Committee, I had tried to get steam back on the main lines, but was beaten to it by others. A career in signalling was prematurely cut short, love for the job being pushed aside by a love far greater. A railway man I had wanted to be, but in both cases fell short.

One adjusts surprisingly quickly. Up till this point the idea of leaving England would have been unconscionable, but when faced with no real alternative, the decision became no more exacting, no more anxiety-ridden than buying a new car. All that remained was to philosophize.

No matter the circumstances, it seems one change will always be counter-balanced by another. Economists tell us if a country's exchange rate falls exports will rise, yet imports will be more expensive. Climatologists tell us latitudinal shift in rainfall patterns might bring drought to one area only to benefit crops in another. I recall in business ruing loss of a contract and a director saying, "When one door closes, another one opens," which it did. So it was with finally meeting a woman with whom to settle down, the job of signalman had to be sacrificed in exchange.

During Birmingham and Liverpool years a war had raged as love of railways and interest in the opposite sex vied for attention, the latter generally claiming victory. In my becoming a signalman the railway at last gained the upper hand. Then marriage brought about a truce. Though I was extraordinarily happy, it were as if two influences of love and railways were fighting it out behind my back. Like an oligarchy of two that cannot last, one had to oust the other, in this case the heart claimed victory.

A further twist in the persistence of equilibrium was that one signalman on the North London Line was an American who had married a British woman; they had consequently settled in London. Perhaps as counterpoise he had to come to Britain so that I could go to America, or I had to go to America because he had come to Britain, one or the other.

To re-visit the earlier analogy between life's journey and an interplanetary space mission, it was the fair sex in Liverpool that drew me towards the city, its railway connections that sped me away. Lo and behold the opposite happened in London. A career on the railway attracted me, a woman took me away. For whatever reason, neither the great city of Liverpool nor the great city of London could provide a marriage partner. That task fell to the New World.

Trading in a signalman's job for emotional security, though inevitable, was delayed. Prior to marriage my wife and I agreed to remain in Britain for the time being, allowing me to relish joy of being both signalman and proud husband. That period lasted four years till 1988 when pangs of homesickness drove my wife to call in a promise. She asked that we bring our stay in Britain to a close and that I implement the procedure to emigrate to America.

Once started, the vehicle of emigration rolled inexorably onward. It seemed at the time that the move was the exchange of much held dear in Britain with the complete and utter unknown of the United States. What I failed to see and failed to appreciate was that a free ticket through marriage to all that America had to offer placed me in a profoundly enviable position.

CHAPTER THIRTY-SEVEN

By the end of what can only be described as a limited career of eight-and-a-half years, I hoped that if nothing else the fine sense of judgement required in all signalmen – a level-headed manner of thinking that is midway between responding too slowly and over-reaction - had been mastered.

In early days at Kensal Green I had sent the Obstruction Danger bell signal, six beats on the bell, to Willesden power box when vandals lit a small fire between rails on the Up City Line. It was pointed out to me afterwards that appropriate action for such minor impediments was a telephone call, not an emergency bell code.

Only one true obstruction ever occurred - when the driver of a freight train reported a fallen tree completely blocked the line between Kensal Green and Gospel Oak. He had fortunately been able to stop his train in time. I immediately sent the Obstruction Danger bell signal to Gospel Oak, not preceding it with the one beat of Call Attention, as is the proper manner. I rang it steadily and deliberately, more like 1-1-1-1-1-1. Timing was propitious, for the signalman at Gospel Oak was able to telephone the next signalman back along the line at Camden Road Junction asking him to hold the next Down passenger train. The signalman at Camden Road in due course re-routed the held train via Primrose Hill.

In the very last week at Acton Wells two dogs strayed onto tracks, one chasing the other till, not far from the signal box, the bitch touched the 600 volts conductor rail perishing instantly. Her pursuer abruptly lost interest and wandered off. An animal now sprawled lifeless over the conductor rail and would likely damage the current pick-up shoe on the next Down passenger train, for which I had already given a Line Clear. I immediately telephoned the signalman at High Level Junction asking him if possible to hold the train whilst I removed the dead dog. He was able to halt the train by throwing back a signal. Using a large wooden paddle supplied to all signal boxes on third-rail electrified lines, I removed the carcase allowing the passenger service to resume. Had the passenger train already left Willesden Junction station with no way of stopping it, then probably the Obstruction

Danger bell signal would have been in order (to which High Level should have responded with 4-5-5 Train Running away in Right Direction) but that of course would do nothing to prevent the train hitting the animal. This was an example where rules and regulations did not cover every single eventuality and where a man on duty had to use discretion.

Later days at Acton Wells saw introduction of locomotives equipped with radios. In other parts of the country motive power had already been fitted with radios in order to work Radio Electronic Token Block Regulations on single-track branch lines, but general use of the technology was new.

The telephone rang one day. When I answered, the voice at the other end seemed hesitant and the reception poor. Thinking it was a wrong number, I was on the point of putting the telephone down when the caller explained he was driver of a train standing at the Down Midland home signal and that he was trying out a new radio system. (A telephone had never been installed at that signal.) Certain engines had been experimentally supplied with radios capable of dialling signal boxes. It was called a ship-to-shore arrangement in that it could only be used one way: the signal box could not dial the radio. There was perhaps one other occasion when a train dialled in by radio; the system advanced no further before I left.

To look at the career overall, if I had the option to re-live time as a signalman, probably nothing would change. Whilst at Kensal Green an opportunity arose to transfer to Marylebone signal box which still operated semaphore signals at that time. What a feather in the cap that would have been to control a London terminus from a mechanical frame! The station was best known to northerners as a square on the Monopoly board game. Perhaps my only regret is that I did not pursue that opportunity, though I do not know whether seniority would have secured the position.

Management considered me over-qualified for the job and endeavoured to prize me out of the signal box. Movements Inspector Henry Knowles invited me at one stage to apply for a post of yardmaster in Willesden. But I was content with fixed hours and an acceptable level of income, even before taking into account love for the job. With typical lack of direction, I had seldom thought about the long term future on British Railways; the only fact I knew for sure was that modern push-button power boxes did not appeal. With emigration looming it was all a moot point of course.

Being a signalman was the best job I ever had. I have never known an occupation where I was so pleased to get to work. The moment I stepped inside the signal box and bathed in the warmth of its welcoming and unique atmosphere, I could not wait to grab the first lever of the day, to tap the first bell signal. There is nothing more rewarding than to feel tension in steel wire as one heaves a cast-iron lever operating a semaphore signal some distance away.

Attachment between men and tools of their trade has no comparison.

So great is the affinity, signalmen sometimes had to chase the man they relieved out of the box. When I was training at Kensal Green, a relief man thought he would do Fred Abbot a favour by having one last lunge at the frame. He put back lever 43 as he made for the door. But a train had not yet passed number 43, so the signal was inadvertently thrown back in front of it, fortunately just a light engine. The problem was easily overcome of course by quickly re-stroking the lever.

Other benefits of being a signalman were not having to deal directly with that despicable commodity, cash, and of generally eluding a menace that lurks in people working in confined spaces such as offices, the threat of emotional turbulence amongst them.

Dan Patterson from Bickle and Fred Abbot and Bob Williams from the North London Line, in their equanimity spiked with a dash of restrained humour, best typified signalmen. A man who spent twenty years trawling night clubs for the right woman consuming more alcohol than he should have done in the process, a man with a zany sense of humour who took thoughts down unexplored avenues of reasoning, was not typical of signalmen.

With departure from Britain looming ever closer, what would I leave behind in the way of railway signalling? For the most part, large cities and trunk routes between them had all been converted to modern signalling. Semaphore signalling and Absolute Block could be found here and there in London, the best example being the line from Acton Wells through Acton Canal Wharf and Neasden Junction to Dudding Hill Junction. Out on the main lines, lever frame signal boxes were however still in control at Stafford, Crewe and Stockport.

Centres of extensive semaphore signalling existed away from large conurbations and principal routes - at Lincoln, Shrewsbury and Worcester. But secondary routes were the principal stronghold of mechanical signalling. The further away from London, the greater the incidence of Absolute Block Regulations. Mile after mile of railway signalled the old-fashioned way lined the edges of the British Isles: Lewes to Hastings on the south coast, the North Wales coast, huge tracts of Lincolnshire, the Cumbrian coast, the York to Scarborough line, Dundee to Aberdeen. Mechanical frames could be found at many seaside towns within and outside the areas just mentioned. Though the elimination of Victorian technology was inexorable, vast tracts remained to delight the enthusiast prepared to hunt them out. And one must not forget the splendid and expanding mechanical installations meticulously restored or built anew on Britain's heritage railways.

Railway signalling is continually evolving, but I saw little change over eight-and-a-half years. A grandstand view from signal box windows of passing trains frequently brought back boyhood memories of Bickle signal box and its men. What I had seen and heard as a lad was no childish irrelevance, for I tried to emulate the 1950s signalmen's spick and span appearance by wearing uniform with collar and tie on most occasions. I did my best to live up to high standards set by them.

Many features of railway signalling had happily remained unchanged. Two beats on the bell for Train entering Section and the stern unambiguous authority of a semaphore arm at danger were just the same in the 1980s as they were in the 1950s, rare examples of the past transported to the present yet still equally relevant in both. If I had remained in close contact with railways the entire thirty years, these two particulars of signalling would have been given little thought. As it was, every 1980s two-beats-on-the-bell and every 1980s horizontal semaphore arm generated a modicum of pleasure. Thus, experiences as a boy were telescoped forward into those of an adult, as if cheating time. This conveyancing of affairs from a previous to a later time would engage in one more example.

When I was eight years old I dreamt I was in America and saw freight wagons going along the track on their own without an engine pulling or pushing them. Those are the only two components of the dream I remember. I do not know what in the dream told of America, but there was no doubt about the location. The dream was not the usual nonsensical collection of disconnected images, but a dream so pellucid it appeared to have really happened.

I was friendly with a railway porter at the time, and told him about the dream. He said, "Well, that means yer gonna go to America and invent trucks that go by themselves." He added, "Dreams always come true yer know."

One half of the dream was about to come true. Concerning the other half, no technology exists to permit railway wagons to move on their own, nor is it likely to be invented by me or anyone else soon. Given the astonishing accuracy of one half of a childhood premonition, what is to be made of the other half? For the present the question must be left hanging.

Whilst I am able to remember quite clearly at a later stage in life essence of the boyhood dream, I do not know to what extent it was recalled in 1988 as emigration drew near, whether it emerged from the subconscious to break into the conscious world as a passing thought, or even if it was remembered at all. If there were any recollection, I am sure it was swept aside in favour of more pressing concerns. At the time I most certainly said nothing to my wife about the childhood dream, for she confirms that to be the case.

CHAPTER THIRTY-EIGHT

Preparations for departure included an interview at the American Embassy to obtain immigration documents. In the summer of 1988 my wife and I travelled north to say goodbye to my sister Pauline, her husband and family. In autumn my brother Rodney and his wife came to London for the same reason. We had lost both parents by this time. Passage was booked for a December transatlantic crossing on board the QE2 ocean liner as I would no longer fly. Tedious chores of moving house included packing, notifying change of address and deciding what to take and what to jettison. Pots, pans, crockery, cutlery and other household effects were sold off cheaply to other residents at our Acton address.

Ah...the filing system. On the verge of the most important move of a lifetime, on the eve of emigrating to a country that promises limitless opportunities for the adventurous, that promises a new start in life regardless of age or skills, an extensive, dusty and largely obsolete filing system now acquired overarching importance. Several cubic feet of folders could not possibly be shipped to the United States. I thinned them out, in many cases holding onto earliest and latest documents – those from the early 1960s and late 1980s – and discarded the rest.

Unbelievably, school exercise books for General Certificate of Education "O" level studies were part of the filing system. They had been stored initially in Yorkshire, then languished in a Liverpool attic, returned to Yorkshire, and finally moved to London. I had clung to the red, yellow, blue and brown-backed exercise books in optimistic belief they could be used as works of reference, but on the solitary occasion I tried to retrieve some geographical information could not find it. All trouble taken to lug them around England for decades had been a waste of time and effort. They were thrown away.

I sat on the carpeted living room floor staring at the last batch of files to be reviewed, those of the Return to Steam Committee. I ought to have contemplated their fate more seriously, but imminent removal abroad reduced to near insignificance anything not directly connected with uprooting. At the time I recognized no historical value, and after postponing a difficult decision for a few days, saw no alternative to destroying them. With hindsight, I should have found a custodian.

As 1988 drew to a close, so did a career as a British Railways signalman. On Saturday 10th December 1988 at 06:40 hours I reported for a last turn of duty at Acton Wells Junction, having handed in my notice to the current Movements Inspector on 9th November. The occasion ought to have been no less a red letter day than had been first appearance at Willesden Junction eight-and-a-half years ago, but the impending transatlantic voyage upstaged everything. The morning proved uneventful from an operational point of view. Inspector Ron Dillington, now occupying a different supervisory position, called by to wish me well in the new venture. He had been there at the start of someone's dream and was now there at its end. His final broad smile and vigorous handshake recognized an association to which we both attached great value.

I photographed the last train signalled, an Up passenger train, sent Train entering Section, then wrote in the train register book "Mitchell Deaver off duty 13:30, emigrating to America". If the final embellishment broke rules, a disciplinary letter could be sent to a forwarding address in the United States.

Dave Smith, myself and two others adjourned to a tavern next to Kew Gardens station on the North London Line for a farewell drink. I would have liked Bob Williams to have joined us, but it would have been too much to ask of the family man. I would also have liked Len Robinson to have been there, but, sadly, a once-in-a-lifetime opportunity to purchase rare block instruments took him elsewhere that afternoon. As tipsy handshakes rounded off the afternoon, Dave Smith and I agreed to keep in touch.

On Wednesday 14th December 1988 my wife and I left England on board the QE2. In one respect I had at last found direction in life, westwards. In all other respects the future was as abysmally uncertain as it had ever been, with no employment waiting for me on arrival in the United States and with no knowledge of the labour market to secure same. What were chances of railway work in the New World? I did not know, did not know to what extent the industry differed on the other side of the Atlantic Ocean, had no comprehension of American signalling, neither did I know to whom an application should be made to pursue a career in the new land. Nevertheless, prospect of an unknown future, like looking at an empty canvas one square mile in size, excited the senses. Anticipatory fever was not unlike bachelor days of embarking on a discotheque night out where anything could happen, except this adventure would be on a global scale. Life hereon, free from historical shackles, could be whatever I made it.

Seventeen assorted receptacles, mostly cardboard boxes, carried our belongings from the United Kingdom of Great Britain and Northern Ireland to the United States of America. A friend kindly rented a van to take us and our chattels from London to Southampton. Dockside officials scanned each container before loading on board the QE2. A cardboard box packed with "00" scale model trains momentarily halted screening as an officer stared perplexedly at the X-ray image of miniature rolling stock. My wife and I elected to hand-carry one container each of our most treasured possessions, she a picnic hamper carefully packed with a Royal Doulton "Giselle" pattern china tea set, I a box of fragile model railway items including a cardboard station building from Liverpool days, its sentimental value far outstripping its monetary worth.

For eight-and-a-half years on the North London Line I had signalled a freightliner train nicknamed either the ol' Southampton or the QE2. Piquantly, here I was now climbing on board the real QE2 ocean liner in real Southampton to leave England for good. We chose to cram seventeen pieces of luggage into our small cabin rather than be separated from them.

Having left last footprints in British soil, we dined on board ship as it slipped quietly in darkness from Southampton docks into The Solent. Dark featureless waters stretched from the huge vessel to the shore as if nothing were there, as if we were floating in space. An even darker land mass sparkled with lights of civilization going about its nocturnal business, this light a street lamp, this light a bus, that light a bedroom window. Illuminations draped the entire shore line as far as the eye could see. Slowly, the coast receded till it became no more than a black ribbon of sequins sown to an endless blue-black curtain that was sea and sky combined.

Time drew near for a last glimpse of England, possibly the last I would ever see of the country. If sentimentality were to rear its head, now would be the time, but I felt no such emotion. Rapidity of change including the novelty of five days on the high seas left no room for mawkishness. The liner nosed further out into the Atlantic Ocean. I had wanted to watch the last trace of England dramatically disappear, but a collection of shore lights stubbornly glistened on the horizon refusing to dip from view. I would look no more. We are going to America. Let's get on with it!

CHAPTER THIRTY-NINE

A Class WD 2-8-0 locomotive stood on the departure track gently simmering. A plume of translucent dusky smoke drifted from the chimney. A small jet of fizzling steam escaped from a cylinder. Coupled to the engine was a grey guard's van, complete with tail lamp and side lights. Close by, three men stood on greasy, wet cinders near the outlet signal discussing the day's work.

"We've gotta call at the yard as usual. There's nineteen empty hoppers to be picked up," began the guard. "Then something unusual, we've gotta pick up a flat wagon for some special out-of-gauge load."

"Where do we pick that up?" asked the driver.

"That's the funniest thing," replied the guard, "they don't know for sure where it is. They've only just realized they needed it. The flat's wanted for an urgent job down south."

"Typical!" said the fireman. "Send us off for something but they don't know what."

"Well, it'll be an interesting day," said the older and wiser driver.

Driver and fireman mounted the locomotive, the guard climbed on board his guard's van. Three blasts on the engine's wheezy whistle told the signalman which route they were to take. A minute later a miniature red semaphore arm sprang upwards to the "off" position, and the short train grumbled along the departure track on its way to pick up nineteen empty coal hoppers.

Further down the line, the guard hooked the WD locomotive to the rake of hoppers. The driver shouted to him, "Where's the flat then?"

"Next yard," came the reply.

The driver tossed his head and rolled his eyes in acknowledgement.

"The yard's full of flat wagons. Can't we just take any one of 'em?" said the fireman.

"They need a special one," said the driver. "Most of those here are for plate, or they're bolster wagons."

After the guard climbed aboard his vehicle, the train made its way, signals permitting, to the next yard down the line. Driver and fireman looked back over their train from time to time ensuring everything was still with them, including the guard's van. At night the guard's van's side lamps would confirm to the footplate crew that it was still attached to the train. The train was not fitted with the continuous brake; if a coupling broke both parts would still keep moving, but not necessarily together.

"These empty hopper trips are nice," said the fireman as the train rocked and rolled along at about thirty miles per hour. "Don't use too much coal or water."

"Easy to stop as well," said the driver in a continuance of the lengthy training a fireman must receive before he, too, can drive. "Now, if they were loaded, that's a different story, you've gotta be really careful running with all that weight and having no vacuum brake."

After seeing a yellow semaphore distant signal in the horizontal position of caution, the driver brought his train to a gentle stand at a home signal. The guard dismounted his van and walked to the front of the train where he met the yard shunter. The guard would handle operations at the front of the train, the shunter would couple to the flat wagon in the yard. The locomotive was uncoupled from the hopper wagons, pulled ahead, and after the disc ground signal cocked forty-five degrees, backed into the yard following the beckoning hand signals from the shunter. It gently buffered-up to the flat wagon.

On receiving the move ahead hand signal – a rolling motion of the forearm - from the shunter, the driver opened the regulator to ease his charge slowly forward. But he stopped suddenly. Something was wrong. The driver had felt undue drag. Both he and the fireman looked back and saw that the back of the flat wagon was lower than the front. It had fallen in. Rails on poorly maintained sleepers had spread causing the rear bogie of this bogie vehicle to drop into the ballast. After a few moments of gazing in despair at the calamity, the shunter walked up to the engine and told the traincrew he was going to speak to authority. Driver and fireman dismounted, took a walk round the stricken wagon, returned to the locomotive and made themselves comfortable.

Fifteen minutes later the shunter returned. "This is what they've told us to do," he said to the footplate crew. "We've got to leave this here like this. We haven't got time to get it re-railed, they're desperate for a flat wagon. There's another on number six road, we've got to take that."

After winding on the flat wagon's circular hand-brake, the shunter unhooked the WD and guided it over to number six siding. As the driver gingerly backed the engine towards the flat wagon, the shunter's arms shot vertically in the air in a sudden message to stop. The locomotive's brakes groaned, and the machine stopped a short distance from the wagon. The shunter walked towards the crew with the explanation. "We can't take this thing. It's chained to the rail! It's a cripple. There's a note on it saying the handbrake doesn't work. I'll have to see what they want us to do *now*."

The shunter walked a short distance to the office to make enquiries. After lapse of a further fifteen minutes, the shunter returned to report: "There's a suitable flat in the exchange sidings. You've gotta go down there to get it."

After much complaining, driver, fireman and guard took their train five miles down the line to stop at the exchange sidings signal box for instructions. "You've gotta back your train in here to clear the Main," shouted the signalman across tracks. "There's a passenger catching up to you, they want you out of the way, so you'll be able to take a break."

"Don't want a break," said the fireman dolefully, "just want to get these hoppers to where they belong."

With the hopper train safely backed into one track, a flat wagon was collected from another track without incident. Engine and wagon arrived back at the signal box, followed shortly by the guard on foot. The signalman slid open a window and eyed the gathering cautiously, before saying, "They're in a bit of a predicament."

"Now what!" said the fireman with agitation.

The signalman continued. "That flat wagon, it's a special flat wagon. It's the only one they've got now that'll do the job. But because of its size, it can't go the same route as the hoppers. It's gotta go the other route. Now, they know you fellahs are not good that way, but if they get you a pilot, they wonder if you wouldn't mind taking it with your guard's van, 'cause they're getting pretty desperate for the flat now. And you'll be running as a Class E instead of Class J. You'll have to leave the hoppers behind, they'll get another crew to take the them." A discussion then took place amongst four men regarding financial advantages to the crew if they took the urgent flat wagon.

The guard was first to make a decision. "Class E, eh. Sounds like a good deal to me. It'll be interesting to see some new territory. And one flat car is an easier train than nineteen hoppers."

The fireman spoke next. "It's nice to stick to yer usual routine. But I suppose when something special comes up like this, it'd be daft not to take advantage of it. I'll get another headlamp and change the headcode."

The driver smiled at the change in inclination of his fireman's mood, then spoke. "Well, we had to go to three different yards before we found the right flat. And now that we've got it, we have to go off along a new route! But it doesn't matter, especially if it's to our benefit. We've been hopping around all day, it's just another hop, really."

BIBLIOGRAPHY

A Pictorial Record of L.N.W.R. Signalling by Richard Foster (Oxford Publishing Company)

British Railway Steam Locomotives 1948-1968 by Hugh Longworth (Oxford Publishing Company)

Buildings of Liverpool by Liverpool Heritage Bureau

Life Adventure in Steam by Frank Mason (Countyvise Limited)

Signalling Atlas and Signal Box Directory by Peter Kay (Signalling Record Society)

Temptations by Otis Williams with Patricia Romanowski (Cooper Square Press)

The Great Book of Trains by Brian Hollingsworth and Arthur Cook (Portland House)

The Last Merseyrail Signal Boxes Part I The Wirral Line by the Merseyside Railway History Group

The Last Merseyrail Signal Boxes Part II The Northern Line by the Merseyside Railway History Group

The Railway Magazine, August 2008, April 2009, June 2009, November 2009

The Signal Box by the Signalling Study Group (Oxford Publishing Company)

The Sunday Times, 20th September 2007

ABOUT THE AUTHOR

Mitchell Deaver acquired a passion for steam engines and for railway signalling during his childhood in 1950s North Yorkshire, all of which he described in his first book *Railway Boy*. Boyhood experiences had a profound effect on adult life, as is revealed in this, his second book.

Following a long and varied working life, a significant part of which was railway employment, Mitchell Deaver is now retired, and lives near Windsor, Pennsylvania, United States. With his wife of twenty-eight years, he enjoys gardening, walking and cycling. In a busy retirement, his spare time is spent building an extensive "00" gauge model railway.

Printed in Great Britain
by Amazon.co.uk, Ltd.,
Marston Gate.